Management App

A Handbook for PAs and Administrators

Helen Harding

PITMAN
150
YEARS

PITMAN PUBLISHING
128 Long Acre, London WC2E 9AN

First published 1987

© Helen Harding 1987

British Library Cataloguing in Publication Data
Harding, Helen
   Management appreciation: a handbook for
   PAs and administrators.
   1. Management
   I. Title
   658.4   HD31
ISBN 0 273 02268 7

Photypeset by Wyvern Typesetting Ltd, Bristol
Printed at The Bath Press, Avon

To Peter

Contents

Preface

I have long felt that there was a need to condense into one book the sort of material which students need to give them an introduction to the complex and fascinating subject of management.

At the thinking stage it seemed relatively easy in that there was no shortage of material which could be considered appropriate in an appreciation level text. Herein lay one of the problems – what to include and, by implication, exclude, and yet still achieve a wide enough coverage to be of general interest whilst providing a useful foundation for examinations such as RSA: Diploma for Personal Assistants (Personnel and Functional Aspects); LCCI: Private and Executive Secretary's Diploma (Management Appreciation and Secretarial Administration); and PEI: Secretarial Practice – Advanced.

A consideration of examination syllabi also revealed that much of the content I had in mind for the book would be useful for some professional examinations of the Institute of Chartered Secretaries and Administrators (ICSA) and the Institute of Administrative Management (IAM). It would also provide relevant introductory management reading for students on postgraduate secretarial diploma courses and certain first level degree courses as well as aspects of the Diploma in Management Studies (DMS) and units of study in the BTEC Higher National Diploma in Business Studies. In fact, the sort of text envisaged would be useful for a wide variety of students on a wide range of courses.

After much deliberation I decided to divide the book into three Parts and to concentrate on areas and topics likely to be of interest and relevance to aspiring personal assistants and administrators. Inevitably some of the topics are weightier or more detailed than others, but such is the nature of the subject matter.

However, what I have tried to achieve is a drawing together of related concepts, as far as was possible, within a principal area of the text. This reduces, at least to some extent, the difficulties which can be experienced when consulting an index and finding references spread literally throughout a book, sometimes apparently unconnected to what the reader had in mind.

I have also included a series of questions at the end of each Part. These have been taken from recent examinations of the bodies mentioned above.

Suggested Further Reading is included in the hope that readers will find their interest aroused sufficiently by this text to wish to explore many issues in more detail. One of the problems for all students studying a range of subjects, particularly over a short period of time, is that of selecting appropriate texts from the extensive catalogues available on a subject such as management. I hope, therefore, that this inclusion may lessen the task somewhat.

The appendices may also provide useful shortcuts to some of the additional reference sources which are useful to students of management.

Acquiring an appreciation of management should not be simply a criterion for passing an examination of one kind of another – it should be a passport to the future. Roles are evolving and traditional boundaries are blurring, so it is important that those wishing to enter careers in public or private enterprise should possess a wide perspective of the role and function of management. Also, there is a growing tendency to view many supervisory roles as first line management. What may previously have been designated as supervision rather than management is, to all intents and purposes – and certainly as far as this text is concerned – treated as one and the same thing.

Acknowledgements

The author and publishers wish to acknowledge the following for permission to reproduce the drawings used in connection with office layout:

Building Design Partnership
DEGW (Space Planners and Architects)
Herman Miller Ltd

My thanks are also extended to the above for their interest and help and to the Facilities Management Group of the Institute of Administrative Management who organize the Office of the Year Award.

In addition I am grateful to Soraya Romano for taking time to read the script in its draft stage and for her comments.

I should like to express my gratitude to the Institute of Administrative Management, the Institute of Chartered Secretaries and Administrators, the London Chamber of Commerce and Industry, Pitman Examinations Institute and the Royal Society of Arts for permission to use specimen questions from past examination papers.

Last, and by no means least, my very warm thanks go to my husband, Peter, without whose encouragement, understanding and advice throughout the preparation of this book, it would never have been completed.

HBH

Notes for Lecturers

Although this book has been written with students in mind, it seems important and appropriate to provide some indication to lecturers of the rationale for its content and structure.

As indicated in the Preface, the intention is to cover a wide selection of material and cater for a range of courses and examinations. Certain features of the resultant text may therefore appear unfamiliar to the lecturer who has prepared a scheme of work based on one particular examination syllabus. However, limiting content to the needs of a single examination can be very restricting and it is often desirable to provide the opportunity to explore a variety of issues whilst developing an awareness of job-related areas of special interest. Lecturers are increasingly required to diversify and extend their teaching repertoire. Consequently, there is a need for a text which reflects the erosion of subject boundaries and the introduction of a holistic approach.

Secretarial studies courses

Where the book is intended for use with secretarial studies students, it is important to appreciate that this area is undergoing yet another metamorphosis. Whilst the arrival of office technology brought with it change in terms of equipment, the scope for change is very much greater and there is a growing awareness of the need to enhance the academic content of the curriculum for advanced level courses in particular.

Practical relevance

Throughout this book, however, the aim has been to provide a balance between theory and practice, recognizing that, in the final analysis, students must be able to apply their knowledge in the work situation if they are to be marketable and capable of making an appropriate and worthwhile contribution as valued and respected members of a management team. Emerging employment opportunities necessitate the creation of new posts, which bring with them changes in emphasis demanding additional and improved skills and expertise. These include:

- better communication skills;
- people skills and teamwork;
- planning and organizational ability;
- decision-making capability;
- problem-solving capacity;
- supervisory and delegating skills;
- business awareness.

Whilst these are all aspects which, it can be argued, will be developed given time and experience, it is essential that there is sufficient underpinning to enable those undertaking first jobs or securing promoted posts to make an effective contribution right away.

Use of examples

In a subject of this kind it is desirable to introduce practical examples in order to bring the topics alive. However, this is preferably done by the individual lecturer in the light of his/her knowledge of the students in a group. Class compositions will vary considerably from post-'A' level students who are undertaking studies straight from school, to more mature students on post-degree programmes, to students attending on a part-time day-release basis. Consequently, some students will have absolutely no practical experience from which to draw whilst others may possess a wealth of relevant material, so finding it relatively easy to apply examples based on their own knowledge and experience. It is anticipated that the text will be used to support formal classes and that elaboration and practical examples will therefore be considered in that context.

Structure

As far as possible, topics are largely free-standing and may be read virtually in isolation from the rest of the book. However, the nature of management is such that one thing is inextricably linked to something else – so much so, in fact, that it can often be difficult to tell where one topic ends and another begins. Really, there is no beginning and no end. Hence the content is structured simply according to what is perceived to be a logical sequence for student reading purposes.

It begins by considering the functional areas of management in the view that most students will already have knowledge of some of these and consequently will not be thrown into a swamp of new subject matter and terminology right at the beginning.

Part I also examines concepts and models used in management and organization theory, and looks at the different ways in which organizations are designed and structured to perform the task of management. Given that the literature of management is extensive, a table of well-known writers on management and organizations is provided at the end of Part I to give the reader a starting point for further study.

Part II is confined to the actual activities of managing whilst Part III selects four particular contexts in which managerial activities are carried out. The choice of areas is obviously conditioned by the preferences of the writer and the relevance seen in relation to current examination syllabi, as well as the likely practical applications which might realistically be encountered in the job situation. These four areas are given more detailed treatment than other topics in the text, but this is not meant to imply that they have greater significance or are more important, simply that they have been selected for elaboration here.

Concluding remarks

The handbook is intended to provide a key to understanding what management is all about. It is hoped that the material will provide a useful foundation upon which students may build – each according to his/her own interests. Management can be an attractive subject since it deals with 'live' issues. No two sets of problems are ever really quite the same. Indeed, one of the intriguing things about management is that there is always another way of looking at an issue and, moreover, always room for another point of view.

Introduction

How many of you see yourselves in a few years' time occupying a supervisory or a managerial position of one kind or another? Possibly quite a few, and those of you who do not are still likely to wish to maximize your potential in secretarial or administrative career terms. Whatever your ultimate aspirations and ambitions, your prospects will be greatly improved and your awareness sharpened when you have an appreciation of organizational problems and management issues.

To be an effective participant in anything requires knowledge of the rules, and so, too, with management. You cannot hope to contribute fully, let alone compete and possess credibility, without knowledge of the subject matter.

Many would argue that success in management activities is a matter of practice and experience, not to mention a stroke of luck along the way. There is possibly a lot of truth in what they say, but theory is also needed. To appreciate the nature of management it is necessary to understand the nature of organizations. But organizations are complex entities, so reliance on pure description will be inadequate. A greater level of analysis and understanding is called for in order to provide explanations and offer practical solutions. Theory provides the tools needed to undertake the analysis and it is fundamental to reaching a workable understanding.

Much of management theory has been around for a long time, and, given the pace of change, the question must inevitably arise as to how valuable and relevant it is today. Practitioners would probably suggest that a lot of theory is a waste of time and energy, but trainers are more likely to suggest that it is valuable as it forms the basis of experience and that we are what we are by virtue of our experience. The argument extends across a continuum and it will be a matter of trying to strike an effective balance. We need to prepare for the future, but one of the ways we can do this is by learning from the past.

Above all, management is an activity, and those indulging in it must be capable of applying their knowledge and understanding in ways which will achieve desired results.

Note: For ease of writing the masculine form has been used throughout with the exception of references made to secretaries. This is not meant to infer masculine or feminine identities, but simply to facilitate fluency. Alternatives may be substituted throughout.

PART I

About Management

'Management is a journey, not a destination.'
Sir Peter Parker, Chairman British Institute of Management
(*Management News*, January 1985)

The business of management is complex for a variety of reasons, but mainly because it deals with imponderables such as risk taking, prediction and human relationships. It is impossible to be prescriptive about what managers should do about such issues. The best approach – or even solution – for one situation may be wholly inadequate for another. Managing is an 'interventionist' activity, which ideally attempts to eliminate or minimize obstacles in favour of establishing effective practice and procedure, conducive to achieving the aims of the organization.

Management, then, is about exercising judgement which is frequently based on inadequate information and prompted by idiosyncrasies external to the organization. This is not to imply that management is continually engaged in one crisis or another. On the contrary, management exists to determine the way ahead in pursuit of organizational goals and to exert control over those factors crucial to the successful achievement of stated objectives.

Managing is a dynamic activity in that nothing stays the same for very long. The scope and pace of change in contemporary society require highly developed managerial skills which are capable of being utilized and adapted to a wide variety of situations.

To study management – and organizations – is to endeavour to make sense of different and often conflicting tensions in a variety of settings and, as a result, to suggest the kind of 'intervention' needed in a particular situation.

1
The Functions of Management

Before looking at the skills and techniques of management, consideration must be given to the functional tasks which managers perform. There is little point in discussing, for example, 'decision making' or 'communication' before taking account of what managers do.

Management functions are the tasks undertaken to enable the organization to achieve its purpose. Their extent and variety are determined by the nature and scope of the organization. For example, a large manufacturing organization will usually have a number of managers in overall control of the various day-to-day activities – viz. marketing (home and export), production, personnel, finance, and research and development. This chapter details the components of the principal functional areas of management typically found in a wide variety of organizations.

Eight principal functional areas are indicated in Fig. 1. Some organizations may give prominence to several of them whilst others may merge different functions in view of the close interrelationships which exist. No hard and fast rules can be applied here because the final outcome will be a

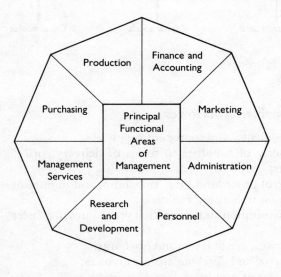

Fig. 1 Principal functions of management

consequence of the impact of factors such as size, ownership, technology and environment, which are discussed below.

The Purchasing Function

In today's highly competitive business environment, effective buying systems and procedures are of critical importance. Marginal increases in purchasing costs can severely affect profitability, particularly in situations where purchasing costs exceed labour costs (areas of high technology) or where very small profit margins operate (retail food outlets).

In simple terms the purchasing function is concerned with the acquisition of raw materials and manufactured component parts essential for **production**. In addition, purchasing may take on a centralized role across an organization whereby **all** items are acquired by a Central Purchasing Department, irrespective of whether or not they are directly involved in production activities. So a Central Purchasing Department would be responsible for securing the most competitive prices for everything bought by an organization, from raw materials, fixtures and fittings, equipment and office consumables to food for the canteen. Figure 2 represents the typical purchasing function.

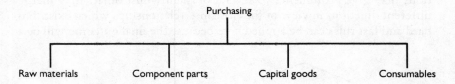

Fig. 2   The purchasing function

The purchasing function therefore involves:

- determining the nature, quality and sources of supply;
- ascertaining the reliability of suppliers in terms of delivery, price, quantities and discounts;
- maintaining stock control procedures – e.g. maximum and minimum holding levels, adequate warehousing facilities;
- devising appropriate distribution and requisition procedures in respect of stock held;
- negotiating purchase prices, credit terms and discounts;
- monitoring goods received and checking against invoices;
- seeking alternative sources of supply.

Purchasing Skills

Although the components which contribute to the purchasing function will be largely similar for all types of purchasing activity, the purchasing skills are not necessarily easily transferable from one type of organization to another. A high degree of specialist and technical knowledge is usually required by those concerned with purchasing activities, and 'buying' is not usually an activity carried out as an extra duty by departmental managers.

For example, a distinctive type of purchasing expertise will be called for in the textile industry. This will be based on knowledge and experience together with a network of contacts in the trade. By contrast, the purchasing function in the motor industry requires different specialist knowledge, experience and contacts, as will be the case for other organizations. Functional management tasks such as Administration or Personnel, on the other hand, will tend to be similar, irrespective of the nature of the organization and its activities.

The Production Function

The production function is primarily concerned with the manufacture of goods or with the provision of services. It is more usual to consider production in terms of the manufacture of goods from the raw material stage but it is important to recognize that other forms of organization – those providing a service (e.g. banks, local authority departments, hospitals, hotels and travel companies) – also have a production function. What is at stake in terms of the production function is the **end product** whether it be in the tangible form of finished goods or the intangible form of the consumer's perception of the quality and reliability of a service provided.

Product or market oriented?

The production function almost represents a business in its own right, so diverse are its roles and responsibilities, with the organizational structure being strongly influenced by the philosophy which determines the end product. For example, a major manufacturing organization which is concerned with producing a particular range of goods, **almost** regardless of demand, level of competition and share of the market, will be product oriented. On the other hand, an organization which produces goods in response to market and consumer needs will be market oriented. It is, however, possible for a company to change from being product oriented to becoming market oriented in order to survive. An example is the case of

Dunlop which originally concentrated almost totally on the manufacture of tyres and which has now diversified into producing sports and leisure goods.

Broadly speaking, production will usually be concerned with engineering, planning and control functions as illustrated in Fig. 3.

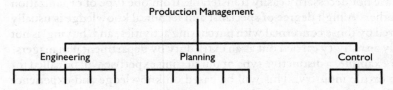

Fig. 3 The production function

In any event the functions of production are likely to include some or all of the following:

- planning in order to balance requirements against resources – orders/ sales forecasts against people, materials and machines;
- sequencing orders to ensure that delivery dates are met;
- batching orders together to achieve economies of scale;
- establishing a balanced mix between different product lines;
- ensuring compliance with legislation affecting the product in terms of both the manufacturing process and the end product – e.g. British Safety Council (safety standards at work), the British Standards Institution specifications and EEC regulations;
- matching manpower skills and training to the demands of the product or manufacturing process;
- using the available labour to maximum effect;
- monitoring plant maintenance, including the capacity, stress, loading or pressure on equipment used;
- liaising with other departments – e.g. Research and Development to determine product range;
- designing special tools for use in the manufacturing process;
- monitoring progress in order to ensure that the right goods arrive in the right place at the right time;
- utilizing technology to ensure the efficient application of methods and techniques in the production process;
- investigating the possibility of subcontracting and estimating the likely cost involved;
- keeping a balance between high and low margin orders;
- keeping customers informed and satisfied;
- controlling the level of stocks;
- taking corrective action to overcome any shortfalls in raw materials, labour and equipment;

- monitoring machine breakdowns;
- rescheduling work as necessary;
- devising strategies in order to respond to changes in demand determined by either external competition or consumer preferences – e.g. discontinuing one model and replacing it with another;
- developing and maintaining quality control systems;
- incorporating the capacity to diversify, given the need to respond to innovation and change.

These examples serve to provide an indication of the areas of activity involved in production and the types of decision which have to be reached.

Service industries

Whilst many of these points are more readily associated with the manufacturing side of production, it is necessary to comment briefly on the production function within service industries. As was suggested earlier, the emphasis will be client oriented where the end product will be a reflection of the customer's personal preference as necessitated by cost, convenience, choice, backup and so on.

The difference is possibly best illustrated by comparing the kind of choices to be made when selecting a piece of office equipment, such as a word processor, to deciding which firm of accountants or solicitors to deal with. In the former the client is able to examine a concrete object, study the data specification and try the machine out, arriving at a fairly definite quantitative assessment. When it comes to selecting professional services, on the other hand, the decision will be much more qualitative, being influenced by the advice of others and the quality of interpersonal relationships established between the client and the professionals.

The Research and Development Function

Irrespective of whether an organization is concerned with manufacturing products or providing services, an important and integral aspect of its activities will be the research and development function. Usually referred to as R & D, this is often an independent section or department in its own right, although it may, in other instances, be incorporated in the production function. The function and location of R & D will depend on the type of organization, the nature of the product or service, the degree of pressure exerted by external forces or competition in the market place and the durability or built-in obsolescence affecting production issues. Figure 4 illustrates the sort of activities undertaken by Research and Development.

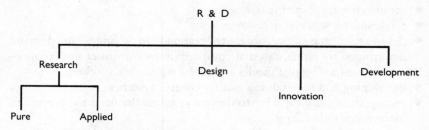

Fig. 4   The research and development function

Need for R & D

Many large organizations concern themselves with product or service diversification, as indicated in the previous section. In order to retain position in the market place, considerable investment is committed to research and development, with the intention of either improving existing goods or services or developing into new areas. Large corporations simply cannot afford to stand still in the face of competition, both from at home and abroad. Consequently, they must seek continually to improve what they offer by modifying existing products in order to attract the interest of customers. For example, few organizations offer the same product range today as they did, say, twenty years ago.

Innovation and change

Research and development is at the sharp end of innovation and change, often being involved in developing products far ahead of their time. The staff located within R & D could be said to represent the 'brains' of the organization, their task being to develop new ideas and to pioneer the introduction of highly competitive, desirable and, therefore, marketable goods. Given the level of investment allocated to R & D and the extended time scale envisaged for a return, it is vitally important to 'get it right' first time! The trick is to be innovative to good effect rather than for the sake of it. Therefore, a great deal of market research precedes the R & D stage, and, indeed, is often built into the entire process in order to ensure consumer interest, so reducing the degree of risk and expenditure.

The R & D function is likely to include the following:

- developing new products (processes or services) in response to market needs or demands;
- making short-term, low-cost product improvements – e.g. 'special editions' or new styling or packaging;
- determining long-term major R & D projects whilst accounting for the cost implications and the likelihood of failure;

- allocating priorities amongst competing project demands;
- designing prototypes for testing purposes;
- developing systems for the flexible and effective investment of resources into R & D projects;
- harnessing the activities of scientists and researchers for the benefit of the organization as a whole, and discouraging, where necessary, self-indulgent 'ego trips';
- setting time limits, where practicable, from the 'first idea' stage to product realization;
- deciding when to risk further investment into a research project and when to stop and cut losses;
- aiming to achieve cost effectiveness in administering and co-ordinating the research programme.

Investing in R & D

The R & D process is complex and expensive; consequently, considerable importance is attached to information gathering through market research in an attempt to substantiate or provide evidence that an idea will ultimately prove to be a worthwhile investment. Organizations are therefore highly cost conscious when it comes to R & D, which suggests that only the larger companies can truly afford it, and even then concentration will tend to be on applied research, leaving pure research to universities. However, many organizations, regardless of size, have developed close links with university research departments and with research organizations such as Professional Technology Centres (commercial organizations which go out and market their expertise to industry) throughout the country. Even so, there still exists a gap between pure and applied research, largely as a result of failure to utilize the knowledge already available by promoting its commercial applications.

Failure of R & D initiatives

Despite the need to innovate and develop new products, R & D is one of the first casualties during a recession as resources are switched in order to maintain current production levels, with fewer companies turning their new ideas into reality on the production line. The effects of underfunding R & D are far reaching, and failure to invest can leave the way open for more commercially oriented countries to take the initiative. Almost certainly it will mean losing out to foreign competitors, especially the USA or Japan, who recognize its importance and maintain a high level of investment in this area of activity.

Risk and R & D

The risk element involved in R & D activities is associated with what must essentially remain as levels of prediction. Usually, short-term modifications to products or services are low risk, whereas major changes (e.g. product replacement) incur long-term strategies and therefore are high risk and prone to failure, due almost entirely to the time factor. After all, no one really knows whether customers will actually buy a product in five years' time – therefore, predicting the volume of sales in the future remains, despite market research findings, an informed guess.

The Personnel Function

Organizations depend on the human resource, i.e. the people they employ to carry out their duties and responsibilities. As a result, management will need to give careful consideration to their general well-being in order that they may meet their obligations and complete their tasks successfully.

In a small organization with fewer than fifty employees, there will be day-to-day contact with the boss, and so it is usually through co-operation on informal lines that the personnel function is carried out. For example, individual employee holiday arrangements, or leave to attend further education or training courses, or starting and finishing times will be negotiated informally, but usually directly, by those involved.

In contrast, the personnel function in a large company will be undertaken by a specialist department working to procedures and company policy applicable to the whole organization. The importance of such a department and its activities cannot be over-estimated since it is a key factor in determining the attitude and commitment of employees to their work. A successful organization will almost certainly have a caring and enterprising Personnel Department whose principal aim will be to motivate staff and help integrate their personal ambitions and aspirations with those of the organization. Personnel activities typically include the specialized functions shown in Fig. 5. However organized, the personnel

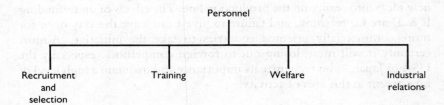

Fig. 5   The personnel function

functions will be mainly concerned with establishing a good working atmosphere and a partnership between management and staff.

Personnel management is therefore involved in some or all of the following, to a greater or lesser extent:

- manpower planning;
- recruitment and selection;
- promotion and distribution of staff;
- implementation of employment legislation;
- motivation through incentive schemes;
- staff development and training schemes, in-house and/or external, directly related to improving skills or acquiring new ones – e.g. leadership, supervisory, communication, machine operation, new technology;
- design of job specifications;
- career counselling;
- staff appraisal and evaluation;
- salary and wage matters – design of pay structure and format (e.g. piece-work, bonus schemes or hourly rates) – following negotiation between management and unions;
- redundancies and redeployment;
- dismissal procedures, including attendance at Industrial Tribunals;
- industrial relations and trade union involvements;
- safety – compliance with statutory regulations;
- health and welfare of employees;
- working environment;
- working conditions, especially with reference to the structure of the working day – starting and finishing times, breaks, the operation of flexitime and holiday entitlements;
- suggestion schemes;
- canteen facilities;
- additional employee benefits – e.g. hairdresser, luncheon vouchers, dental and chiropody services, and profit-sharing schemes;
- recreational and sporting facilities.

Quality of personnel service

The scope of provision will depend on the size of the organization. A large company employing several thousand people could provide many, if not all, of the services and functions outlined above, whilst smaller organizations would provide only a few. It is the quality of the service which matters, together with the amount of care seen to be given to employees, their preferences and their work situation.

Identifying staff training needs

A significant part of the functions of the Personnel Department is to maintain up-to-date information on staff by conducting a staff audit to assess and identify weaknesses and thereafter make recommendations regarding up-dating and retraining. Furthermore, the Personnel Manager in particular should be aware of the highly talented members of staff working within the organization in order to attempt to keep them rather than lose them to rival organizations. Staff interviews, staff reports and assessment procedures are useful tools to spot confident and competent personnel and thereafter to seek ways of keeping them.

Many of the functions of Personnel highlighted above are dealt with in more detail in Part III.

The Marketing Function

Central to any organization is the marketing function. In its simplest form it refers to selling goods or services. Nevertheless, marketing is a complex process involving a number of key decisions which need to be taken in close association with the Production and Purchasing Departments. Policy decisions involve what to sell, how to sell, where to sell and how much to sell for. To a large extent these will depend on the nature of the product(s) produced or service(s) provided, and the extent of competition and market forces generally.

A well-defined market is a prerequisite for producing goods or services. It will indicate whether to specialize or diversify; whether to sell direct, via retail outlets or by mail order; whether to restrict sales locally, regionally, nationally or expand internationally; and how to arrive at a price. Marketing is therefore about selling the right products, in the right place, at the right price, at the right time, in the right way to the right people.

A range of expertise is therefore required by staff operating within Marketing Departments, and the overall marketing function is likely to be split along the lines indicated in Fig. 6.

By subdividing the marketing function it is possible to identify more precisely the elements which are included and the type of work involved.

Research is concerned with finding out who the customer is likely to be, what he wants, how to reach him and how satisfied he is with the product or service.

Market research activities will be likely to include:

- analysing previous sales records;
- studying published statistics;
- reading technical and trade journals;

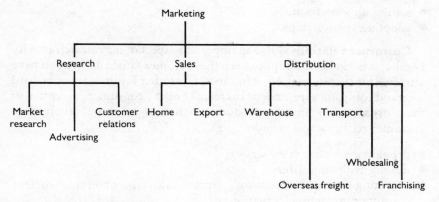

Fig. 6 The marketing function

- comparing and contrasting competitors' products and specifications;
- conducting interviews;
- preparing questionnaires;
- distributing samples;
- carrying out tests;
- identifying age and sex groups together with income levels;
- studying purchasing frequencies;
- establishing regional/geographical variations in terms of product/ service demand.

Advertising is concerned with informing potential customers of the nature and availability of the product or service, in a manner fitting the company's corporate image and in line with its advertising policy. The activities and ways in which this is likely to be done will include:

- identifying the appropriate media;
- appointing a Press Information Officer;
- preparing press advertisements and releases;
- utilizing radio and television commercials;
- designing publicity posters;
- featuring on hoardings and on public transport;
- setting up point-of-sale displays;
- devising publicity stunts;
- distributing sales literature and leaflets;
- introducing free samples and gifts;
- running sales promotion exercises – e.g. road shows;
- running competitions;
- attending exhibitions and trade fares;
- giving demonstrations;

- setting up showrooms;
- adopting sponsorships.

Customer relations is also an important aspect of the research activity because it is vital to attempt to keep the customer satisfied once you have attracted his custom in the first instance. Customer loyalties are often hard won and companies are anxious to create a healthy consumer perception of their organization and its products. Activities of those involved in customer relations will include:

- providing an 'after sales' service;
- dealing with complaints;
- operating within the statutory framework – e.g. observing current consumer protection legislation;
- establishing a consumer advice service;
- setting up a Customer Services Department, where appropriate;
- monitoring customer opinion;
- responding to customer preferences;
- developing customer loyalty;
- co-ordinating and disseminating information gathered throughout the relevant departments of the company.

Sales is the central aspect of the marketing function and is concerned with the actual transmission of goods or services to the consumer. It involves the effort of finding the customers and persuading them to buy the product. Effective sales management will result by obtaining optimum value from market research and advertising activities and good consumer relations. Dependent upon the nature of the organization and the product or service being marketed, actual sales management is likely to fall into one of the categories identified in Fig. 6 above.

Home sales refers here to the sales processed within the Sales Department *per se*. Sales office work involves:

- recording and processing all documentation concerning orders and invoices;
- dealing with customers and enquiries;
- routing certain queries to relevant sales force personnel;
- preparing quotations;
- maintaining customer records;
- liaising with sales representatives;
- analysing salesmen's records and co-ordinating their paperwork;
- preparing sales statistics based on product, sales area and representative;
- comparing and contrasting sales figures with those available from competitors.

Export sales will form a major part of the business of some organizations. Successful exporters are encouraged by the Government because they bring revenue into the country. However, the problems of exporting goods are infinitely greater than those of selling at home, for a variety of reasons. These are mainly due to the different standards required by the importing countries in terms of both specifications and health regulations, not to mention the documentation and paperwork involved. Also, there can be language difficulties and fears of political unrest, economic instability and inhibiting currency regulations. Companies involved in exporting must familiarize themselves thoroughly with the wealth of information which is available on foreign trade from sources such as the Department of Trade and Industry and the EEC.

The functions of an Export Department, in addition to those listed for home sales, will be likely to include:

- processing all necessary special export documentation – e.g. bills of lading, certificates of origin, shipping notes, declarations, insurance certificates;
- specialist packaging and dispatch;
- keeping up to date and ensuring that all essential regulations are complied with;
- communicating with branches, agents and consignors overseas;
- handling all financial and insurance matters.

All the work achieved in producing the goods and finding a buyer can be lost if the distribution channel fails. Effective distribution techniques are essential if stock levels are to be reduced, so freeing working capital and reducing the need to borrow.

Fast delivery by low-cost transport is a necessary element of the overall product price. At product launch stage it may even be necessary to employ express carriers, but once demand for the product is established it should be possible to switch to a less costly means of distribution. All organizations need to use resources to their maximum potential, and consequently there is frequently conflict between time and capacity.

The principal channels of distribution are indicated in Fig. 6. Warehousing refers to the distribution of finished goods to strategically placed warehouses where large quantities may be held at any one time awaiting dispatch. Sometimes goods may be passed on (sold) to a wholesaler who acts as an intermediary between the manufacturer and the customer. This may often enable a supplier to reach a larger number of clients than might be possible if he were to sell the goods direct.

Franchising is the ultimate channel of distribution where the rights to sell or even to manufacture are transferred to another within a given marketplace. Typical examples of franchising are Wimpy Bars and other fast food outlets such as Pizzaland. They all conform to set standards and have a predetermined pricing structure although success or failure in the final analysis will rest with the owner of the franchise. Another area of activity where this distribution technique is also practised is in recruitment consultancies such as Alfred Marks which now operates on a franchise arrangement, particularly in the Provinces.

Characteristics of successful marketing

Successful marketing – whatever the commodity, whether it be a product or a service – will depend on a combination of some or perhaps all of the functions referred to above. Although it is undoubtedly simpler to associate the concept of marketing with goods, it is important to recognize that considerable attention is also given to marketing all manner of services and less tangible commodities such as places, holidays, entertainment, education, political parties and ideologies, and even people.

However, getting it right depends on striking the right balance of knowledge, skill, expertise, experience, flair, instinct, energy, imagination, timing and, of course, luck. It is interesting to reflect how fickle the customer can be and how swayed by fad and fashion. Sometimes the most unexpected, under-resourced and poorly marketed product can prove to be an enormous success, whilst another product, which may have undergone an elaborate and costly sales campaign, involving double-page advertisements in the national press, extensive television coverage and various other publicity exercises, may still fail to achieve the desired and anticipated results.

Promoting product or service awareness

The marketing activity is closely connected – and, indeed, dependent – on the ways in which potential customers perceive the product or services offered. Consequently, marketing departments often go to considerable lengths to persuade people as to the 'quality', 'durability' or 'efficiency' of their particular goods.

The medium they select to advertise their wares will depend on the nature of the product and on the particular type of consumer they wish to attract. Hence television is used for soap powder, beer, telephones, summer holidays, paint and food but not for exclusive watches, Rolls Royce cars, mink coats or educational establishments.

Company images

Surprisingly, perhaps, not all large organizations promote their goods or services through extensive advertising campaigns. Compare and contrast typical retail outlets on the average main shopping street. Some advertise extensively, whilst others (e.g. Marks & Spencer p.l.c.) scarcely advertise at all and yet remain an outstanding example of success in retailing. Conversely, British Rail (a nationalized industry) frequently mounts a national advertising campaign despite public awareness of its availability and services, and still runs at a loss.

Marketing is the quintessential activity of all commercial organizations which thrive or survive on latest sales figures. This is what makes marketing so pressured and so stressful yet potentially highly rewarding for its sales executives and marketing managers who have high risk functions and who occupy what might be termed the 'hot seats' of the organization.

The Administration Function

The administration function, irrespective of the nature and size of the organization, is the one concerned with the paperwork and day-to-day running of what might loosely be termed office-type activities. Administration is always secondary to the principal *raison d'être* of the organization. Nevertheless, its existence is intrinsic to operational success and effectiveness in that its activities both complement and control the primary activities of the organization.

Without administrative support, organizations simply could not survive in a modern world which demands the submission of returns, the maintenance of records and the myriad other routine paper-based activities that are essential in organizations whether they be manufacturing companies or hospitals or local authorities.

What might be classified as administration will vary from organization to organization but is likely to include those illustrated in Fig. 7.

The administration function will be determined by the nature of the organization, but responsibilities are likely to include:

- providing centralized administrative support in respect of internal collection, sorting and delivery of mail;
- providing telephone service via a centralized switchboard;
- providing a duplicating and photocopying service via an in-house print room facility;
- providing a centralized filing system for the storage and maintenance of company records and files;
- providing a complete secretarial support service in the form of shorthand and audio dictation, typing, word processing and committee support and attendance;
- ensuring the effective operation of a stationery and stock control system for all office supplies;
- designing standard forms for use throughout the organization;

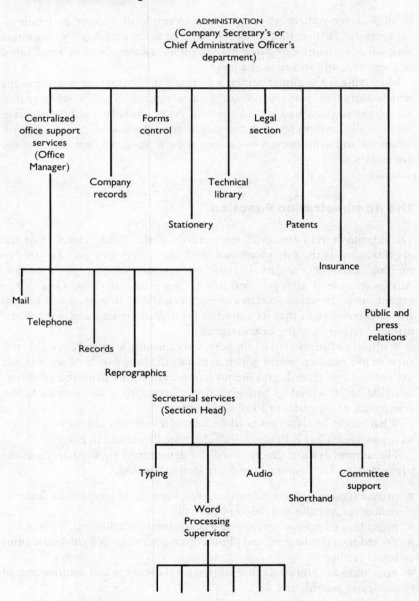

ADMINISTRATION
(Company Secretary's or
Chief Administrative Officer's
department)

Centralized
office support
services
(Office
Manager)

Forms
control

Legal
section

Company
records

Technical
library

Stationery

Patents

Insurance

Mail

Telephone

Public and
press
relations

Records

Reprographics

Secretarial services
(Section Head)

Typing

Audio

Committee
support

Shorthand

Word
Processing
Supervisor

Fig. 7   The administration function

- devising a system of forms control which operates throughout the organization;
- maintaining company records as required by the Companies Acts;
- handling all work in connection with the allocation, registration and transfer of shares;
- maintaining a comprehensive and up-to-date technical library;
- representing the organization on legal matters;
- providing legal advice as required – e.g. contracts, trades description, company law, employment legislation, health and safety legislation, working conditions, data protection;
- ensuring that new ideas and inventions are patented as appropriate;
- providing insurance protection in respect of accident, fire, theft, fraud, damage to persons and property;
- presenting company information to the public and publicizing company activities;
- developing a corporate image;
- preparing press releases;
- advising company personnel on media coverage and appearances;
- keeping staff informed of company plans and developments, perhaps via the publication of a house magazine.

Many of the functions indicated above will be transacted on an organization-wide basis – i.e. they will be centralized. Centralization of activities is both economical for the organization in terms of staff utilization, equipment, materials and space and will facilitate specialization of tasks.

This in turn has the effect of producing many line management roles within the framework of administration. For example, Centralized Office Support Services may come under the general control of an Office Manager, accountable to the Chief Administrative Officer (CAO), but so diversified are the activities of the services provided that specialists will occupy supervisory positions within the different sections. Therefore, the Mail Room may have a Senior Mailing Clerk, whilst the Records Section may have a Chief Filing Clerk and the Head of Secretarial Services may even require the support of yet another supervisory tier in the form of a Word Processing Supervisor (see Fig. 7).

The Finance and Accounting Function

The success or failure of any organization is ultimately reflected in its financial position as evidenced in the publication of its annual Report and Accounts. All organizations, but particularly those in the public sector, where there is an increasing emphasis on value for money, must be accountable in financial terms. This means that attention has to be given to finance at all stages, from the raising of funds, through the application of resources and the accompanying accounting procedures, to the results achieved, together with corresponding profit margins and hence the potential for the future.

Management has a corporate responsibility to shareholders and all others who may be said to have a vested interest in an organization's activities to make the best possible use of all funds which are at their disposal, as well as making adequate contingency plans for raising additional resources should they be required.

The financial activities of any organization are likely to be split up into three main areas, as indicated in Fig. 8. Many aspects of finance will be concerned with more than one area; e.g. the accounting procedures relating to different departments will be concerned with both financial accounting and cost accounting. Similarly, capital and revenue expenditure will be significant in the preparation of budgets but will also be represented in Final Accounts.

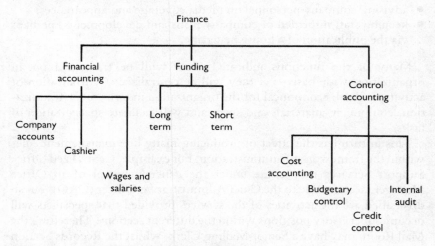

Fig. 8   The finance and accounting function

Finance and accounting are important and highly specialized management activities which command considerable significance and associated power within any organization. The overall functions are likely to include:

- the preparation of company accounts;
- the maintenance of accurate records in respect of accounts payable by the company (i.e. its creditors) and accounts due to the company (i.e. its debtors);
- an account of how money is used departmentally;

- a detailed analysis of all receipts and payment of monies handled by the company, including those internally sanctioned – i.e. wages, expenses, petty cash;
- the calculation and preparation of all wages and salaries due to staff, including payments in respect of overtime, incentive schemes, bonuses and allowances;
- the preparation of departmental budgets – annual, monthly and weekly;
- the analysis of departmental capital and revenue expenditure set against budgets;
- complete cost control exercises to assess expenditure incurred at the different stages of production – e.g. the cost of materials, work (wages and salaries), overheads and other expenses;
- the operation of a system of credit control to assess the credit worthiness of prospective customers;
- the vetting of financial transactions via a series of internal audits and checks – e.g. ledger entries, posting and cash handling;
- ascertaining possible sources of long-term funds for the organization – e.g. share issue, debenture holdings, loans, government grants, mortgaging;
- identifying medium-term borrowing facilities – e.g. bank overdrafts, finance and discount house arrangements, extended credit facilities, leasing arrangements;
- assessing the appropriateness of alternative sources of funds;
- investigating the possibility of securing financial assistance from the European Economic Community (EEC);
- investigating the potential of securing central and local government grants and incentives – e.g. Regional Development Grants (RDGs);
- comparing and contrasting different forms of investment;
- applying different analytical techniques to financial and accounting procedures as a means of assisting financial decision making – e.g. cash flow analysis, profitability ratios, break even analysis, cost/benefit analysis;
- introducing computerized methods – e.g. spreadsheets.

Given the highly specialized nature of these activities, it is outside the scope of a general text on management to provide a more detailed analysis of the functions and techniques which are applied. The synopsis above is intended to provide useful guidelines.

The Management Services Function

This functional area of management is a more recent inclusion as a principal area and centres around the specialist services and provisions which the management of an organization may call upon to support planning and policy-making activities and to improve organizational efficiency. It serves to draw together, often in one unit, a range of expertise provided by specialists.

An organizational awareness on the part of departmental managers of the existence of such a provision is vital in order that the services may be used to the full. Where such a provision does exist it is unnecessary for all managers to attempt to become experts in everything. All they need is the knowledge that such support skills are available to them together with an understanding of how and under what conditions they might find it appropriate to call upon them.

The diagrammatic presentation in Fig. 9 indicates the kinds of expertise which might be found within an organization in respect of management services. As with the functional areas already considered, the extent of

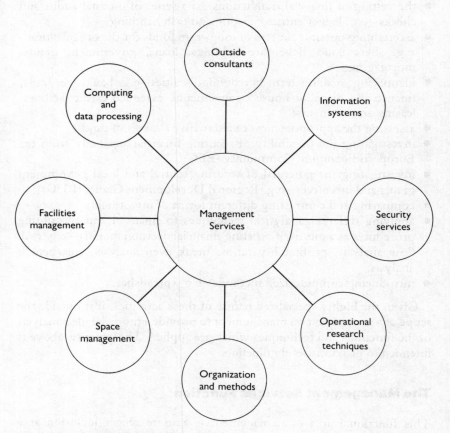

Fig. 9 The management services function

involvement will vary according to the type and size of organization, with smaller companies making greater calls on outside consultancies.

The activities undertaken by the different service units suggested would be as follows.

Organization and methods

Organization and methods (O & M) is the application of work study techniques to the office. It operates on an internal consultancy basis with the intention of improving office and administrative efficiency throughout an organization. It is a service which requires careful and diplomatic implementation. Otherwise it may be met with hostility and opposition from the staff involved, who may well feel threatened and frustrated by what they perceive as an invasion of their privacy and management criticism and lack of confidence in present procedures. However, where advance notice and due consultation and participation are included the results can be effective. Organization and methods involves:

- analysing current work patterns;
- reviewing clerical procedures;
- studying the forms currently in use;
- examining individual procedures;
- timing tasks;
- assessing machine usage;
- monitoring staff movement;
- examining office layout;

and is aimed at:

- setting standards of performance;
- devising new forms and often reducing the number of existing ones;
- reducing paperwork and paper flow;
- eliminating redundant activities;
- speeding up routines;
- maximizing use of office equipment;
- recommending the introduction of new equipment where necessary;
- eliminating unnecessary staff movement;
- improving office layout.

Specialists in O & M may be called in where there is a change in organizational structure, where productivity is considered to be low, where new systems and equipment are to be introduced or where there has been a move to new accommodation.

Computing and Data Processing

The introduction of a computer and computerized manipulation of data will have a major impact on any organization, especially on the speed, quantity and quality of information which it is able to put at the disposal of management. It brings about a greater degree of centralization within an organization. In fact, many functional areas of management have been virtually taken over by computer – e.g. accounting procedures and payment of wages. Computing is an extremely specialized area of activity and as such is handled by experts at all stages from design and programming through the control phase to the operational aspects. This has meant that many routine jobs previously undertaken by clerks are now performed on the computer. Therefore, certain middle management functions which involved the supervision of such staff have virtually disappeared, being replaced by computer specialists who interpret the computer results and pass them directly to top management. This has the effect of 'flattening' the organizational pyramid (see page 45) by removing a tier and pushing authority and responsibility further down the line. The work of the Computer Section or Electronic Data Processing (EDP) as it is often called will involve:

- designing effective and efficient systems (the systems analyst's function)
- programming the computer to perform the tasks (the programmer's function)
- preparing the raw data for input to computer
- loading the appropriate programmes   } the operator's function
- supervising the running of the programmes
- ensuring that the right information is sent at the right time (the processing controller's function)
- maintaining an accurate library of information (the data base controller's function).

In terms of business applications the possibilities are limitless throughout literally all departments and sections of an organization. The advantages to management are:

- the speed with which information can be processed;
- the accuracy of the information produced (errors are few and far between and will usually be the result of bad programming ('rubbish in, rubbish out');
- the ability to up-date information constantly and quickly;
- the ability to standardize procedures;

- the flexibility of computers in handling different tasks;
- the problem-solving capacity;
- the ability to simulate real situations.

There are relatively few disadvantages for management, the principal problems being:

- the pace of technology and the computer market, and hence the dating of equipment;
- the danger of becoming inundated with more information than can realistically be handled, given the capacity of the computer to produce it so quickly and easily;
- the need for specialist staff at all stages of operations.

Operational Research Techniques

These involve the use of mathematics in management decision making, and as such are useful only where problems are quantifiable. Certain areas of work do, therefore, lend themselves more readily to such applications – stock control, production scheduling, machine loading, investment decisions and the like. The use of these techniques does not require advanced knowledge of mathematics and statistics but relies on an understanding of simpler techniques such as the proper use of tables and graphs, together with the ability to assess their validity and relevance in reaching decisions based on their application.

Typical of the sorts of techniques used are:

- linear programming;
- network analysis – e.g. Critical Path Analysis (CPA) or Programme Evaluation and Review Technique (PERT);
- probability theory;
- queuing theory;
- simulation activity.

Information Systems

Management information systems are formal mechanisms set up to provide relevant information throughout organizations for all those who need it. In establishing an information system, an organization must consider:

- what information needs to be held;
- who will use the information;
- in what form it will be required;
- who will receive it;
- the purpose for which it is intended.

The potential within any organization to make use of information is enormous. Consequently, the volume of information which needs to be handled and processed will require a computer.

Information is held on computer data bases and is accessible to any authorized person in an organization for whatever application, in whatever format they wish. The data base is organized in such a way that it will allow a large number of users simultaneously to draw information from it for a variety of purposes. The data bases may be internal to the organization and/or external and capable of access by any company wishing to make use of the information.

Imagine a management information system operating within a large local authority. Information would be held on the data base in respect of all ratepayers – e.g. their names and addresses, the rateable value of their properties, their method of payment of rates, whether they had put forward requests for planning permission or changes of use of premises, to name but a few possibilities. Without computers, collection of data on this scale would be virtually impossible without an army of clerks and multiple hard copies of the necessary information.

The advantages of well-conceived management information systems are:

- the ability to produce accurate, up-to-date information at high speed;
- the provision of increased efficiency throughout the organization;
- the improved use of resources;
- enhanced management decision-making capability;
- the potential to introduce additional checks and controls with the minimum amount of effort;
- the ability to utilize the system to reduce the traditional constraints brought about by distance and time factors;
- more efficient administration;
- increased profit-making potential.

Three less obvious and more peripheral areas which none the less provide a valuable management services function are as follows.

Space management describes the management and control of an organization's accommodation in respect of the siting, planning, building, structure, design, layout, maintenance and allocation of space within an organization. This may be closely linked with operational research at the planning and construction stages when critical path analysis may be applied to the activities in order to minimize the time to be taken on the whole project.

Facilities management is also an increasingly important specialist area, concerned with the total provision of all facilities used within a building – heating, lighting, ventilation, communications, furnishings, fittings and equipment.

Security systems will also be centralized and controlled by an expert to whom management can refer as and when necessary. Security is a major concern for all organizations in that there is no such thing as 'total security', only a concerted effort to achieve as near to it as possible. Security will encompass both security of information and confidentiality and aspects of safety as it applies to health, fire, accident and damage to persons and property.

These three aspects of the extended management services function are all discussed in more detail in Part III.

The organization of management services

The way in which a Management Services Department or Unit is organized will depend on several factors:

- the nature of the organization to which it belongs;
- the extent of centralization which exists within the organization;
- the range of activities within its remit;
- the level of importance attached to the different activities – e.g. has one specialism assumed more importance than all the others?
- the status of the department within the organization;
- the inter-relationships which exist between it and other departments;
- the calibre of the staff.

Summary

Each of the management functions discussed will be in evidence to a greater or lesser extent in all organizations. The larger the organization, the more likely it is that the functions of management will co-exist and be readily identifiable as discrete departments, units or sections. For smaller organizations the functions may be merged, with managers having more diversified roles leading to fusion rather than separation of functions.

What is important to bear in mind is the interdependency of functions, departments and people. Nothing happens in isolation. There is always the need for close liaison because decisions made in one department will frequently affect another. Also, it is important to recognize that the titles used to describe different functions will vary dependent upon the nature of the industry, as will the type of work carried out within the different departments or sections.

Nevertheless, a consideration of management functions does provide an insight into the managerial and supervisory activities actually carried out whilst, at the same time, pointing out the complexities involved.

2
Concepts, Theories and Models

'Analysis is an important prerequisite of action.'

Charles Handy
Understanding Organizations

Concepts

'Concepts', 'theories' and 'models' of organizations and management represent ways of looking at how organizations work and what makes them tick. A change of gear is required in order to move from a description of what managers do towards the analytical perspective which homes in on the organizational setting and the interplay of variables which affect the behaviour of both managers and staff. Concepts, theories and models are the essential tools for such analysis.

Concepts are no more than ideas which may be evaluated alongside ongoing work situations. In turn, they may generate a series of propositions about the way in which things might be improved. This, however, is more likely to emerge with the application of **theories**, which are combinations of groups of concepts brought together to explain a particular problem or phenomenon. Theories tend to belong to a particular school of thought – e.g. classical, action, system or contingency. The main value of theory is that it deepens understanding of complex issues and enhances the quality of judgement required to implement effective strategies of management in relation to any given set of circumstances. Organizational and management **models** are intended to be used as the basis for comparison with 'live' situations. Their value lies in the explanation given for the differences between the two.

Aims, objectives and policies

An organization may be defined as the bringing together of resources, both human and physical, with the deliberate intention of securing specified outcomes. An essential element of management activity is the setting of aims and objectives to help establish and sustain a sense of direction in order to guide the enterprise over a period of time. Given the rate of change and innovation in contemporary society, aims should be kept under scrutiny and revised if necessary in the light of developments.

Aims are broad statements of general intent which provide a backcloth against which more precise objectives may be formulated. They should be general enough to enable wide interpretation and maximum flexibility, but should, nevertheless, be capable of attainment. Aims are the ultimate goals to which an organization wishes to aspire.

Aims are brought into sharper focus when they are translated into objectives, which are clearly definable, readily achievable and understood by all those sharing the activities of the organization.

Objectives should provide a sound indication of *where* an organization is hoping to go and *what* it hopes to achieve, whilst **policies** will determine *how* the objectives are to be realized. It is only when objectives are specified that policies can be formulated and plans drawn up. Objectives provide a useful benchmark against which progress can be monitored, problems anticipated and success evaluated. Policies will be formulated taking into account the time scale, so any change in long-range objectives will necessitate policy modifications *en route*.

Ultimately the responsibility for formulating objectives rests with the Board of Directors of an organization, and the preparation of these will help form the basis of a Corporate Plan. Where a company is limited, the 'Objects' will be listed within the company's Memorandum of Association but these are not the same as objectives and would be too vague and wide ranging to be of real value.

Identifying aims and objectives

The identification of aims can be relatively easy. For instance, an organization can indicate that its aims are to produce high-quality merchandise, create good opportunities for employment and raise a high level of profit for its shareholders. However, when seen in the context of a dynamic market and all the external constraints which affect organizations (see Fig. 10) the need to determine more precise objectives becomes readily apparent.

Identifying the aims of the organization is not the same as achieving them; consequently, what is required is a strategy for implementation in the first place and a mechanism for continual evaluation in the second place. Formulating objectives helps provide specific and practical guidelines, taking account of a number of internal and external factors as shown in Fig. 10.

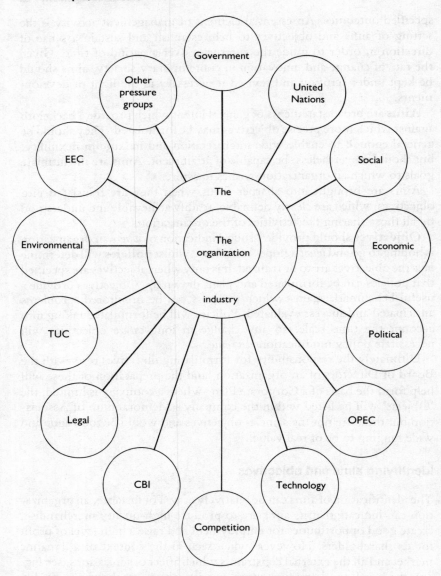

Fig. 10   Factors/agencies influencing organizations

Factors determining objectives

What are the considerations which need to be taken into account when formulating objectives? These will be a mix of internal and external factors, and will include:

- the ethos or identity which the organization has – i.e. whether it is economically, socially or aesthetically oriented;
- the organization's past history;
- the organization's future prospects;
- external interests and pressure groups;
- economic viability;
- the size of the organization;
- scope for development and product diversification;
- the element of risk which exists;
- the possibilities for structural change – e.g. takeovers, mergers, internal rationalization, new internal organization;
- the impact of technology;
- the state of the market generally;
- the extent of competition from other organizations;
- the adequacy of existing resources – physical (accommodation, plant and equipment), human and financial;
- the potential to raise additional capital;
- the legal framework within which the organization operates;
- the capacity to change objectives.

It is important to recognize that setting objectives need not be confined to the organization as a whole. Departments, units or sections will often need to identify their own objectives in order that they may work closely and consistently within the organizational framework.

Policies

Objectives are transformed into action via policies. Policy making is also a function of top management and will broadly be concerned with decisions affecting, for example:

finance
personnel
marketing
production
accommodation

aspects of which are considered throughout this book. Policy decisions may be defined as choosing between alternative, practicable courses of action, and it is from these that organizations will form a Corporate Plan (see Part II). Once determined, policy decisions need to be communicated down the organization to all levels of staff, where they must be clearly understood if they are to be translated into action, strategies and techniques which enable the organization to realize its objectives.

Power

Power is a concept frequently associated with people in high places and is a significant feature of all role systems. However, it is possible to possess power by virtue of specialist knowledge or expertise or personal charisma, irrespective of position within the hierarchy of the formal organization structure. In simple terms, power is the capacity which one individual possesses to influence the behaviour of another, in a particular set of circumstances. Often this will mean getting people to do things they don't really want to do. Individuals acquire power, and thus the ability to affect others, through:

- position or status;
- expertise – e.g. the specialist nature of the role;
- the possession of information (perhaps through access to the more powerful);
- authority vested in them;
- proximity to someone in a high level position – e.g. PA to the Managing Director;
- physical presence;
- being seen in the 'right' places;
- by making the 'right' decisions – e.g. joining the department that is on the up rather than on the decline.

Reference is often made to the term 'power game'. This is really a sort of 'power one-upmanship' activity which is likely to be encountered in the upper echelons of management hierarchies where rivalries and jealousies will exist as they do elsewhere. Participants develop 'the arts' of the game; for example:

- the art of learning the niceties of organizational games;
- the art of successful 'name dropping';
- the art of being seen at all the 'right' places with all the 'right' people;
- the art of taking credit for departmental successes;
- the art of reporting all the good news and leaving others to deliver the bad news;
- the art of discrediting the opposition.

Power can be both productive and destructive, and it is always important that managers handle it to the advantage of the organization. A healthy power struggle – which suggests that power may be more than one sided – can be useful in terms of developing the competitive instinct and so increasing productivity, creativity and teamwork. Too much conflict, however, may be destructive. It is a question of striking an effective balance and recognizing 'the games people play'.

Authority

It is important to recognize the distinction between power and authority. Authority is the legitimate right to do something, and it is the possession of the authority which brings about the power. Allocating authority is an essential aspect of any large organization which operates on formal lines. Authority is conferred upon individuals by those in positions of superiority and can therefore be delegated (see page 153). The extent of authority must be made clear to the individual, who is then required to operate within the limits of that authority. When an individual accepts the authority to do something, he also accepts the fact that he will be accountable to a superior for the way in which he uses the authority and the results which prevail. Individuals will be given authority where it is felt that their skills and qualities are commensurate with the responsibility inherent in the task. Authority is most useful in an organization where it is given to the person who can make any accompanying decision most expertly.

Lines of authority flow downwards throughout an organization whilst accountability operates upwards. For example, lines of authority may run from the Chief Executive to the Marketing Executive to the Sales Manager to the Assistant Sales Manager and ultimately to Sales Representatives. This is often referred to as the 'scalar principle' whereas the hierarchical structure is the 'chain of command'. Additional reference is made to the concept of authority in Chapters 3 and 12.

Co-ordination

Co-ordination refers to the synchronizing of activities within an organization. Its success depends upon the ability to dovetail the often disparate operations in a harmonious and integrated way in the pursuit of common objectives. Effective co-ordination is one of the primary goals of a manager and will call upon a wide range of skills and abilities:

- a clear understanding of objectives and policies;
- careful planning;
- accurate definition of duties;
- good organization;
- well-designed procedures;
- effective communication of all kinds, both formal and informal, oral and written, lateral, horizontal and vertical;
- best use of all available resources;
- consistent techniques;
- a highly tuned sense of timing.

The essence of effective co-ordination is time. Time will be crucial at all stages as independent activities of different sections, departments, groups and individuals are drawn together to form an integrated whole.

Control

Control is the final step in what might be termed the 'management cycle' of basic management tasks – viz. planning, organizing, directing, supervising, motivating, co-ordinating and controlling – which are fundamental to all management activity. Control mechanisms will, in fact, be in operation throughout the cycle of activities in order to assess whether plans are working effectively or whether adjustments need to be made to correct any shortcomings or weaknesses. Without such interim mechanisms, all manner of minor inefficiencies would go unchecked and overall standards would drop. Controls are therefore 'calls to account' and are essential to the effective and efficient operation of any organization. The types of controls instituted by different organizations vary but usually include:

- the setting of quantity standards – e.g. sales quotas, production targets;
- quality controls;
- work scheduling;
- reporting mechanisms;
- progress reviews;
- internal audits;
- procedural manuals;
- monitoring activities;
- visual presentation of data;
- monthly statistics;
- budgetary control;
- stock control;
- time sheets;
- staff discipline.

Formal Organizations

Formal organizations are concerned with who is in charge and who is responsible to whom. This is usually represented diagrammatically in the form of an organization chart (see page 48) outlining the allocation of staff and resources across the various divisions, departments and sections. Such charts also serve to indicate the roles of individuals within the organization (e.g. managers, supervisors and general employees) and superior/subordinate relationships which exist within these roles along with the various levels of responsibility and authority associated with them. See also 'Weber's bureaucratic model', below.

Informal Organizations

Despite the existence of formal leadership roles based on rank or grade, informal influences may predominate. For example, the formal leader (superior) may be weak and ineffective, irrespective of his formal managerial position, and an informal leader (subordinate) may emerge and take his place in the eyes of his peers (fellow subordinates). Managers do not have a monopoly on leadership qualities. Lower ranking individuals may possess personal qualities which are viewed as superior in leadership terms, and this may give rise to conflict in that it is contradictory to the picture of the formal organization as portrayed in an organization chart.

Negotiation

This is an extension of the informal organization in that it determines who does what. A secretary's original job description will, at the time of appointment, indicate the nature of the work, what is involved and the pattern of relationships intrinsic to the task. However, in any dynamic work situation things change as the organization adapts and responds to external pressures and technological advances. Therefore, job descriptions soon become outdated and it is too time consuming and difficult to keep them up to date. What will happen is that the secretaries will negotiate their roles with their bosses, perhaps losing some of their original duties and taking on new and additional ones. By such an informal process, demarcation will soon become blurred and roles will gradually change. There may even be role reversal with the secretary taking over duties previously associated with the boss!

Satisficing

This is not concerned with what is done and who does it but with how much is done. Formal organizations attempt to secure maximum efficiency but in reality, according to Simon,* staff tend to 'satisfice' rather than 'maximize' in terms of how much work they do. Workers have their own perceptions of what a job comprises, and of how much or how little

*Simon, H A (1957) *Administrative Behavior*. New York: The Free Press

effort they need to make. This leads to the establishment of working norms, and staff will know what constitutes working above or below the norm. Peer group members will be just as likely as management to remonstrate with the laggard but, unlike management, will also complain where someone is seen to 'overwork'. Pressure by peer groups is always on workers to conform to the accepted pattern of behaviour as established by custom and practice over the years.

Theories

As different techniques and research procedures on organizations have developed, distinct schools of thought have emerged, each providing a broad perspective characterized by a unique emphasis. Four schools of thought are briefly outlined here: classical theory; the action perspective; the systems approach; and contingency theory.

Classical Theory

As the name implies, certain theories are regarded as 'classical' accounts of the ways in which organizations work. Like all forms of study, theories need to be developed to help students find their way around the focal point of study, to develop a language and a series of propositions or observations capable of widespread application to provide a starting point for subsequent investigations. Classical theory has focused on the formal organization – e.g. structure, departments, rules, regulations, authority – and to a large extent has pushed people out of the analysis. Weber's bureaucracy (see below) is a prime example of this where little or no account is afforded the idiosyncrasies of individuals, their beliefs and aspirations. The emphasis is on rank, chain of command and specialization. This is the weakness of the classical approach since structures require people if they are to work at all, coupled with the fact that the approach tends to remain rather static. The names of some classical writers and the approaches taken are presented in the Table at the end of Part I (page 58).

The Action Perspective

This focuses attention on human behaviour. Accounting for behaviour is never easy because what determines it is difficult to define. People working in organizations are assigned tasks, duties and responsibilities, and it is a combination of these which determines role. The role in turn determines the nature of the individual's action in any given set of circumstances; e.g. it is the nature of the role of the secretary or manager which helps influence the actions taken.

Role theory provides a useful means of explanation in terms of the individual in the organization, and is closely tied to action. There are a number of influences which help define the role of the individual and therefore the nature of the action. The following are examples:

status
seniority
experience
formal qualifications
training
age
career paths
background
aspirations
goals
personal relationships
working environment
degree of commitment
ambition

It is the organization which prescribes the roles with the intention of producing certain types of action, enacted to fulfil the expectations of the organization consistent with its aims and objectives. It is a function of management to attempt to secure and sustain the willing co-operation and commitment of employees; this will best be achieved by harnessing the aspirations of individuals and matching them to the needs of the organization. Individuals tend to comply with role expectations. It is the acting out of the role and the interaction which takes place which provide the basis for the term 'action perspective'.

The Systems Approach

This attempts to account for organizational behaviour by making direct reference to the systems and procedures which constitute the framework within which people must work. To use the systems view is to emphasize the interaction between, for example, information systems, communication systems, technical systems and financial systems and to minimize the influence accorded to individuals.

All organizations have complex systems intended to harness the work of individuals to the pursuit of organizational goals. There are different kinds of systems applied to the study of organizations and management, and three approaches are discussed briefly here: open and closed systems; management by objectives (MbO); and planning, programming and budgeting systems (PPBS).

Open and Closed Systems

Open systems extend beyond the boundaries of the organization to include a variety of external influences and conditions, some of which may be of crucial significance to organizational survival. Such systems are usually based on input, throughput and output factors and the wider environment, including social, political and economic conditions (see Fig. 11).

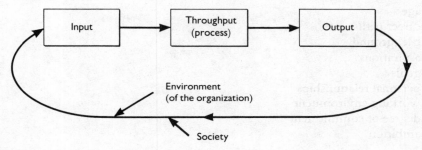

Fig. 11 A systems model
Key: *Input* refers to the raw materials (manufacturing) or the clients (service) entering the system.
Throughput: refers to the technology used in the production of goods or in bringing about changes in individuals.
Output: refers to the finished product or the condition of the individual on leaving the organization.

Closed systems tend to concentrate solely on internal factors. Attention is given to in-house organizational processes and procedures geared to securing the compliance of the work force. The value of the closed system perspective lies in the fact that it provides a sharp focus on intra-organizational procedures – e.g. communications, delegation of duties and working practices. Ironically, this strength is also its weakness, for the closed system fails – deliberately – to take into account the myriad of external influences which impinge upon the work of organizations.

Management by Objectives (MbO)

Since managers and staff working in any organization have only a limited amount of time at their disposal, MbO systems prescribe the essential activities to be undertaken by individual workers. Routines are developed which are centred on the attainment of specific objectives which might, for example, take the form of determining the production of so many units or the performance of particular tasks according to predetermined procedures. MbO systems require personal, individual involvement by everyone. They attempt to integrate individuals into working groups committed to attaining the goals of the organization. The main advantage is that, having determined the objectives to be achieved, it is possible to assess the extent to which they have been met. Therefore, MbO offers an effective evaluation tool, especially where the processes are readily quantifiable. However, ultimately, MbO systems can only be as good as the quality of the decision making which preceded the introduction of the system.

Planning, Programming and Budgeting Systems (PPBS)

Large organizations require major systems in order to co-ordinate their activities effectively. PPBS represents a comprehensive strategy centred on the formulation of plans (including the setting of goals and sub-goals), the creation of a programme (including the designation of appropriate processes and procedures) and the establishment of a budgeting system capable of responding effectively to the demands of the plans and programme. PPBS has been largely used by, though not restricted to, government departments at both national and local levels. Major corporations such as Imperial Chemical Industries (ICI), British Aircraft Corporation (BAC) and British Nuclear Fuels Limited (BNFL) also use forms of PPBS.

Essential elements of any PPBS scheme include:

- identification of goals;
- time factor problems – e.g. five-year plan;
- effective communication network;
- co-ordinating procedures;
- corporate decision making;
- alternative decision strategies;
- impact of change and innovation;
- research and development;
- cost effectiveness;
- efficient financial controls.

This list is not exhaustive, nor is it in any order of priority. Whatever system is used, it is assumed that the essential task of management is to allocate the minimum level of resources (both financial and human) for the optimization of organizational goals. Contrast this with Simon's 'satisficing' mentioned above.

Contingency Theory

This adopts a middle ground position in that it offers a variety of explanations dependent on the circumstances prevailing at a particular time. It takes full account of the fact that organizations are different, having developed their own working practices and procedures, and adapted to the unique environments in which they are located. The impact of the environment is a key factor in contingency theory, the others being size, technology and strategic choice – all discussed within Part I.

Contingency theory does not **prescribe** what management should do. It **demonstrates** and **predicts** likely outcomes as a consequence of the interaction between certain variables. Therefore, to apply contingency theory to a problem would be to predict the impact of, for example, size as a determinant of organizational structure. Here the larger the organization the greater would be the number of divisions, departments and sections. In short, when contingency theory is applied to a management problem, what is being said is that 'It all depends'.

Models

Models have a specific and practical use in that they are often used as the basis for comparison. Models of organizations are abstract, being used to promote the 'ideal', and are devised to fulfil the same purpose as the architect's or planner's model – viz. an approximation of reality or a solution to a problem. However, it must always be remembered that models do not need to contend with the complexities of living entities and are not constrained by such things as financial restrictions.

In the literature of organizations and management, consideration is given to many different kinds of models and their application to a range of problems. The following are some examples:

decision making
motivation
job satisfaction
innovation and change
communication systems

all of which are discussed elsewhere in this book.

The model chosen here for the purposes of elaboration is Weber's Model of Bureaucracy, based on studies of the Prussian Army. Most writers tend to agree that the bureaucratic model is a useful means of explaining and accounting for aspects of organizational behaviour (see below).

Weber's Bureaucratic Model

Criteria of bureaucracy	Examples of effect on organizations
Well-defined hierarchy of authority	Line management system – chain of command 'top down'. Extent of authority related to rank or grade in the organization
Specialization and division of labour	Staff appointed to perform specific tasks, in clearly identified areas of work – e.g. secretary to work in Personnel Department; designer to work in Marketing Department; accountant to work in Finance Division
Rules covering the rights and duties of position	Contract of employment, indicating the obligations of staff member to the organization and of employing organization to its employees
Procedures for dealing with work situations	Custom and practice indicate how tasks are to be dealt with and distributed across the organization. Who does what, where and how
Impersonality of interpersonal relations	Personalities secondary to the role undertaken by individuals. Working for the organization is paramount – not working for specific individuals, the concept of loyalty
Employee selection and promotion on the basis of technical competence	Appointment and promotion to be based on ability – what you can do rather than 'whom you know'

The application of the criteria may result in most of the elements of the model matching strongly with the organization(s) being analysed. Alternatively, the matching may be weak on some of the dimensions but strong on others. For example, prisons, the armed forces, the police force, hospitals, government departments, educational institutions and some local government services will tend to conform closely whilst other types of organization such as small businesses, consultancy organizations, theatre companies and research and development agencies, will approximate bureaucracy only weakly, and then on only a few of the dimensions.

3
Organizational Design and Structure

'To the manager his organization is unique; but only by comparing it with the experience of other organizations can he learn much about it, and to do this he must generalize.'

Charles Perrow
Organizational Analysis: A Sociological View

The term 'organization' hides more than it reveals. On the one hand, all organizations might be seen to be the same whilst, on the other hand, they are all different if not unique. This chapter is concerned with the factors which make organizations different in terms of the condition of the organization and the ways in which the relationships of both management and staff are affected, the quality of relationships and the capacity to get things done.

Managers will be required to respond to a number of variables which will themselves differ in terms of the extent to which they are susceptible to control by management in any precise way. For some variables, then, managers will only be able to 'make the best of things' rather than bring about change – the influence of the environment is a good example of sources of pressure which managers can only react to or accommodate.

Management style (see Part II) with reference to decision making serves to illustrate an area in which management can and does exert its own influence – i.e. it is both proactive and autonomous in the procedures adopted. Factors likely to affect the organizational condition include ownership, function, scale and structures. It is to these factors which reference is now made.

Ownership

Ownership of organizations in a mixed economy – i.e. a system which comprises both state and private ownership (as in the UK) – is one source of influence on organizations and the personnel working within them. The fact that British Steel is a nationalized organization owned by the State suggests that there will be different if not contrasting constraints and implications from those of a public liability company such as Marks & Spencer which is financed by shareholders. Both will be keen to make a profit but whereas this will be a primary objective in the case of Marks & Spencer, for British Steel it may be secondary, especially when the market for steel-based products is depressed.

Private companies are very concerned with profit making in order to survive in the face of severe competition, whereas in the public sector attention is increasingly given to efficiency. Ownership is becoming less critical, during a time of economic restraint, as a factor likely to influence the survival of the organization.

Function

Most organizations are concerned with the manufacture of goods or the provision of services. 'Product producing' (i.e. manufacturing organizations) are usually public liability companies or limited companies, and as such are motivated by profit-making considerations. Competition will be fierce, and an important objective for organizations will be to survive, especially during a recession.

'People processing' organizations are usually concerned with 'people changing'. Schools, colleges and universities aim to educate and consequently change or modify student behaviour, while hospitals and welfare agencies provide remedial, curative and supportive services. They have little or nothing to do with profit making since provision is held to be for the benefit of society.

There are also service organizations which are neither product producing nor people processing. Here the profit motive may or may not be a prime consideration, depending on the nature of the service and the ownership of the focal organization. Examples of such service organizations are British Rail, hotels, libraries and museums, the leisure industry and retail outlets, whether multiple chain stores or corner shops.

Scale

The scale of organizations helps determine the level of their importance. The bigger the organization, the more likely will be its influence on society and the economy. Multi-national corporations (e.g. Shell and Ford) operate on a world-wide basis and have considerable impact on the economies of different countries. A decision by Ford Motor Company to cut back or close its UK operation would have severe – if not drastic – implications for the British economy. Conversely, a decision by Ford to extend its UK business would, to say the least, be highly beneficial.

At national level both public and private enterprise exist. On the manufacturing side, there are nationalized industries such as coal and steel, whilst the private sector has its own large corporations such as ICI, Unilever and GEC. At local level there is a wide variety of small businesses, typically managed and owned by small groups (often partnerships) of manager/owners or even by individuals (sole traders). There are also small organizations owned by the State, although most government and local authority services are large and complex – e.g. the Department of Health and Social Security (DHSS) and the network of schools and welfare organizations.

Whilst categories of ownership, function and scale can only be general and illustrative, they do provide a quick summary of some important organizational characteristics. For example, State ownership **tends** to be associated with loss making and a general indifference about the quality of service offered, whilst 'big' organizations, once considered to be 'beautiful' and 'efficient', tend now to be viewed as impersonal (bureaucratic) – i.e. wasteful – and occasionally even vulnerable. Consequently, medium-sized companies are often taken to be ideal and efficient with considerable attention being given to staffing aspects, the quality of working life and the service provided to the consumer.

Design

Organizational design is not accidental but emerges as a result of pressures exerted by determinants of structure, discussed later. Although different and often unique, organizations have a number of characteristics in common regarding the ways in which they manage, control and exercise authority, distribute or delegate the work to be done and co-ordinate their activities. A useful starting point is the organizational pyramid (Fig. 12).

Organizational pyramid

This structure or design may be applied to many different kinds of organizations and is typically known as a **hierarchy**. Not all organizations have the same extended hierarchy as that shown in Fig. 12. Some will have a narrower base line and be even taller, whilst others will tend to be flatter, having only a limited hierarchy (i.e. most staff will share the same or a limited number of ranks or grades).

The organizational pyramid provides a straightforward description in that at the top of the pyramid the boss presides as the overall leader whilst a

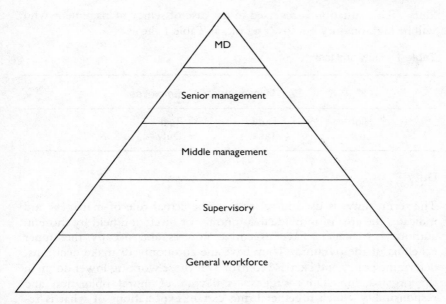

Fig. 12 Organizational pyramid

variety of tasks are distributed downwards throughout the organization. As the pyramid opens out towards the base, more individuals occupy similar, complementary or even low grade identical roles. Conversely, as the pyramid narrows and gains height towards the apex there is the suggestion of a rarified and lonely existence for 'the man at the top'. In the last resort it is the supreme boss who alone is in complete charge of the organization – the Chairman or Managing Director (MD). As the formal legal executive, all staff are ultimately accountable to him.

Allocation of duties and tasks

Whatever the design of the organization, it is people who carry out the variety of duties and tasks which make it tick. The organizational pyramid says something about where people are to be located, as well as providing some indication of their importance within the organization, but it also determines distribution of duties and tasks according to position in the hierarchy.

The lower down the structure, the more likely it is that the roles will be highly functional – i.e. centred on the actual manufacture of goods or provision of services. The staff at the lower end of the organizational spectrum fulfil the *raison d'être* of the enterprise (e.g. nurses nurse and teachers teach) and are very high on 'task-centred' activities but low on 'duty'. This situation is reversed in the case of senior management who will be high on duty but low on task, as Table 1 shows.

Table 1   Duty and task

	Management	Employee
High	Duty	Task
Low	Task	Duty

Duty

The term 'duty' is used in relation to the actual role of managers and indicates the area of individual autonomy or discretion held by those in authority. Managers have executive powers and occupy the upper echelons of the pyramid. They have the autonomy to make decisions, determine policy and exercise control over those working lower down in the organization. Duty suggests a flavour of moral obligation and responsibility which together bring certain expectations of what is required without being written down, as in a job description. Duty requires flexibility in modern business where there is a need to determine priorities, re-think and make appropriate changes as new circumstances emerge.

It is unlikely that the executive will work to normal office hours; he may take days out, work in the evenings or entertain clients at home during weekends. These are all duties or expectations arising from the role of manager, where there is an overriding commitment to the success and well-being of the organization as a whole.

Task

'Task' suggests something different from duty. Staff working on the 'shop floor' or in a public office are likely to be tied to a limited number of routine, specific and mundane tasks. They will be located at the bottom of the pyramid, have little or no autonomy, no power (other than collective), virtually no say on what is done yet will be expected to comply with rules and regulations. The workforce in a department or section will be under the control of a manager or supervisor and will have specific routine functions (tasks) to perform within set time periods. Expectations will be confined to doing the job.

The vertical dimension

As the organizational pyramid demonstrates, consideration also needs to be given to the vertical or 'top down' aspect of organization structure.

Managers communicate down to members of staff using a one-way system of communication or flow of information. However, attention must also be given to the intermediaries – i.e. those occupying the middle management positions. These positions will be allocated either on the basis of seniority (rank) or on the basis of expertise. In either case, staff occupying middle management positions will be expected to maintain and support the hierarchy. An easy way to look at the vertical dimension is to think in terms of the overt (observable) hierarchies of staff grades in different organizations such as, for example, the armed forces, the police or nursing. Other hierarchies and their grading structures are more obscure (at least to the public), as, for example, in the Civil Service, banks and educational institutions.

The horizontal dimension

As the organizational pyramid progressively opens out towards the lower end, opportunities arise for horizontal or lateral design structures to be introduced in order to maintain the coherence of the enterprise. The horizontal 'across' the organization dimension thus helps to fill in the detail of the organization. The larger the organization, the greater will be the division of labour. Such divisions will be expressed in terms of departments, sections or units, where staff will be engaged in some form of collective activity, whether to produce goods (or parts of goods) or to provide a service. Examples are departmental stores such as Harrods or Debenhams, where the type of organization is based on a number of departments each dealing with a particular aspect of the retail trade. The names given to departments denote the functional nature of the work and the roles enacted by staff.

Organizations create divisions or departments as they grow. Comprehensive schools will have departments, whilst a university or polytechnic is likely to have a very large overall subject division such as a Faculty structure. Faculties are broken down into Schools, which in turn may be further split into Divisions (e.g. the Faculty of Business and Management may include the School of Law which may be further subdivided into the Divisions of Company Law, Criminal Law and International Law, to name but three possibilities). Hospitals will also divide their services in a number of ways according to specialist functions, as will large manufacturing companies such as ICI and British Leyland.

Organization Charts

Organization charts illustrate the dimensions of organizational design by showing the patterns of interrelationship which exist between divisions, departments, sections and individuals within an organization. They show at a glance the distribution of authority, the specialist tasks performed and the spans of control. Figure 13 shows the vertical 'top down' command network as well as the lateral distribution of labour across the organization as a whole.

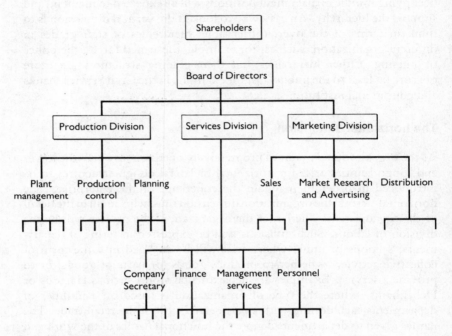

Fig. 13   Organization chart

Departments

Departments have the following advantages:

- areas of work (functions) are easily identified;
- staff develop a feeling of loyalty to the department;
- autonomy and entrepreneurial activity can be developed;
- career structures are established on the basis of specialization.

There are, however, a number of possible disadvantages:

- a disproportionate distribution of power;
- competition and conflict cause unnecessary divisions;
- a tendency to empire build;
- co-ordination can be difficult;
- inflexible use of staff.

Division of labour

The fact that the design or structure of organizations tends towards the creation of departments (sometimes called units or sections) is indicative of the need for a division of labour as organizations develop and grow. In short, specialized staff need to be recruited to perform the variety of tasks intrinsic to any organization.

There are always a number of problems to be resolved in the management of complex organizations. Separating tasks into manageable units is one way in which management attempts to control and co-ordinate activities. However, this does not resolve the problem, and what is required is a further refinement of the division of labour to provide for more detailed control of groups of individuals working in departments.

Span of Control

Span of control is the extent to which a manager can control and direct those under him. It is obvious, however, that it should be easier for managers to manage two or three individuals in the work situation rather than eighteen or twenty. As Fig. 14 shows, seven is held to be the magic number of individuals a manager, controller or supervisor can effectively

Fig. 14 Span of control

manage. Even seven will be problematic when throughout the working week the manager has to know what No. 7 is actually doing, as well as the other six members of staff. In reality, of course, the manager does not really know: he satisfices and makes certain assumptions – acceptable to him – in terms of what Nos. 1 to 7 are doing.

Line Management

In many organizational designs or structures a chain or pattern of command is developed – usually called a line management structure (Fig. 15). At its simplest, this is a military-type formation and is designed to provide a clear indication of the chain of command – i.e. who is responsible and accountable to whom.

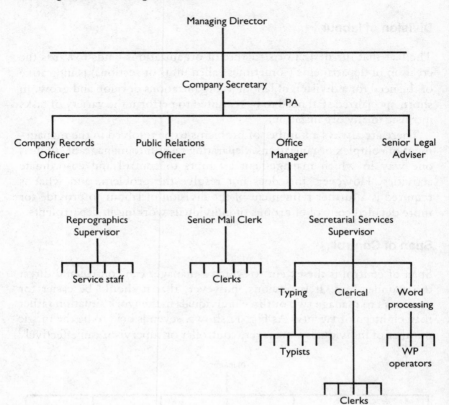

Fig. 15 Line management

Extended Line Management

The line management principle is often extended beyond the rather limited application explained above, in recognition of the different kinds of expertise available at management level. For example, the Chief Training Officer will, in addition to his line management role, have an 'across the organization' role based on his specialist area of work. Training matters will be referred to him from anywhere within the organization, including those holding higher managerial positions. It will be unnecessary for the Chief Accountant, for instance, to refer initially to the Personnel Manager. He may approach the Chief Training Officer direct to arrange training for one of the clerks within his department. This is normally referred to as **Line and Staff** structure, and is illustrated in Fig. 16.

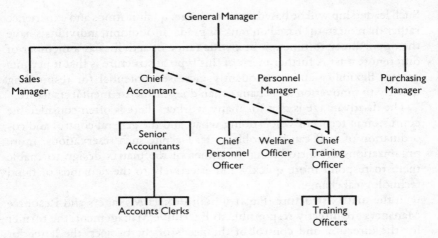

Fig. 16   Extended line management

Alternative designs and structures

As distinct from departmentalism, there are two main alternative approaches to design and structure – matrix and functional. Both are concerned with bringing about a fusion of the different operating systems and procedures, whilst emphasizing the need for shared decision making or corporate management.

Matrix

The development of this form of structure is based on a problem-solving approach, whereby the different and often disparate functions of an organization are brought together in an attempt to provide a solution. This form of design originated in the North American Space Agency (NASA) which had initially one specific overall objective – to land a man on the moon!

Everyone working for NASA had specific skills or knowledge and expertise. Instead of being assigned to a department or section, individuals were assigned to the 'programme'. Staff moved around the 'project' according to the needs of the programme as it developed. For example, an expert in fabrics would be assigned to different teams dealing with different fabric problems – space suits, seating, interior design and so on. Sometimes the expert would be a project or team **leader**, at another time simply a **member** of a team.

The major advantage of the matrix design is that it allows for a larger number of individuals to become leaders in their own area of expertise.

Such leadership will be based on knowledge, qualifications and experience rather than on status based on rank or grade. In addition, individuals have the opportunity to function in a wide range of activities as a member of different teams. A further merit of this type of structure is that it permits greater flexibility and consequently increased potential for responding quickly to innovation and change than does the departmental structure.

The disadvantage is that for many workers there is often considerable confusion in terms of who's doing what, and the general control and co-ordination of staff can be problematic. Despite such reservations, more organizations are introducing variations of the matrix design to enable them to respond more quickly and effectively to the demands of rapid technological change.

In the matrix structure (Fig. 17) both Project Managers and Resource Managers are directly responsible to Executive Management: the former for the direction and control of the needs of the project; the latter for

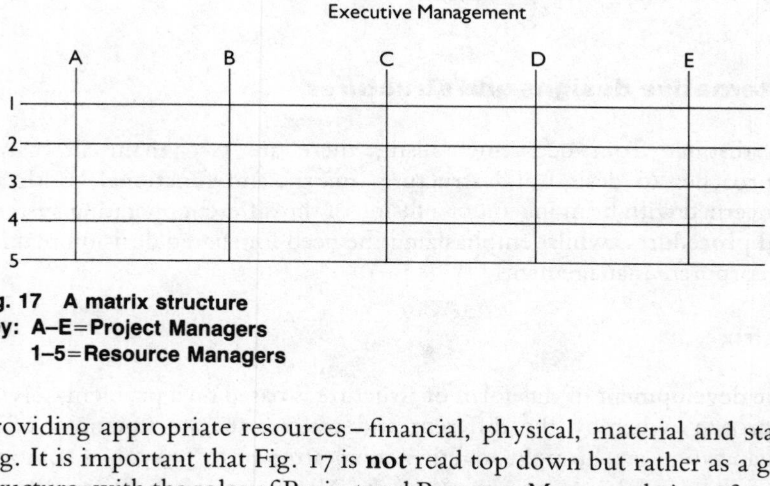

Executive Management

Fig. 17   A matrix structure
Key: A–E=Project Managers
1–5=Resource Managers

providing appropriate resources – financial, physical, material and staffing. It is important that Fig. 17 is **not** read top down but rather as a grid structure, with the roles of Project and Resource Managers being of equal status.

Functional

Functional structure is based on an executive or management team, with each manager having functional authority 'across the organization'. Policy is determined by functional managers on the basis of corporate or collective decision making. Control of the critical functions of the organization are thus highly centralized, often located at Head Office.

The actual title given to each of the Directors will depend on the nature and type of organization. Figure 18 illustrates a functional directorate of a manufacturing organization.

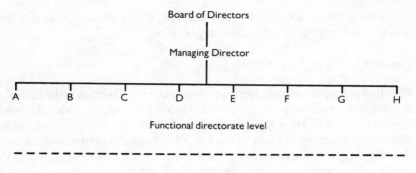

Fig. 18   A functional structure
Key: A=Production   E=Personnel
       B=Purchasing   F=Accounting and finance
       C=Management services   G=Research and development
       D=Marketing   H=Administration

This form of structure has several advantages – principally that it produces, at senior level, a significant increase in the number of managers with an interest in the activities, development and success of the **whole** of the organizational enterprise. Also, functional structures tend to reduce the span of control, concentrating functional authority and, therefore, increasing control and co-ordination. Functional directorates operate at the most senior level within organizations. Below that level (see Fig. 18) there may be either departmental or matrix organization. In other words, the application of a functional directorate has the effect of introducing a top tier of management, inserted between the Managing Director and the existing managers of departments or matrix structures.

Departmental heads or project leaders tend to benefit from this type of structure in that they are able to concentrate on the specialist tasks related to their sections. In this way, duplication of functions – often a major disadvantage of the departmental or matrix structure – is minimized.

Increase in staff responsibilities

One other effect of functional structures is that they increase responsibilities of individuals working in specialist areas because they remove additional non-specialist activities. For example, an employee working in a traditional hierarchical departmental organization will have specialist tasks plus general administrative tasks as delegated by the Head of Department, whereas an employee in a departmental organization headed by a functional directorate will be able to concentrate the bulk of his efforts on the specialist task. The wider organizational tasks will be taken over (i.e. managed) by the functional directorate who will have allocated the work to the appropriate specialist department.

Benefits to the organization

One immediate benefit arising from the functional structure is the increase in managers with organization-wide responsibilities. Functional directors, by virtue of their functional authority, are clearly in a position to overview the activities of the entire organization and so can plan for future developments, research initiatives and resource allocation for the benefit of the organization as a whole, whilst simultaneously having the effect of mediating the often conflicting interests of specialist sections.

Whatever the structure, it is important to recognize that its effectiveness will depend to a large extent on the quality of interpersonal relationships and the suitability of communication systems.

Determinants of structure

Organizations adopt different structures and some explanation is required to account for this. Contingency theory refers to a number of factors, each having a predictive value or impact on organizational design and structure. Such factors are therefore held to be 'determinants of structure', which is not meant to convey inevitability but rather to suggest a level of conditioning or influence which has an impact on the organization and its design and consequently accounts for differences across organizations. Four aspects of contingency theory are considered:

- size;
- technology;
- environment;
- strategic choice.

Size

This is perhaps the most obvious determinant or influence on the structure or design of an organization, but care must be taken because aspects of organizational design are often ascribed to the size factor when other influences are likely to be more significant.

A company employing around fifty workers can be organized rather more informally than one employing 1500 workers. Individuals working in a small organization tend to have more flexible roles than those working in large companies. In large organizations problems tend to centre on control issues, the co-ordination and distribution of work, delegation of responsibility and the accountability of employees.

The size factor can also determine actual working practice. Consider communication systems, for example. In a small organization, it is likely that the manager will communicate directly with his employees. He may even work along with them in certain circumstances. Therefore, less emphasis will be placed on maintaining a hierarchical position or presence. The procedures adopted and the distribution of work according to expertise and seniority will also be managed informally. Communication will be direct – personal, face to face – and open to negotiation.

By contrast, communication in a large organization will be largely formal and impersonal in order to maintain control. Memos will proliferate down the organization, these often being the only 'system' of communication. Where this form of communication becomes excessive (i.e. it generates memos on trivia), communication tends to break down rather than become more effective. In fact, if this procedure is adopted by a manager, it is often copied by individuals lower down the organization, and it is not uncommon for memos to be exchanged by people working in the same room! Hence such a system, which may at least in part be attributed to the size factor, frequently becomes dysfunctional to the extent that staff may choose virtually to ignore memos.

In short, size of organization suggests either the presence of bureaucracy in the case of large organizations, or, in terms of smaller organizations, a level of informality.

Technology

'Technology' here refers to the nature and function of an organization (i.e. what it does), not to computers and automated systems. The indications are that the nature of work helps determine design and structure (see Woodward 1965).

The impact of technology will be more visible in the case of manufacturing organizations, where a production line process imposes constraints on structure and the allocation of jobs and patterns of control. Mass production implies a large scale complex manufacturing process, characterized by work on impersonal, systematic production lines. Whilst there will be a high degree of predictability involved (largely due to the product process), with routine being preferred to change, it is impossible to discount the idiosyncratic pressures generated by both internal and external factors. For example, the methods and techniques utilized by a car manufacturer will be subjected to all manner of market forces and pressures, but will, none the less, represent the organization's technology, indicating the nature of the enterprise along with the functional tasks of its employees. In an educational organization the technology will be teaching and learning, which again reveals something about the nature of the organization, what it does and the kinds of tasks entered into.

From these two examples it can also be seen that the technology influence can either be fairly specific (i.e. it relates to practical situations involving production) or vague (i.e. it refers to a process involving the development of human behaviour). The extent to which technology has an effect on organizational design – whilst difficult to determine, there being few conclusive studies – is likely to be quite considerable since what is done can hardly fail to produce working practices which must ultimately be accommodated in the design.

Environment

'Environment' here refers to the variety of external factors which impose, influence or determine organizational structure and design. It is necessary to take account of the fact that the effects of environment on any organization are significant only to the extent to which working practices and procedures are modified to cope with external demands.

Environmental factors and influences can take many forms, from government legislation to consumer preferences, market demand and competition. All organizations work within a complex network comprising a variety of other organizations, often leading to a situation of mutual dependence. Environmental networks may be steady and reliable or turbulent and uncertain.

Strategic Choice

Strategic choice, developed by Chandler* – 'structure follows strategy' – takes on a rather different form from the other determinants of organizational design. It refers to the area of choice or discretion available to management to make modifications. Managers can and do make decisions affecting organizational design or structure. Indeed, they have the authority to do so by their very positions. Strategic choice suggests that management is not continually confounded by size, technology and environment. If it were, it would be questionable whether management would be needed at all. The 'decision residual' (i.e. the area of discretion open to management) suggests that the effects of the other factors can be manipulated or even ameliorated.

For example, management could re-design the organizational structure, deciding to open new departments, close or merge existing ones, re-define the line management structure, introduce a new tier of management or even scrap the existing design altogether and replace it with a new one (e.g. a matrix or functional structure).

Similarly, a formal organization will have rules and regulations and a

*Chandler, A D (1962) *Strategy and Structure*. Cambridge, Mass: MIT Press

variety of working procedures. It is the actual application of the rules by management which is open to discretion – whether to turn a blind eye or whether to enforce the rule and deal with the consequences (e.g. possible industrial action).

It is often the quality of such strategic choice decisions which distinguishes similar organizations from each other.

Conclusion

The structure or design of organizations is not just a matter of choice. Often the nature of the structure is determined by external factors and consequently organizations will often be in a situation of reacting to events rather than having a free choice to do this or that. Structures are seldom produced by logic or systematic design, since organizations are about people at work, their attitudes and response to their working environment.

When looking at organizations from the outside it is sometimes possible to identify faults in the design which could be easily and quickly remedied to improve the effectiveness of the enterprise. However, when considering the situation from within, there can be a number of personal factors present which will be critical enough to dissuade management from making a change.

For example, it may well be apparent that the organization needs to diversify the roles of its managers instead of relating them to the narrow, functional demands of departments. But what can be done with those managers who may be too old to adapt to the new roles or with those who would find it difficult to take on a wider cross-organizational function? Clearly individuals can 'get in the way' of making what appear to be, on the surface at least, obvious adjustments to organizational design and structure.

The implication is, therefore, that organizational structures are never truly finalized. Organizations are involved in a complex, dynamic process, conditioned by a wide variety of forces within and without, which are themselves complex and dynamic entities. With the present pace of innovation and change, many organizations are adapting new designs as management seeks to maintain effectiveness in order to survive and possibly diversify to meet new and changing demands. There will be no best or ideal structure, but there are designs which are more or less appropriate for particular organizations.

Writers on Organizations and Management

The literature on organizations and management is extensive and it will be useful to have, at least, a point of reference with regard to those writers who are well known in the field. The following outlines a selection of the better known and gives a brief synopsis of their particular area(s) of interest. Specific Further Reading references are given at the end of the book.

Writer	Area(s) of interest
Argyris, Chris	Prolific writer on the psychology of individuals in organizations. Investigates topics such as personality, attitudes, opinions, leadership and motivation.
Barnard, Chester I	Psycho-social aspects of organizations based on co-operation and unity of purpose rather than economic and technical factors.
Blau, Peter M	Bureaucracy; organizational structure and formal organizations.
Buckley, Walter	The application of models and systems.
Burns, Tom and Stalker, G M	Accepted classic study on forms of organization and management styles in relation to the organization's responsiveness to innovation.
Child, John	Specialist writer on organizational structure and design, as well as general introductory texts on organizations. Member of the Aston Group.
Drucker, Peter F	Well-known writer on management practices and one of the first to emphasize the importance of 'managing by objectives'.
Etzioni, Amitai	Sociological explanations of complex organizations in contemporary society.
Fayol, Henri	A French industrialist, he is described as 'the father of management theory' and as such was one of the earliest exponents of a general theory of management.

Writer	Area(s) of interest
Follett, Mary Parker	Wrote widely on governmental and business administration and addressed issues such as leadership, conflict and control. Emphasized the psychological and sociological aspects of management.
Goffman, Erving	Writer on the sociological effects on the formal organization.
Gullick, Luther	Administrative management theory (classical).
Herzberg, Frederick	Attitudes of people towards their work; determinants of job satisfaction and dissatisfaction.
Hickson, David J	Contingency theory; decision making. Member of the Aston Group.
Katz, Daniel and Kahn, Robert L	Social psychology of work; leadership roles; motivation.
Knight, Kenneth	Examines alternative management structures with particular reference to matrix design and the future of organizations.
Lawrence, Paul R and Lorsch, Jay W	Focus attention on the organization as a system. Identify ways of reducing differentiation and increasing integration with specific reference to the demands made by the environment.
Lewin, Kurt	Personality theory – Gestalt psychology.
Likert, Rensis	Organization structure and design; development of systems of management and measurement criteria; study of human behaviour in organizations.
Lindblom, Charles E	Decision making as 'muddling through' rather than as a systematic, logical process.
McGregor, Douglas	Theory of motivation and consequent effects on management style – Theory X and Theory Y.
Maslow, Abraham H	Social psychology of motivation based on hierarchical model of human needs.

Writer	Area(s) of interest
Mayo, Elton	'The Hawthorne Experiments': a human relations study underlining the value of group interaction in the workplace.
Mintzberg, Henry	Explains how organizations work, with particular reference to what managers actually do and the decision-making process.
Parsons, Talcott	Structural–functionalist theory; systems analysis.
Silverman, David	The action perspective based on human relationships in organizations.
Simon, Herbert A	Decision making based on the idea of 'administrative man'.
Stewart, Rosemary	Management's understanding of organizational problems; analysis of different types of managers' jobs.
Tannenbaum, Arnold A	Study of hierarchies, patterns of control and levels of participation in management decision making.
Taylor, Frederick W	'Father of scientific management' movement. Attempted to define 'a fair day's work' and led to the creation of work study techniques.
Toffler, Alvin	Resumé of contemporary technological change and predictions for future development.
Urwick, Lyndall	Public administration and business management based on a series of logical principles following Fayol.
Weber, Max	Originator of the 'bureaucratic model'.
Woodward, Joan	The relationship between technology and organizational structure.

Questions

Explain the term 'span of control'. How useful is the term in analysing the management structure of an organization known to you?

(ICSA, June 1985)

Describe the skills required of a manager responsible for the effective running of a functional department within an organization. State the type of functional department you are considering.

(ICSA, June 1985)

Your organization is thinking of setting up a Management Services Department. You have been asked to address a meeting of departmental managers on the possible servicing which such a department may provide for other departments. Provide an outline of your address.

(IAM, Summer 1984)

(a) Briefly outline the characteristics of a formal organization structure.
(b) Discuss the disadvantages to an individual joining or already belonging to such an organization structure.

(IAM, Summer 1985)

What are the principal factors which influence the 'span of control' in an administrative situation?

(IAM, Summer 1985)

Indicate and comment upon the *basic* functions of management.

(PEI)

Identify and explain the principal management information requirements associated with the marketing function of an organization.

(IAM, Winter 1985)

Mr Newman, the Production Director, has asked you to enumerate the benefits to Comlon International p.l.c. of introducing a system of 'management by objectives' and the action to be taken by individual managers.

(LCCI, 1983)

How may the activities of different departments in an organization be co-ordinated?

(ICSA, Summer 1985)

Explain briefly what you understand by the following management functions, and relate them to a working environment:

(a) organization;
(b) direction;
(c) control.

Further illustrate your answer with diagrams where appropriate.

(LCCI, 1981)

Without a planned procedure for managing product design a number of serious problems can arise. What are these?

(LCCI, 1982)

(a) What is an organization chart? Give four advantages and four disadvantages of such a chart.
(b) Draw a simple organization chart for the following people in the same firm: Sales Manager, Managing Director, Works Manager, Board of Directors, Chief Accountant, Company Secretary.

(PEI)

(a) You are required to construct an organization chart for a medium-sized single-establishment manufacturing company which has a Personnel Department. The Personnel Manager, who has a direct line relationship with the Managing Director, has a Personal Assistant.
(b) Explain the formal relationship that the Personal Assistant in your illustration would be expected to have with others in the organization.
(c) For what purposes might the Personnel Manager or his Personal Assistant need to communicate with persons in other departments, and what channels of communication would you expect to be used?

(RSA, 1983)

What advantages does the use of external O & M specialists have, compared with the use of internal O & M personnel?

(RSA, 1984)

Specify four possible limitations of organization charts.

(RSA, 1984)

(a) What do you understand by 'an organization'?
(b) Discuss, with an example, the main characteristics of informal organizations within a work environment.
(c) Why may a knowledge of informal organizations be useful to an administrator?

(IAM, Summer 1984)

(a) What is understood by the 'contingency' approach to organization planning?

(b) Explain, with reference to research findings, if possible, the importance of *either*:
  (1) technology *or*
  (2) environment
  in determining the most appropriate organization structure for a given enterprise.

(IAM, Winter 1985)

An organization may be considered as comprising four elements: tasks, structure, people and technology.
(a) Describe one strategy that may be used to effect change in respect of *each* of the four elements.
(b) Show how a change in one element may affect the three other organizational factors specified above.

(IAM, Winter 1985)

'Unless "policy" is clearly defined it is not possible to frame an "organisation" because it is not possible adequately to determine the appropriate executive responsibilities and "relationships".' (Brech)
(a) Define each of the three items (in quotation marks) in the above quotation.
(b) Name and distinguish the main characteristics of *three* types of formal relationships which may be identified within an organization structure, and state how these characteristics are conventionally shown on an organization chart.
(c) In the organization shown below, the work of all the managers A–J is interrelated. Comment on the chart and suggest how it might be redrawn to conform to sound management principles.

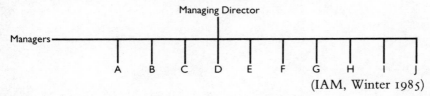

(IAM, Winter 1985)

You have been asked to comment and report on the organization structure of an undertaking.
(a) What are the most important factors you would consider in deciding on the suitability or otherwise of the existing structure?
(b) Comment on how your approach to organizational design is likely to differ according to whether you adopt a classical or a contingency approach to management.

(IAM, Summer 1984)

The reprographic services within a single–establishment, moderate-sized industrial company have to date been provided in a decentralized, somewhat unregulated fashion. It is now proposed to set up a centralized unit offering a high level of expertise and including the latest facilities. It already has been decided that the unit will be headed by a senior supervisor but it has not yet been decided where the unit will be placed within the structure of the organization.

(a) Suggest, with reasons, where the unit might suitably be placed within the structure of the organization and indicate to whom the unit supervisor would be directly responsible.

(b) Explain, with examples, how and why this change in organization could affect the implementing of work decisions and control of work throughout the organization.

(c) Briefly suggest how, under the new arrangements, the confidentiality of certain sensitive categories of information might reasonably be ensured.

(RSA, 1983)

PART II

Management in Action

'*Management is a much less tidy, less organised and less easily defined activity than that traditionally presented by management writers or job descriptions.*'

Rosemary Stewart (1976)
Contrasts in Management

Theorizing is all very well, but management is a practical thing and it is about 'doing'. This Part sets out to examine some of the principal activities which make up the essence of managing, whilst drawing from theory and management literature to support observations made.

The significance of each of the areas discussed will vary between organizations, each of which will be engaged in different activities in pursuit of different goals, whilst adopting individual management styles. Organizations represent something of a conundrum in that they are, on the one hand, all alike and yet, on the other hand, all very different. Whatever the case, however, a number of universals may be applied and it is to these that Part II turns.

Emphasis is firmly placed on the activities of managing and the problems typically encountered along the way. Where appropriate, suggestions are made in relation to resolving problems and smoothing the path towards achieving improvements. What works in one situation or set of circumstances cannot be guaranteed to work in another, so no prescription is intended. Rather, it is hoped that levels of awareness may be raised in terms of what courses of action might be tried, in what circumstances and to what effect.

4
Forecasting and Planning

'But tomorrow always arrives. It is always different. And then even the mightiest company is in trouble if it has not worked on the future.'

Peter Drucker
Managing for Results

Forecasting

Forecasting is like educated guesswork. However, it is not purely speculative in so far as it is based on information, much of it technical and sophisticated. The weather forecast provides a good example of short-term forecasting based on a wealth of information provided by satellite and interpreted by experienced experts, yet it is often inaccurate! This is the nature of forecasting since it seeks to control the future on the basis of today's information.

Complex Forecasting

Organizations use forecasting for a variety of reasons. For a manufacturing organization, forecasting levels of output required over the next three to five years will be of crucial importance in determining resources, both physical and human, whilst for a hospital forecasts will be made of how many patients can be treated during the next twelve months. Such processes are both complex and dynamic, and rely on a synthesis of information which, realistically, can be supplied only by computer.

Techniques of forecasting

Many organizations use forecasting in relation to the volume of sales or services or the costs of production – vital information for the manager. The need for forecasting is closely related to the need to know, for example, the quality, type or colour which is required by customers for particular products. The mathematical technique used to provide such information is **extrapolation** – i.e. the use of past values to predict future sales or level of services. The intention is to determine the variables – factors – upon which trends depend. For example, price may be the dependent variable upon which sales of a chocolate bar may be forecast; or the dependent variable may turn out to be the colour of the wrapper. The difficulty with extrapolation is that it remains largely predictive and may take no account of sudden change. **Regression analysis** – an extension of extrapolation – is where the impact of the dependent variable is isolated and analysed along with its effects on volume of sales. However, it may be an oversimplification to rely too much on a single dependent variable. Usually it is a combination of variables which affects sales potential, and this leads to **multiple regression analysis** – i.e. an evaluation of the combined effects of specific features associated with the product or service and its sales potential.

Need for forecasting

The problem with forecasting is that it is dealing with events before they happen and consequently runs the risk of being inaccurate. This will tend to be more prevalent with long-term rather than short-term forecasting as more intervening and often unpredictable variables can emerge and distort the forecast. Whilst the unexpected can and does happen, organizations which do not forecast tend to be passive and reactive to events, and are more likely to move through a series of crises of one kind or another. Forecasting is a proactive, interventionist, positive activity aimed at reducing uncertainty and risk in order to help secure the survival of the organization. For Henri Fayol the fundamental *raison d'être* of management is to 'forecast and to plan, examine the future and draw up the plan of action'. Forecasting, then, is the antennae of the organization.

Factors of forecasting

Successful forecasting relies heavily on the quality and scope of information. It is surprising how much of this is already available and easy to assemble in a form most suited to the exercise. The following list details the kind of information likely to be of value in the forecasting activity:

- size of labour force, the distribution of skills and anticipated needs for the future;
- skill shortage areas and new techniques required;
- future labour costs;

- quality of relationships between managers and employees;
- adequacy of existing organizational structure;
- systems available to monitor quality control;
- levels of output already achieved and prospects for the future;
- quality of staff morale, loyalty and commitment to the organization;
- customer demand for product or response to service and future trends – i.e. declining or increasing;
- state of the market at home and abroad – boom or slump;
- share of the market and potential for or desirability of increasing this in the future;
- adequacy of premises, site and location – currently and in the light of future developments;
- level of profit being maintained and future outlook;
- relevance of the organization's goals to future development;
- ease with which product or service diversification can be introduced;
- availability of adequate and appropriate levels of investment for future expansion;
- extent of integration and cohesion within the organization as a whole;
- public image – satisfactory or in need of improvement;
- nature and significance of competition both at home and abroad;
- anticipated legislation likely to affect future activities;
- age of product or service and its relevance to the future;
- extent and level of investment required for new technology and plant;
- experience available for negotiating change.

Why use forecasting?

Priorities need to be established and connected to a rationale for forecasting. The list below provides an indication for management of the benefits to be derived from forecasting activities.

- Reduction or elimination of risk.
- Production forecasts which help determine resources – e.g. the need for new machinery.
- Sales forecasts.
- Labour forecasts which help identify staffing needs and shortages.
- Potential for diversification of goods or services – e.g. the suitability of the plant, the skills of the staff, market demand.
- Cost forecasts which identify expenditure on materials, labour and plant.
- Profits forecasts which identify levels of return to investors and surplus for reinvestment into new products.

Much of the activity of forecasting is interrelated in that there will be a knock-on effect from one forecast to another. For example, production will affect resources and thus help determine labour forecasts, whilst sales forecasts will be inextricably linked to what the consumer wants and consequently will help to identify future potential – which will necessitate forecasting what should be produced and how it should be produced, so coming back to production forecasts, and so on.

Planning

Planning is different from forecasting in that it is concerned with goal setting, the organizational design to achieve those goals and the formulation of evaluative techniques to monitor progress.

Put a group of managers in a seminar situation and sooner or later the question of planning will be raised followed by a general consensus of its importance. A few days later and all will be forgotten due to the fact that planning is concerned with tomorrow rather than today. Nevertheless, planning remains important, the main purposes being to:

- establish the goals of the organization;
- provide a sense of security for managers and the workforce;
- establish a sense of direction for the future activities of the organization as a whole;
- co-ordinate activities in pursuit of objectives;
- be able to respond effectively to unanticipated events;
- intervene and act positively in situations rather than simply react to them;
- synthesize and utilize data for the future;
- reduce the gap between objectives and performance;
- handle change and innovation;
- establish criteria against which performance may be evaluated;
- review objectives and determine priorities.

Kinds of planning

There are four different kinds of planning: strategic or corporate, tactical, operational and contingency.

Strategic (Corporate) Planning

Strategic planning, sometimes known as corporate planning, is distinguished by the following features:

- it is long term;
- it is located at top management – i.e. board room level;
- it is centred on 'what to do' type questions;
- all aspects of the organization are included, hence the 'corporate' flavour;
- it is closely connected with the overall goals of the organization;
- it has remoteness and distance from other levels of planning, due to its status within the organization;
- it determines policy priorities from a number of options.

Tactical Planning

The main characteristics of tactical planning are:

- it tends to be short term;
- it is undertaken by middle management;
- it is distanced from strategic planning;
- it is closely related to operational planning;
- it is concerned with 'how to' type questions in pursuit of problem solving and consequently requires a research base;
- it identifies strengths or weaknesses in present processes or the service provided;
- it modifies the organization structure in order to achieve that most appropriate to securing the overall goals.

In addition, tactical planning deals with resource allocation across the organization as a whole, anticipating and providing for conditions conducive to maintaining production or service levels by developing schemes – tactics – to secure workforce participation and commitment.

Operational Planning

The main functions of operational planning are:

- it tends to be short term;
- it is undertaken by departmental managers or section supervisors;
- it is distanced from strategic planning;
- it relies on collaboration with middle management and is closely connected with tactical planning;
- it is centred on functional problems involved in the production process – e.g. working practices or availability of the service;
- it monitors the level of production, cost effectiveness, quality control and profitability;
- it creates conditions for an effective response by the workforce.

Contingency Planning

Although the label 'contingency planning' appears to be ambiguous in that it implies planning for uncertainty as if the nature of that uncertainty could be evident in advance, its very purpose is to cope with the unexpected and unpredictable. For contingency planning to be effective, it requires:

- the formulation of plans for alternative courses of action when things go wrong;
- a capacity to respond quickly to emergencies;
- creativity on the part of the planners;
- flexible working procedures;
- well-understood procedures to guide the actions of managers and members of the workforce;
- an effective system of communication;
- clear lines of responsibility or chain of command.

Contingency planning reacts to the unanticipated and will usually, but not necessarily, be short term in nature. The level of involvement (e.g. board room, middle management or supervisors) will be determined by the nature of the crisis.

The need for planning

The more volatile the environmental setting of the organization, the more the need to reduce uncertainty and turbulence in an effort to guarantee future survival. The growing need to plan has emerged as new techniques have been formulated to handle the information potential generated by computer technology.

Planning is an essential part of the manager's role in that it is closely associated with the attainment of the organization's goals. The closer the organization comes to matching its goals – or objectives – the more likely it is to be effective. The problem is that goal identification is seldom straightforward since most organizations are engaged in numerous activities, some of which may even compete with each other in that the attainment of some goals may be at the expense of realizing others. For example, where an airline company advertises holiday flights at a competitive price but is committed to providing quality and comfort, it risks being overwhelmed by demand and then has two options open to it – increase the price or limit the number of tickets. Either way, company objectives will be in conflict in that it is impossible to satisfy all criteria – viz. increased volume of sales, greater margin of profitability, low price and comfort for passengers. Consequently, the 'goal fulfilment equals organizational effectiveness' proposition is somewhat unrealistic when it . is realized that most organizations cannot achieve them all.

Levels of planning activity

The planning problem is compounded by the fact that all tiers of the organization will have different goals. Board room managers will have a set of self-interests conditioned by their situation. They will tend to see things from the top of the organizational pyramid and, as a result, have an extensive view of the whole organization, the direction it is taking and its overall prospects for the future. By contrast, the workforce, located at the bottom of the pyramid, have a limited view brought about by the insularity of roles, narrowness of activities and restricted network of contacts. Planning as an activity is largely removed from them, leading to accusations that management has 'kept them in the dark'. Figure 19

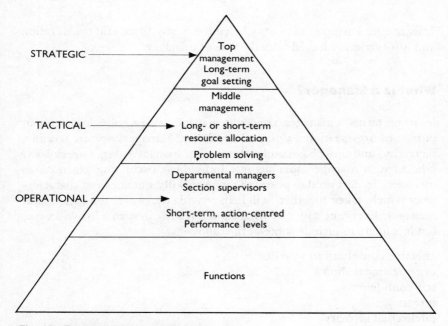

STRATEGIC ──────────→ Top management
Long-term goal setting

Middle management
TACTICAL ──────────→ Long- or short-term resource allocation
Problem solving

Departmental managers
Section supervisors
OPERATIONAL ──────→ Short-term, action-centred
Performance levels

Functions

Fig. 19 Types and levels of planning

illustrates the levels within the organization at which the different planning activities described above are taken.

Although plans promise to bring about a sense of direction and order, there can be a real danger in believing them! Also, too much planning can stifle human ingenuity, whereas too little can lead to uncertainty if not outright chaos.

5
Leading

'Leadership is the ability to persuade others to seek defined objectives enthusiastically.'

Keith Davis
Human Behaviour at Work

Effective leadership is an essential element of any successful organization and is inextricably linked with the role of managers.

What is a Manager?

In simple terms, a manager is one who manages and provides leadership in pursuit of organizational aims and objectives. Managers operate within a hierarchy, and most have under them other managers (e.g. supervisors) who in turn manage other people. Individuals occupying positions as managers/leaders need to possess a range of skills, qualities and characteristics which, taken together, will help provide the profile for a successful manager. Everyone's idea of what should feature in such a list will vary, but it is likely to include some of the following:

effective communication skills
organizational ability
self-confidence
integrity
intellectual capacity
sound judgement
a strong constitution
creativity and inventiveness
motivational skills
a willingness to delegate
the ability to co-ordinate
experience
expertise
honesty

a good judge of character
fair-minded
respected by others at all levels
able to inspire confidence and trust
decisive
adaptable
flexible
charismatic
dependable
persuasive
constructive in criticism
objective in settling disputes
prepared to praise
willing to recognize and develop potential in others
interested in people

Dependent upon the nature of the organization the type of leadership role required will vary. For example, leadership qualities required of a leader in the armed forces would be different from those required of a departmental manager in a manufacturing company or an account executive in an advertising agency. Basically, items on any list will fall into two broad categories – those concerned with the task and those concerned with the people performing the task.

For ease of reference, Table 2 below suggests typical attributes which would be considered appropriate in a manager.

Many writers have attempted to identify what managers really do; two particularly noted for their research are Rosemary Stewart and Henry Mintzberg.

Dr Stewart (1967) conducted diary exercises (see also page 160) where she analysed the working days of 160 British managers. Her analysis enabled her to produce five basic profiles as follows:

- **emissaries** (e.g. sales managers and public figures) – i.e. those who spend a lot of time away from their desks;
- **writers** – i.e. those who spend a lot of time in desk-bound activities such as reading, writing, researching;
- **discussers** – i.e. those who spend a lot of time talking and who fit well into the category of what might be termed 'average managers';
- **troubleshooters** – i.e. those who cope with crises (typically production managers) and spend a lot of time with subordinates;
- **committee men** – i.e. those who spend a lot of time sitting on committees (usually found within larger organizations).

Henry Mintzberg (1973) conducted similar empirical studies in the USA in an attempt to come up with an answer to the question which had

Table 2 Managerial skills, qualities and responsibilities

In relation to the job	In relation to subordinates
Competence	Authority
Co-ordination	Communication
Evaluation	Delegation
Experience	Discipline
Knowledge	Fairness
Methods	Help and advice
Monitoring	Motivation
Organization	Respect
Planning	Supervision
Technology	Training

In relation to colleagues	In relation to superiors
Confidence	Accountability
Co-operation	Link person
Liaison	Loyalty
Reciprocity	Responsibility

puzzled him from childhood and which he had addressed as his doctoral research, viz. 'What do managers do?' The evidence he produced enabled him to identify ten working roles for managers:

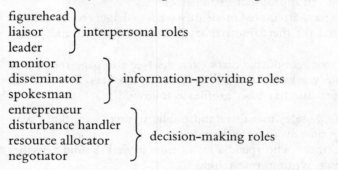

Useful synopses of other studies undertaken in this area of research activity are provided by Mintzberg in one of the appendices to his own book (1973, *The Nature of Managerial Work*).

The Basis for Leadership

There must always be a basis for leadership and this will usually take one of two forms – viz. common assent or legitimacy. Common assent is where there is a consensus that a particular individual is the leader, for whatever reason, whereas legitimacy rests on entitlement to lead on the basis of any one or combination of the following:

- statutory requirement (e.g. a Company Secretary);
- status within the organization;
- position within the hierarchy;
- job description;
- education/qualifications;
- expertise;
- special knowledge of the organization *per se*;
- birthright;
- reputation and respect in the outside world.

Additionally, individuals may find themselves occupying leadership roles for a variety of other reasons, which could include appointments made on the basis of:

- opportunity (where, when and how the vacancy arose);
- default – e.g. the internal appointment of the person most suitable and available;
- organizational expediency;
- budgetary implications – e.g. no funds to advertise for someone new, or insufficient funds to get what is really wanted;
- the need to present a certain image;
- the compliance of the individual – e.g. someone who will not 'rock the boat';
- 'better the devil you know';
- nepotism.

Styles of Leadership

Styles of leadership will vary from person to person and from organization to organization dependent upon the values and personalities of the leaders and on the needs of the organizations. What is important is that the style adopted is appropriate in that it will ensure managerial effectiveness in the pursuit of organizational aims and objectives.

Differing styles of leadership based on the personality of the individual and on the situation in which he leads include: autocratic, democratic and laissez-faire.

Autocratic

This is the traditional view of a leader where what he says goes and where the leader's word is literally 'the law'. There will be little, if any, room for collaboration or discussion. Decisions will be taken by the leader and subordinates will be expected to carry them through unquestioningly. In certain circumstances such a style will be very effective. For example, where the manager is extremely competent, possessing a wealth of knowledge and experience whereas the subordinates are, by comparison, inexperienced and unwilling to accept responsibility, it will make sense for the manager to 'tell' them what to do. However, such a style will be likely to result ultimately in resentment by subordinates in that it is very dictatorial in its approach and fails totally to provide them with the sort of experience which is vital for personal advancement. Also, from the point of view of management, such a style – whilst capable of achieving good results – is too dependent upon the individual in charge. No allowance is made for failings or inadequacies on the part of the individual.

Democratic

This is the co-operative, participative approach where the workforce is given the opportunity to discuss the issues and problems involved and share in the decision-making process. The adoption of such a style does not, however, remove authority or ultimate responsibility for the decision – right or wrong – from the manager. A democratic style is one of co-determination rather than abdication. Such a style leads to joint involvement and will be likely to foster greater commitment to the task whilst improving the standard of industrial relations generally. However, it can be extremely time consuming to operate, difficult to unscramble once set in motion (the individuals concerned will assume the 'right' to be consulted) and the quality of decisions can be diluted in an attempt to please everyone.

Laissez-faire

This is where there is complete freedom afforded to the workers to take decisions without collaboration with the leader. Here the leader virtually assumes the role of group member. The theory is that workers will perform better when left to find their own solutions to problems in the interests of their own needs and wants. However, the danger lies in the lack of direction and control which may result in uncertainty, leading to frustration on the part of the workers and chaos for the organization.

Other ways of looking at leadership style

Another way of looking at leadership style would be to view it as: **task-centred** or **people-centred**.

This view conforms with McGregor's Theory X and Theory Y (see the next chapter – 'Motivating'). When the style is task centred it concentrates on the significance of the job itself rather than on those fulfilling the task and would most closely resemble the autocratic style discussed above. Where the style is people centred the approach is a consultative one more in keeping with the democratic style.

Burns and Stalker also suggested two alternative 'opposites of style' – the **mechanistic** and the **organic**. Mechanistic managers will tend towards autocratic leadership, whilst the organic manager will value the opinion of subordinates according to their expertise, technical skills and qualifications. Burns and Stalker concluded that the predictable, routine organization would incorporate a mechanistic style more easily than an organization which needed to be flexible, innovative and creative, which would be better served by an organic style.

Other theories

Other theories on management/leadership style are offered by:

- Tannenbaum and Schmidt – the decision-making continuum.
- Blake – the managerial grid.
- Hersey and Blanchard – situational leadership based on 'maturity' of subordinates.
- Reddin – the effectiveness dimension (3D grid)
- Adair – action-centred leadership
- Fiedler – contingency theory

The Decision-making Continuum

Tannenbaum and Schmidt* held the view that leadership styles could be seen as stretching across a continuum (see adapted version in Fig. 20). At one end of the continuum there is the authoritarian style, closely resembling McGregor's Theory X, whilst at the other end is the participative style, closely resembling Theory Y. In between is a range of distinct styles which can be identified as follows:

Tells	Here the manager makes a decision and tells subordinates who simply follow his instructions.
Sells	Here the manager will be more selective in his choice of words when giving instructions. There will be an element of persuasion in order to encourage subordinates.
Explains	Here the manager takes the time and trouble to explain to subordinates, so allowing for greater personal exploration of the decision he has reached whilst increasing the involvement of the subordinates.

*Tannenbaum, R and Schmidt, W H (1958) How to Choose a Leadership Pattern, *Harvard Business Review*; **36**: 95–101

Tests   Here the manager will put forward a tentative decision but will provide the opportunity for subordinates to offer their opinions. The tentative decision may be subject to change according to whether or not alternative suggestions or ideas put forward are accepted or rejected, but the manager will still make the final decision.

Selects   Here the manager presents the problem, asks for suggestions from the subordinates but makes the decision himself, based on the suggestions offered.

Consults   This is much more participative. Here the manager outlines the situation, explains the limits within which the decision must be made and asks for suggestions. A rational decision will be reached following a process of consultation with subordinates who have the opportunity to express their views.

Joins   Here total participation comes into effect as manager and subordinates consider the situation jointly and discuss possible alternatives until a mutually acceptable situation is reached. Here the manager commits himself to abiding by the decision.

With this model managers have a range of styles available to them and on the face of it may select an appropriate one from the seven which are represented across the continuum (see Fig. 20) and adhere to it. This is, however, an over-simplification in that management is a dynamic activity and something which may pay dividends in the short term, e.g. an authoritarian approach, would soon lose the commitment of workers in the long term. What will tend to happen is that managers will modify their styles to fit differing circumstances.

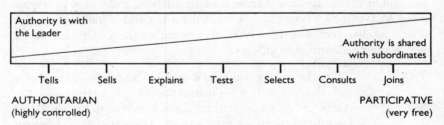

Fig. 20   The decision-making continuum (based on R Tannenbaum and W H Schmidt)

The Managerial Grid

The work of Dr R Blake and his colleague Dr J S Mouton looked into the application of human resources (i.e. people) to achieve organizational goals (i.e. production). Leadership style was determined by the extent of the concern for people and for production; the results were plotted on a grid from which five leadership styles were identified, ranging from 1.1 which indicated a low concern for both people and production to 9.9 (the 'ideal' approach) which indicated a high concern for both, with 5.5 occupying the mid-way position with a balanced concern for both (see Fig. 21).

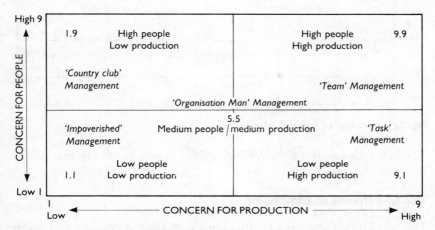

Fig. 21 The managerial grid (based on R Blake and J S Mouton)

Situational Leadership

In their *Life Cycle Theory of Leadership** Hersey and Blanchard put forward the view that leadership style can be directly related to the extent to which subordinates are willing and able to tackle a task. They refer to the degree of willingness and capability as 'maturity' and suggest that different leadership styles are required according to whether subordinates have high or low maturity. An illustration based on Hersey and Blanchard's concept of 'maturity' is given in Fig. 22.

What they call 'maturity' does not refer only to age but to the duration in a particular job situation and the capacity which an individual has to undertake a particular task. Hence individuals require less task structuring as they 'mature' in a job, but will need more task structuring where they take on a new job or responsibility. Therefore, it is highly probable that while a manager may adopt a delegating/participating style for one task where an individual displays high maturity, he may have to adopt a selling/telling style for another task where low maturity is in evidence.

*Hersey, P and Blanchard K H (1969) Life Cycle Theory of Leadership, *Training and Development Journal*; May: 26–34

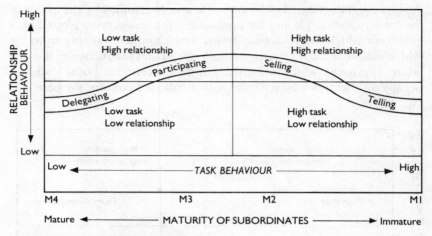

Fig. 22   'Maturity' of subordinates

The key to a situational leadership style is flexibility on the part of the manager.

The Effectiveness Dimension

The best known approach to situational leadership is possibly that taken by Reddin* who uses the grid formation as a base but adds a third dimension (see Fig. 23) in the form of Effectiveness.

He believes that the performances of all managers can be measured on the basis of three characteristics which all managers possess:

1   Their level of desire to get a job done, i.e. **task**
2   Their level of interest in people as individuals, i.e. **relationships**
3   Their ability to achieve a high level of productivity, i.e. **effectiveness**

He labels eight different types of manager who fit into the different boxes of the 3D grid (see Fig. 23), ranging from what he refers to as the Deserter, who is low on both task and relationships and is consequently less effective as a leader, to the Manager (Executive) who is high on task and relationships and is thus very effective in leadership terms. The different types may be briefly characterized as follows:

The Deserter

● wishes to maintain a low, almost horizontal profile;
● seeks the quiet life with minimal involvement;
● has a low level of perseverance when faced with a problem;

*Reddin, W J (1970) *Managerial Effectiveness*. New York: McGraw Hill

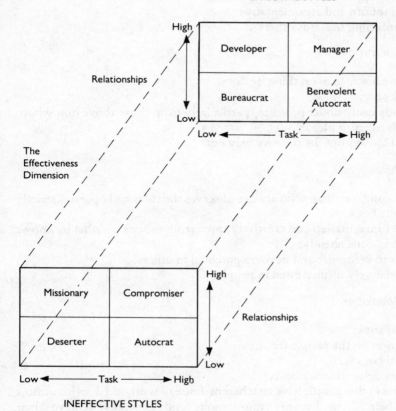

EFFECTIVE STYLES

The Effectiveness Dimension

Relationships

High — Low

Developer | Manager

Bureaucrat | Benevolent Autocrat

Low ◄——— Task ———► High

INEFFECTIVE STYLES

Missionary | Compromiser

Deserter | Autocrat

High — Low

Relationships

Low ◄——— Task ———► High

Fig. 23   The three-dimensional grid (based on W J Reddin)

- is resistant, and even hostile, to change;
- has a poor effect on the morale of others.

The Missionary

- only sees good in people;
- avoids conflict of any kind;
- is easy going;
- prefers to change his view rather than face any sort of confrontation.

The Autocrat

- has a poor view of people, believing that they dislike work and so need to be forced into it (similar to Theory X);

- is self-opinionated and domineering;
- is stubborn and argumentative;
- is unfeeling towards others.

The Compromiser

- is mediocre in everything he does;
- lacks decisiveness;
- bends easily under pressure, particularly from those above him whom he is eager to please;
- will always opt for the easy way out.

The Bureaucrat

- is a company man who always observes the rules and operates strictly to the book;
- lacks imagination and creativity, preferring to stick to what he knows or has done already;
- fails to recognize and develop potential in others;
- is relatively disinterested in people.

The Developer

- is creative;
- is good on the people front;
- motivates well;
- takes delegation seriously;
- believes that people have an inherent desire to work and does his utmost to help them become autonomous and generally achieve their aspirations;
- tends to be a low profile person within the organization.

The Benevolent Autocrat

- is a confident and competent organizer;
- has the ability to produce results without building up resentment from those who do the work;
- has total commitment;
- is uncertain about how to get the best out of subordinates.

The Manager (Executive)

- scores well on all fronts;
- has high standards;
- appreciates the need to have good working relationships if he is to secure the sort of commitment necessary to achieve good results;

- is an exponent of team building;
- knows when to take a decision by himself;
- contributes to the high level of morale of those who work with him and for him;
- encourages commitment to the work of the organization.

It follows that any of these basic styles could be effective or ineffective depending on the situation in operation. The difference is not in the behaviour but in its appropriateness to the situation. The manager once again needs to be extremely flexible and 'sensitive' to the situation.

Action-centred Leadership

Adair produced another model for leadership when he developed the concept of 'action-centred leadership'*. He devised it initially for training with the armed forces but it has since been applied widely by the Industrial Society in many of their courses.

It emphasizes the interdependence of three sets of needs which are usually illustrated by the overlapping circles of a Venn diagram (see Fig. 24).

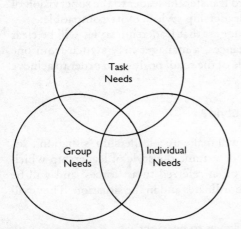

Fig. 24   Action-centred leadership (based on Adair)

Fiedler's Contingency Theory

Fiedler† conducted studies into leadership styles in a wide range of organizations and concluded that three factors contributed to the effectiveness of a leader:

*Adair, J (1968) *Training for Leadership*. London: Macdonald
†Fiedler, F E (1967) *A Theory of Leadership Effectiveness*. New York: McGraw Hill

- The relationship of the leader with the working group.
- The clarity with which the task undertaken is explained.
- The power of the leader in terms of the rewards he could provide and the punishments he could mete out with the approval of the organization.

His studies suggest that leaders need to adopt different approaches depending on the extent to which these factors predominate in any given situation. Different combinations of the three will call for different strategies on the part of leaders.

Fiedler's idea was that 'leadership effectiveness depends on the appropriate matching of the individual's leadership style . . . and the influence which the group situation provides. . . . Hence almost everyone should be able to succeed as a leader in some situations and almost everyone is likely to fail in others.' (p 247).

His contention is, therefore, that dependent upon the situation prevailing at a particular time any leadership style can be effective. What is required is the ability of the leader to adapt his style to the needs of the situation as no one style will suit all. Fiedler accepts that this is virtually to ask for the impossible in that it infers altering personality at will. A more feasible solution, he suggests, is to transfer the leader to the supervision of a group with whom his natural leadership style is more compatible.

In practice it is unrealistic to suggest that leadership styles will be clear cut. Depending on the circumstances, a manager may switch from one style to another or adopt a 'middle of the road' position in order to achieve the desired results.

What are the determinants of style?

Just as there are elements which will make up a leadership 'situation', so, too, are there factors which will determine the style of leadership which any manager adopts. These are often referred to as 'forces' and will be present in the manager, in the subordinates and in the situation. They will include:

- personal ideology (what he believes to be 'right');
- view of self (whether he sees himself as an initiator, a facilitator, a supervisor, a motivator or whatever);
- personality (introvert or extrovert);
- how pressured he feels (e.g. by the job or the problem);
- how much he needs security and predictability;
- manner (calm, communicative, confident, courteous, critical, considerate, cautious);
- how he views his subordinates (positively, negatively, with uncertainty);

- how competent or incompetent the subordinates are;
- how subordinates view him (with respect, with contempt, with admiration, with caution);
- how ready subordinates are to assume responsibility;
- the extent to which subordinates expect to share in decision making;
- how cohesive the team or working group is;
- how tight the time constraints are;
- the organizational climate (see below);
- how the organization expects him to be.

Any combination of such factors will have a bearing on the style a manager feels he must adopt to achieve his objectives.

Whatever leadership style is chosen will be significant to both organizations and individuals, in terms of:

- organizational efficiency;
- organizational effectiveness – how well the goals are achieved;
- organizational flexibility – how well it can handle different tasks and respond to change;
- organizational growth;
- individual motivation to do work desired by the organization;
- individual job satisfaction;
- individual growth and career development.

Organizational climate

This refers to all the factors which influence behaviour within organizations, irrespective of function and structure. Different departments or sections may, of course, have individual climates. In a nutshell, it reflects the way things are done within an organization and can best be identified by seeking answers to the sorts of questions posed here:

- What kind of behaviour is most likely to be rewarded?
- What kind of behaviour is discouraged?
- How important is status?
- How are decisions reached?
- How high or low is morale?
- How is conflict handled?
- How are errors dealt with?

Answers to such questions will provide vital clues as to how the organization goes about its business, its values, principles and ideals and will be highly relevant in terms of the leadership styles adopted. Managers can respond to the situations in which they find themselves by applying different strategies to the ways in which they handle people and problems.

Often it will be possible to adopt a process of trial and error and to modify techniques to take into account new tasks and procedures, changing personnel, differing circumstances and the time constraints which will be in operation at any time.

Leadership roles

In addition to the leadership styles presented above, managers have positive roles to play – i.e. they are required to apply their talents, knowledge and abilities (as suggested at the beginning of this chapter) to the work situation.

To occupy any role is to attempt to meet the expectations of others. In the case of an organization the 'others' will range from superiors in the board room to subordinates.

The role of leader will be geared to attempting to fulfil the following expectations:

- establish a clear sense of direction and purpose in the form of well formulated and achievable aims and objectives;
- make forecasts and develop plans;
- develop a systematic pattern of quality control over all aspects of work under his jurisdiction;
- formulate a pattern of effective communication, both top down and bottom up;
- create opportunities for the expansion of the business or service;
- negotiate working practices and conditions conducive to employee needs and morale;
- incorporate evaluative procedures to monitor standards of performance – e.g. level of output, consumer preferences;
- originate new techniques in the light of such monitoring and evaluation to improve the quality of the product or service;
- represent the organization as required both within the organization and with external agencies;
- inspire the continued confidence of directors, peer group colleagues and subordinates;
- establish appropriate reward mechanisms for committed and successful workers;
- operate within the constraints of any budget imposed;
- liaise, as necessary, with trade union officials in an attempt to foster and maintain good industrial relations.

The multi-dimensional nature of the role

The role of leader is multi-dimensional since the manager has to fulfil a variety of expectations, some of which may even be contradictory in nature. For example, realizing the expectations of the Board of Directors and achieving the goals of the organization may necessitate taking steps which are unpopular with subordinates. It is not only a leadership role within the organization, but also the role expectations perceived for a manager by the outside world – viz. shareholders, clients, family, associates and the community.

Role conflict

This occurs where the demands and expectations of different individuals/ groups are at variance. For example shareholders will be interested in securing the best return on their investment. This might best be achieved if the organization were to merge with another company which might, in turn, undermine or damage the manager's present position. Alternatively, productivity might be greatly improved by the introduction of robots but this would necessitate redundancies and changes in work patterns which would meet with hostility from the workforce.

Another situation producing role conflict would be where the demands of the job (e.g. the need to put in overtime) conflict with domestic responsibilities such as attendance at a parents' evening at the children's school. The potential for conflict is virtually endless and survival for the manager will be dependent on his ability to strike an effective balance and maintain a sense of perspective.

6
Motivating

'Motivation is not what you do to people, it is what you allow them to do to themselves.'

Bill Reddin
from *The Best of Bill Reddin*

Motivation is about 'getting the best out of people'. It is concerned with what causes an individual to act, and an understanding of it will be important to any manager who is anxious to ensure that his subordinates are giving of their best and helping to achieve the desired results.

Motivation is not something which can be learned or handed out. It is something which comes from **within** an individual and expresses itself in what might be termed 'commitment' to something or another. This 'something or another' can be anything, and may or may not be related to the work situation and the task in hand. Also, it may have negative rather than positive connotations and can be disruptive. What is vital for management is that the commitment is to the task, or that it can be brought to the task by some type of incentive or reward. Only that way can the organization hope to achieve its goals.

Motivation is a complex subject, and what motivates one worker may have absolutely no effect on another. Many researchers have carried out investigations but results are inconclusive in that they were not always comparable and were often carried out in laboratory conditions, with relatively small samples and a limited time scale. Nevertheless, a number of competing theories have emerged to pose some interesting questions for practising managers today. The following are some of the better known examples of motivation theory.

The Behaviourist Approach

Research by the Behaviourist School centres on the belief that individuals are driven to act in a certain way in order to achieve a goal (Fig. 25).

Theories were developed as the result of work undertaken by Pavlov,

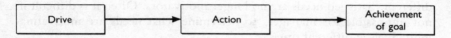

Fig. 25 Model of individual behaviour

Skinner, Watson, Thorndike and others (mainly with animals). At its simplest the research was concerned with providing a stimulus and soliciting some sort of response. If the response was followed contingently by something 'nice' there was said to be 'positive reinforcement'. Whereas if the stimulus was followed contingently by something which was 'nice when it stopped' this was said to be 'negative reinforcement'.

This approach is often referred to as 'carrot and stick'. If, in modern management terms, we substitute for 'positive reinforcement' a reward of some kind (e.g. a large bonus or a free holiday) for behaving the way the company wants – i.e. achieving good results – and for 'negative reinforcement' substitute sacking the least successful workers, we have applications of the theory which will act as examples to other staff as to the way they are expected to behave to receive the reward or positive pay-off.

Abraham Maslow

Maslow (1943) formulated one of the most popular theories of motivation, based on the belief that man's needs can be arranged in a hierarchy (Fig. 26) of importance and that it is not until one need is satisfied that the desire (need) will exist to satisfy the next. It is important to recognize that

Fig. 26 Maslow's hierarchy of needs

higher order needs should not be read as 'better' than lower ones. It is the order in which individuals are motivated to satisfy need which is important. Also, needs change according to circumstance; what may have been a strong motivator will, once satisfied, give way to something quite different. Satisfied needs are no longer motivators. Often it is difficult if not impossible for managers to determine what needs are motivating individuals at different times.

Douglas McGregor

McGregor, on the other hand, believed that the key to motivation lay in the fact that there were two conflicting views of work, both of which were based on instinctive assumptions about people.

The traditional assumption (which he developed as his Theory X) is that people are naturally lazy, will avoid responsibility whenever possible, have a tendency towards lack of co-operation, are unambitious, not very intelligent, require a lot of control and in many cases have to be literally coerced into working towards the objectives of the organization.

Set against this he introduced Theory Y, where work is seen as second nature, enjoyable for its own sake (given favourable working conditions), where workers are anxious to share in problem solving and to take responsibility, and where they actively seek to improve their position.

Frederick Herzberg

Herzberg further developed the thinking of Maslow and McGregor through a series of experiments conducted in 1966 with a wide range of working groups. In his experiments he asked workers to identify three occasions when they felt satisfied in their work and three in which they felt dissatisfied. They were then asked to categorize the causes under a number of headings and Herzberg drew up a distribution frequency for the group.

He identified the characteristics which brought satisfaction – referred to as 'motivators' – and were related to the job content:

- a sense of achievement in a job well done;
- a job worth doing well in the first place;
- being given responsibility for the job;
- being recognized for one's achievements;
- being afforded the opportunity to advance.

Dissatisfaction – referred to as the 'hygiene' factors (in that Herzberg believed in the need to have them reasonably well 'cleaned up' before they could provide satisfaction) – stemmed primarily from the working environment and organizational conditions:

- adverse company policies;
- poor working conditions;
- poor supervision;
- lack of status;

- deficient interpersonal relationships;
- inadequate salary.

Elton Mayo

One of the pioneers of scientific management, Elton Mayo, born in Australia and ultimately Professor of Industrial Research at the Harvard Graduate School of Business, was the first researcher to point out the inadequacy of studying workers in isolation and postulated the significance of employee co-operation.

His major research, which came to be known as the Hawthorne Experiments, took place at the Hawthorne Plant of the Western Electric Company in Chicago during the 1920s and 1930s. The research was related to the physical environment of work and was originally designed to test the effects of lighting on fatigue and production. The first tests involved conducting parallel observations of two working groups. In one group the intensity of the lighting was varied periodically whilst in the other it remained constant throughout the experiment. The results showed increases in production for both groups despite the differences in lighting. This implied that something other than improved lighting was the key to increased productivity.

Further experiments followed in an attempt to clarify the anomalies of the lighting experiment, and the main feature of the follow-up programme was the establishment by Mayo of a Relay Assembly Test Room in which he could observe the 'total human situation'. Experiments were carried out over a five-year period. A test room was specially set up and occupied by six girls selected for the research, who carried out their work (assembling telephone relays) seated at a long bench. During the experiment a series of changes were introduced – some improving the work situation (e.g. the introduction of piece-work, shorter hours and longer breaks), others reverting to previous less favourable conditions. Throughout the experiment the girls were observed and their production levels recorded. The interesting outcome of the study was that, irrespective of the experimental changes introduced, production levels rose continually. The conclusion was that production rose due to changes in the attitudes of the girls towards their work and their environment, together with the fact that they felt flattered at the interest and attention shown in them by management and wanted to prove how good they were. Their attitude to authority changed in that they no longer felt threatened by the supervisor. Morale rose and there was an atmosphere of co-operation and group identity, with self-discipline generating from the group and enhancing productivity rather than decreasing it, irrespective of the working conditions prevailing at any given time.

The significance of these experiments lay not so much in their scientific value – there were methodological faults and weaknesses – but in the fact that socio-scientific research in an industrial context had received its first notable publicity.

Chris Argyris

Argyris proposed that despite the natural desire of individuals to act responsibly, be self-reliant and independent, the climate of typical organizations tends to be such that it stifles these facets of human behaviour. This results in apathy and inertia. He maintained that, where jobs are insufficiently stretching and demanding, results will be poor, leading to worker frustration and the adoption of indifference as a defence mechanism to self-respect. He recognized the importance of providing stimulation via the dignity of work and the satisfaction of accomplishment in a job well done rather than relying wholly on financial reward and fringe benefits.

Another facet considered by Argyris is the distinction between happiness and motivation. He recognized that just because an employee is happy does not automatically ensure that he is motivated. Nor is a motivated employee necessarily a happy one. Argyris pointed out that employees need to be shown trust and confidence by managers, and that where their personal involvement is increased, employees can make a unique contribution, so increasing their intrinsic motivation and ensuring their commitment to organizational objectives.

Rensis Likert

Likert (1967) focused on leadership style to explain effectiveness and motivation within groups. One aspect of the Institute of Social Research studies at the University of Michigan suggests that, where organizations get into financial difficulties, there is a tendency to attempt to cut back by placing pressure on the workforce to work harder and exercise economy. This strategy is likely to generate more money but it ignores the human factor. Likert referred to this as Human Aspect Accounting, and maintained that failure to recognize it as a force is likely to result in resentful, distrusting employees who complain constantly, work carelessly, apply their own restrictions to productivity and de-motivate the competent and committed members of the working team, perhaps to the extent that they will leave to seek alternative work. The ultimate effect of this may well be to reduce organizational effectiveness still further, so losing even more money.

Likert's studies indicated that leadership style is significant in securing positive motivation and sustaining high productivity. Styles were classified into four groups – referred to as 'Systems' – according to the degree of freedom which employees had to communicate with the manager or supervisor and the level of confidence and trust they felt the manager or supervisor had in them. Briefly, the styles highlighted were:

System 1 – Exploitive authoritarian
System 2 – Benevolent authoritarian
System 3 – Consultative leadership
System 4 – Participative leadership

The results of the studies stress that, whilst System 1 might be successful in producing results in the short term, it had serious long-term disadvantages. At the other end of the scale, System 4 will be beneficial in the long term but will be extremely demanding in that it requires substantial commitment on the part of management. Time will be needed to educate and develop supervisors and managers in motivational techniques and participatory skills.

Intrinsic and Extrinsic Motivation

The number of factors which are believed to motivate individuals is extensive and they are frequently referred to as 'satisfiers'. In considering the motivation of employees, it is useful to group these 'satisfiers' as intrinsic or extrinsic.

Briefly, **intrinsic** satisfiers are those which come from within the individual, and are related to the job itself and the satisfaction which an employee gets from the job or elements of the job situation. Such factors are difficult to categorize because much will depend on the nature of the job. **Extrinsic** factors are more readily identifiable and include:

pay
working conditions
status
job security
relationships with fellow workers
promotion prospects
fringe benefits

It is difficult to assess the precise significance of pay as a motivator, but current thinking would seem to indicate that it is rarely the sole motivating agent and may even feature well down a job satisfaction rating.

Organizations will attempt to provide incentives (i.e. rewards) over and above standard rates of pay, to encourage employees to improve their performance and so achieve greater productivity. The aim of any incentive scheme is consequently designed to secure employee commitment in pursuit of organizational goals.

Incentives and Incentive Schemes

A wide variety of incentives together with carefully conceived incentive schemes may be applied by management at any time for motivating purposes. These will range from **fringe benefits** such as:

company cars
dress allowances
subsidized restaurant facilities
on-site banking
special sports and recreation facilities
social events
subsidized company holidays abroad
free medical and dental treatment
subsidized hairdressing and chiropody
flexitime

to specially devised incentive schemes such as:

group bonus schemes
organization-wide bonus schemes
profit-sharing schemes
productivity agreements

Where the company wishes to appeal specifically to the intrinsic motivation of employees, emphasis will tend to be placed on:

staff development
job rotation
job enrichment
job enlargement
job autonomy

in an attempt to enhance satisfaction with the job itself through a feeling of increased accomplishment, greater participation in decision making, more direct control over the work and feedback in respect of results achieved. Many motivational theorists believe that intrinsic satisfiers produce greater job satisfaction in the long run than the more obvious external reward mechanisms.

It should be noted, however, that not all schemes will be advantageous. Disadvantages can arise from ill-considered incentive schemes – e.g. those based on performance levels difficult to achieve – because they can produce the opposite effect to that intended by lowering morale and consequently reducing the likelihood of achieving the goals of the organization.

Despite the doubts which exist about the connections between motivation and job satisfaction, there does seem to be a positive link between motivation and performance in that the higher an individual's motivation, the better will be his performance.

Motivation is a complex process and many of the issues involved are far from clear. Motivation theory does, however, provide many valuable clues which can help understanding of the relationships which exist between motivation, performance and job satisfaction.

7
Improving Morale

'. . . indicators of morale, the degree of attachment to, or satisfaction with one's organization, its goals, its traditions, one's work and the people one works with.'

C J Lammers and D J Hickson
Organizations Alike and Unalike

One motivational aspect with which all managers will be concerned is that of morale. Morale is something about which most individuals have an instinct but which tends to be difficult to define with any degree of precision. Many would define it as being equivalent to job satisfaction, and indeed it has much to do with it, but others stress the group dimension which morale has in that it is often associated with phrases such as, 'the morale of the troops was high'.

One possible definition for consideration in the context of the work situation might be, 'Morale is the attitude of individuals and groups towards their work and working environment which serves to condition how well or how badly they perform'. This suggests that workers who like their work and the company they work for and enjoy the companionship of their fellow workers, will be highly motivated and will wish to work co-operatively in the pursuit of a common purpose – viz. achieving the goals of the organization.

Things are rarely as ideal as this, and part of the manager's role is to develop an awareness of the myriad of employee attitudes, feelings and sentiments which can colour their views and affect morale at any time.

Used by itself the word 'morale' is rather like the word 'health' in that it has neither a favourable nor an unfavourable meaning until it is placed in context. What morale does is provide an indication of the general condition of an organization, and an effective management approach will include recognizing its existence and attempting to identify those factors on which employee job satisfaction will be most likely to depend. This is necessary if good human relations are to be sustained, so facilitating greater efficiency and increased productivity.

Morale in the workplace

The study of morale in the workplace is therefore a tentative, almost philosophical, activity which is hard to describe, with evidence being difficult to assemble and evaluate. Accurate measurement of morale indicators will often be difficult. Factors which are external to the organization and have nothing to do with the work situation can be influential. For example, an individual's morale may be adversely affected by family or domestic problems, the state of the world, or even by the demise of his local football team! The range of external factors is endless, and the degree to which they may influence behaviour and attitude is consequently difficult to determine.

Morale factors which can be identified and measured

However, there are within an organization certain factors which may provide valuable insight as to the state of morale. These include:

- labour turnover;
- level of absenteeism;
- timekeeping;
- accidents;
- quality of work;
- quantity of work;
- number of grievances;
- number of disciplinary proceedings;
- number of disputes;
- level of participation in company schemes;
- extent of the use of company facilities.

All these factors can be measured and the results tabulated to provide statistics which may be indicative of the level of morale. However, it must be remembered that such statistics can only be **indicators**, as other factors may be more significant in determining the results.

For example, a high labour turnover may be an indication of low morale within a company but it may equally represent a reaction to some external factor such as housing shortage, poor education provision or changed personal circumstances. What labour turnover does provide is a trend, but the trend should be assessed in the context of the industry both locally and nationally, and comparisons should be made with other years. Turnover may remain low, however, in times of high unemployment irrespective of the fact that morale may be at an all-time low.

Accident statistics, on the other hand, may provide a valuable and reasonably reliable indicator of morale: accidents often occur as a result of carelessness or distraction, which may well be indicative of the individual's attitude of mind rather than the result of unsafe working practices. On the other hand, the number of accidents will be governed by the nature of the work – how potentially dangerous is the workplace – and the degree of importance managers give to the whole question of safety and the implementation of the Health and Safety at Work etc. Act 1974. Pros and cons could be provided for each one of the items listed above.

Whilst the factors considered above provide useful indicators, studies into morale suggest the following principal influences:

- the adequacy of supervision;
- the job itself;
- the organizational climate;
- the economic and related rewards;
- the promotion prospects;
- the working relationships;
- the working environment.

Adequacy of supervision

This is perhaps the most important factor affecting employee morale since it represents the point of contact between the organization and the employee. Dissatisfaction with supervision can arise for a variety of reasons:

- lack of leadership;
- poor delegation;
- poor knowledge of the job;
- poor interpersonal skills;
- lack of caring and support;
- inadequate communication skills;
- expression of favouritism;
- victimization;
- personality conflict;
- excessive disciplinary measures.

Procedures exist within organizations to handle some of these problems. For example, certain issues will come to light during appraisal exercises and may well reflect staff development deficiencies in the preparation and training of those holding supervisory positions (see Chapter 15 for 'Appraisal'). Grievance procedures also serve as an official channel for airing justifiable complaints. However, where the problem may be rooted in personal factors based on emotional reactions, it will be more difficult to provide a solution. One answer might be to separate the individuals concerned.

The job itself

Most people find intrinsic satisfaction in a job which they particularly like and where they know that they do it well. Dissatisfaction arises when:

- there is too much work;
- there is insufficient work;
- the work is of the wrong calibre;
- there is inadequate training;
- the nature of the job is fragmented;
- the job becomes de-skilled;
- there is little aesthetic pleasure.

Such criticisms will usually indicate an absence of job analysis and evaluation together with inadequate staffing levels. They will also be likely to highlight the need for staff development activity whilst casting doubt on the quality of recruitment and selection procedures. Individual dissatisfaction with a job will often be indicative of staff who are either under- or overqualified for the position they hold. In any event such problems may be resolved by introducing organization and methods (O & M), sharpening up selection procedures (perhaps by introducing some form of testing) and giving more thought to job evaluation.

Organizational climate (see also page 87)

Organizational climate – the 'feel of the workplace' (see also Chapter 5, 'Leading') – will be reflected in:

- the organizational structure;
- the communication network;
- the extent of participation and consultation;
- the way in which change is introduced;
- the team spirit engendered throughout the organization;
- the number of disputes.

Modern management practice encourages participation and collaboration at all levels of the organization. A sense of commitment to the purpose of the organization is fostered and all employees are encouraged to make a contribution to and become part of a collective endeavour to achieve a successful enterprise. A healthy organizational climate will be present where attempts have been made to reduce hierarchical and lateral differentiation and to increase the level of integration. For example, in new forms of organizations, barriers to status and position have been greatly reduced by the introduction of shared restaurant services for all the workforce rather than divisive staff dining rooms and works canteens. Also, both employees and management wear the same company uniform where appropriate – e.g. protective clothing on the shop floor.

Economic and related rewards

The salary or wage factor will always be significant, to a greater or lesser extent, in affecting morale. Where elements other than money contribute to a high level of job satisfaction the financial side may be less significant, but individuals will still expect to be adequately rewarded financially for their efforts. Where salary and related reward issues **will** tend to dominate is when:

- salaries are low in comparison to others doing the same or similar work within the organization;
- salaries are poor compared to those paid by other employers;
- salaries are disproportionate to the level of responsibility held;
- other organizations offer additional 'perks'.

These problems will be more likely to be prevalent where an organization does not operate a realistic wage/salary structure. Organizations need to ensure that the rates they pay are compatible with other employers in the area and/or in the labour market generally. The position will tend to be simplified where jobs are graded and salary scales published. Employees then know precisely where they stand and what will be required of them if they are to move from one grade to another. Many organizations choose to operate pay incentives for the acquisition of additional qualifications or improved skills, and these will tend to encourage employees to seek to better themselves.

Where a wage 'freeze' is in force or a very minimal pay award, possibly as a result of government pay policy, organizations may introduce incentive schemes of some kind – e.g. employee profit-sharing schemes or preferential share purchase. Alternatively, they may opt for the introduction of perks such as free medical and dental care, subsidized hairdressing and canteen and reduced rate holidays (see also Chapter 6, 'Motivating'). Where organizations make special provisions to treat their staff well, they are likely to increase the loyalty of existing staff whilst gaining the sort of favourable reputation which will always make it easy to recruit new staff as and when necessary.

Promotion prospects

Most ambitious workers will desire to be promoted in recognition of their skills and abilities. Where promotion prospects are limited, perhaps due to financial restraints or a depressed economy, morale may be adversely affected and management will be faced with the problem of sustaining interest and commitment on the part of their workforce. At such times, management needs to give particular attention to making such promotion appointments as are available; otherwise the problem may be compounded in that morale may be adversely affected yet again when staff consider that the 'wrong' people are promoted!

A procedure for promotions needs to be devised and staff must be assured that any appraisal exercises which are conducted have a direct relationship to their prospects. When internal promotions are being considered it will be usual for staff to go before a Promotions Panel made up of a representative cross-section of the company and not just the Personnel Manager and immediate superior (e.g. departmental head or section supervisor).

Working relationships

Man is by nature gregarious and the acceptability of the working group will influence his morale. Indeed, one of the main factors contributing to an individual's job satisfaction will be pleasant superiors and colleagues. Conversely, one of the reasons for people changing jobs may be the poor quality of the interpersonal relationships which exist in the workplace. Reasons for problems will be varied but are likely to include:

- the wrong mix of individuals;
- the wrong size of working group;
- inability of individuals to operate as a team;
- personality factors.

Each point lies within the domains of industrial psychology and organizational analysis, and requires due consideration when an appointment is to be made or a promotion given. Where any vacancy arises it must be viewed in context, and the context will not only be job related but also people related. Success will depend to a large extent on the human relations involved. Sometimes it may be simply a matter of adjusting the size or composition of a working group (i.e. adding one or taking one away or switching between groups), but where personality factors come into play, problems can be more difficult to solve.

Working environment

A wide variety of studies has been conducted into the numerous effects of the impact of the working environment on the morale of staff. These include:

- the relationship between environment and output;
- the significance of office layout to work flow;
- the effect of colour;
- the relationship between fatigue, morale and productivity;
- the benefits of ergonomically designed furniture;
- aspects of health and safety at work;
- the introduction of new technology;
- lighting, heating and space considerations.

Finance permitting, the working environment is one area where change can be instituted reasonably easily. In recent years increased attention has been given to this, with many advances in technology and the introduction of different work patterns. Also, living conditions in general have improved dramatically, so raising people's thresholds in terms of what they consider to be acceptable.

How all the factors considered above could be represented on a 'Morale Factor Scale' is difficult to determine in that their degree of significance will change according to different circumstances and variables operating at any given time, both at the level of the individual and in the context of the organization.

The morale issue needs to be approached on a broad front because concentrating on one or two factors will not suffice. Successful enterprise comes from the pursuit of common aims by sincere, straightforward individuals who have a group spirit and shared sense of commitment and who believe in one another's capabilities.

8
Communicating

'The interest in life does not lie in what people do, nor even in their relations to each other, but largely in the power to communicate with a third party . . .'

Virginia Wolf
On Not Knowing Greek

The ability to communicate is central to our very existence and is something which is now receiving more attention than it ever did. There is a growing realization of its importance in the business context in that, if managers can't communicate, they can't manage people – and people are the key to making any organization tick.

Communication is concerned with transmitting and receiving information which is the key to all aspects of organizational life, whether it be planning, controlling, problem solving, decision making, motivating, interviewing or any of the other management activities discussed in this book.

Given the importance of information, it is vital that communication is effective: many of the problems encountered by management today are aggravated by poor communication. Communication enables management to get jobs done and yet business disasters are frequently attributed to breakdown or failures in communication.

What causes communication breakdowns?

Communication is more than speaking or writing or signalling in some way to a third party and hoping that they 'get the message'. It isn't as simple as that and, despite the fact that a high percentage (something in the region of 70 per cent) of our time is spent communicating in one way or another, remarkably little real attention is given to the acquisition of effective communication skills and techniques.

The basic dilemma in communication is that the meaning of the message received may not be that which was intended by the sender. The 'transmitter' and 'receiver' are two individuals separated by **communication barriers** which are capable of distorting the messages which pass between them. The reasons for distortion may include any one or a combination of some of the following:

failure to hear or see (physical barriers)
language difficulties
lack of knowledge
external interruption or interference
non-verbal signals or cues
tone of voice
pre-judgement
differing perceptions
reference group identity (status, position and function)
superior–subordinate relationships
stereotyping
emotional reactions
indifference
prejudice – on grounds of race or sex
'filtering out'
mental closure

Some of these barriers speak for themselves – e.g. deafness, interruption from outside noise, tone of voice, indifference or sexual prejudice – but others may require a little more explanation.

Language difficulties

This will not simply be a question of foreign languages but will also include dialects, accents, the use of technical language or specialist jargon. Also, given that there are in excess of 600,000 words in the English language and that the average person survives on about 2,000, language problems should not be so difficult to appreciate. The meanings of words also present problems when the Oxford Dictionary records an average of 28 separate meanings for each of the 500 most frequently used words! Words come into their own in context but this merely emphasizes the need to provide the appropriate 'background' in order to reduce any likelihood of confusion. Words can also be emotive and symbolic in certain circumstances; consequently, their use will either stress the impact or provoke an unwanted reaction, so the choice of words is vital to successful communication.

Non-verbal signals or cues

Sometimes referred to as 'metacommunication' (meaning that which is additional to basic communication and therefore something which will provide valuable clues), this includes what is often referred to as 'body language' or, to give it its technical term, 'kinesics'. The comment that 'actions often speak louder than words' is significant, and such cues can convey to the trained observer a lot about both the transmitter and the receiver. Non-verbal signals can provide a lot of valuable feedback. They will include:

facial expression
posture, whether seated or standing
gesture, particularly hand movements
eye contact
where people stand in relation to others – the use of space
nodding of head
shrugging of shoulders
appearance and dress

Pre-judgement

This may result from the 'I've heard it all before' syndrome. What we hear or understand when someone speaks is conditioned by what we know already, by our background and experience. So instead of hearing what we are told, we hear what our minds tell us has been said.

Differing Perceptions

People interpret the same stimulus in different ways according to their previous experience. Therefore, criteria such as age, sex, nationality, culture, education and personality will all have a bearing on the way a situation is perceived. Figures 27 and 28 are well-known examples of

Fig. 27 Rabbit–duck figure (used in 1900 by psychologist Joseph Jastrow)

Fig. 28   Young girl—old woman. This was created originally by cartoonist W E Hill in 1915 when it was published in *Puck* as 'My Wife and My Mother-in-law'. It was later brought to the attention of psychologists by Edwin G Boring

differences of perception and awareness. Initial reactions will be different in different people, dependent on those factors.

Similarly, thirty managers attending a management seminar, all listening to the same speaker, may each interpret what is said in thirty different ways.

Reference Group Identity

People often react according to the group they identify with at any given time. For example, when one workmate laughs, the others will often join in. In the job situation, individuals tend to interpret and react to messages and adopt stances according to their status, position and functional role within their organization.

Superior–subordinate relationship

The barrier here will be that each will tend to tell the other what he wants him to know rather than what the other wants to hear. The standpoints will therefore often be different, and it will be up to the superior to try to build the confidence of the subordinate in order that the message/instruction/command will be received accurately and in the spirit intended.

Stereotyping

This is an extreme example of letting expectations determine communication content and validity. It can happen even before an individual has opened his mouth. It is the 'all brawn and no brain' or 'dumb blonde' comment which is often stubbornly preserved even in the face of conflicting evidence.

Emotional reactions

These arise out of insecurity, worry, fear or anger, and can only be successfully overcome by an individual when he controls the display of emotion and is sensitive enough not to wish to upset others. When emotions run high, it is usually better to wait until they subside before trying to get a message over.

'Filtering out'

This is one of the reasons why management can find it very difficult to introduce change. People tend to be naturally resistant to change in that it conflicts with what they already believe. They don't want to hear it, so they either 'filter out' the new piece of information or they twist the meaning to make it fit with preconceived ideas or attitudes.

Mental Closure

This is to do with our ability to 'fill gaps', when we will almost certainly be prepared to accept a full square or circle or read unjoined dots as a triangle (Fig. 29) or even accept incomplete words in a written text. This also

Fig. 29   Mental closure

happens with verbal communication: when the receiver tries to close the gap before the total message is put across, he may jump to the wrong conclusion and two and two will make five. Once such a mental 'set' is established, it can take considerable effort on the part of the receiver to make the necessary mental adjustment to rectify the situation.

If, then, there are so many possible barriers to effective communication, one thing should be crystal clear – that it can never be assumed that every message sent will be received in the manner intended. A classic example of distortion and one worthy of repeating here is the one from the trenches during the First World War: it started out as 'Send reinforcements, we're going to advance' and ended up as 'Send three and fourpence, we're going to a dance'.

Why is communication so important to management?

Communication is a two-way activity, and successful management depends on its ability to gather and to assimilate the information it receives as well as to transmit efficient and accurate information, to convey clear instructions and to consult with its workforce. It can achieve these ends only when its channels of communication operate effectively.

Communication needs to be managed both within the organization and with the world outside. Sometimes it will be of a formal nature whilst at other times it will be informal – e.g. relying on what is popularly referred to as the 'grapevine' (see page 114).

Internal Communication

Within an organization, managers will need to communicate with all levels of personnel from the Board of Directors to whom they are ultimately responsible, to their immediate superiors, to colleagues in the management team, to subordinates and to trade union representatives. Communication will therefore take place vertically, horizontally and diagonally (Fig. 30).

In what circumstances is internal communication essential?

Literally every action taken within an organization will involve communication of some kind, irrespective of the level at which the communication is taking place, the medium adopted and the identities of transmitter and receiver. In an attempt to categorize communicating situations, it may be helpful to consider the following:

giving instructions
keeping people informed
solving problems

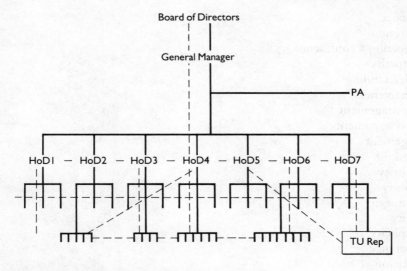

Fig. 30 Internal communication network
Key: ---=lines of communication
HoD=Head of Department
TU=Trade Union

negotiating
airing differences of opinion
providing constructive criticism
affording praise
reprimanding
disciplining
handling grievances
soliciting opinion and points of view
offering advice
evaluating results

Any of these situations needs to be seen in the context of a two-way process, and the factors referred to as barriers to communication must be borne in mind at all times if the communication is to be effective.

Skills and qualities

Additionally, communicating is more than simply speaking or writing to a third party. It is, rather, exercising a range of skills and qualities which include:

tact
diplomacy

patience
discretion
respecting a confidence
sympathy
understanding
assertiveness
encouragement
discouragement
judgement
foresight
integrity
honesty
openness
clarity
simplicity
coherence
precision
conciseness
decisiveness

Indeed, effective communication is largely dependent on attitude of mind, which, ideally, requires the acceptance of the need for others to be 'in the know' and to have sufficient information to enable them to understand what is going on.

Communication strategies will vary according to circumstances. Sometimes it will be necessary to prepare formal written reports whilst at other times an informal chat will be more appropriate. It is therefore more than what is actually said or written – it's the way managers **are** which makes them good or bad communicators.

Sharing information

The preparedness to share information with the workforce will be the key to good industrial relations (see Chapter 15).

Management must communicate through its managers, who need to talk to their subordinates at regular intervals about things which are of interest to them and are likely to affect their work. Many managers adopt an 'open-door' policy and will also try to circulate freely in the workplace in an attempt to encourage a positive attitude to the interchange of information and to generate good lines of communication generally. This is the essence of 'participatory management' where there is continual, constructive dialogue between management and the workforce on matters of mutual concern.

Formal mechanisms will be used to set up, for example, consultative groups, joint committees, briefing meetings and the establishment of worker directors in decision-making processes.

Informal means of communication will provide information on such issues as:

- plans for the future and the reasons for them;
- external events which are affecting the organization;
- problems which the organization is facing;
- opportunities which exist for the organization to expand or diversify;
- where the organization stands in relation to its competitors;
- future trends;
- union negotiations as they affect the organization;
- where the individual sees himself and his future within the organization.

Such dialogue can greatly enhance industrial relations because it allows the workers to air their feelings freely and to get first-hand information on matters of company policy and future plans, whilst alerting management well in advance to any issues and problems which are likely to come to the surface at a later date.

External Communication

Many organizations will have extensive contacts with external agencies. Managers will then require to apply different strategies and adopt different roles dependent upon the audience/recipient and the message they wish to convey.

External communication links might be with any or all of the following:

clients/customers
shareholders
suppliers
representatives from competing organizations
financial advisers
consultants
accountants
banks
insurance companies
lawyers
tax inspectors
local government officers
government ministers
media representatives

All external contacts will require different skills and, sometimes, the mastery of different specialist languages in order to communicate effectively on something approaching an even footing.

It will often be necessary for those representing the organization to place personal feelings and attitudes to one side when adopting a 'company line'. It may even necessitate making 'no comment', directing an enquiry elsewhere in the organization or fending off questions which either they are not at liberty to answer or which the organization would prefer to be left unanswered. On other occasions it will be essential to represent accurately the image of the organization and do a good public relations job.

The Grapevine

The grapevine or 'bush telegraph' comes into operation when the correct procedures and lines of communication are not used. Usually it is a vehicle for spreading rumour or gossip and distorting the truth (Fig. 31). The

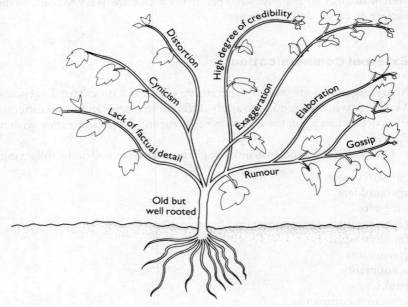

Fig. 31   The grapevine

speed at which information travels along its branches or lines can be alarmingly fast. An active grapevine can do an organization a lot of damage by spreading false or incomplete information, so causing concern, cynicism, fear and low morale which may ultimately reduce productivity and affect staff turnover by creating an unsettled workplace. Like any underground organization, its hold can be a strong one and difficult to destroy. It is also dangerous in that it will often be believed in preference to the 'official line' – even when it is wrong!

It is interesting to note that a MORI (Market and Opinion Research International) poll carried out into how employees got their information revealed that in one particular company as many as 45 per cent of the workforce considered that they got the vast majority of their information from the grapevine although only 2 per cent admitted to actually preferring the grapevine as a source.

Such findings suggest that organizations must be mindful of the way in which information is disseminated – particularly during times of turbulence or uncertainty – when the trust and confidence of employees is of paramount importance. It will be vital in such circumstances that workers do not find that they have to rely on the grapevine.

How is effective communication achieved?

Organizations ultimately depend on their ability to transmit efficient and accurate information. The starting point for achieving this will be to seek answers to some fundamental questions:

- What is the purpose of the communication?
- Who needs to receive the information?
- Where will the communication take place?
- When will the communication take place?
- Is there a deadline?
- What precisely needs to be communicated?
- How important is accuracy?
- Are there legal implications to be considered?
- Is the information confidential?
- How will the information be communicated?
- What tone needs to be adopted?
- What is the range of communications options open?
- Are there cost implications and considerations?

Well-considered answers to these questions will go some way towards ensuring the success of communication in the organization. It will be very much a matter of planning the communication, thinking it through thoroughly and then acting. It will also be useful to see the situation from the point of view of the receiver(s), in an attempt to gauge likely reaction and so be better prepared to respond effectively.

What methods of communication are available?

Basically, the method employed will be a matter either of written and graphic presentation or of oral communication which will frequently be supported by the non-verbal. These are two broad categories, and choices will have to be made according to the dictates of circumstance.

Written and graphic communication

This includes:

letters
circulars
memoranda
reports
notices
agendas
minutes
booklets
leaflets
press releases
manuals
handbooks
forms
questionnaires
charts, graphs and pictograms
diagrams
statistical tables
maps
flow charts

Irrespective of the form of written communication selected, attention must be given to:

content
structure
style
purpose
accuracy
clarity and coherence
tone
precision
impact
courtesy

identity of recipient
layout and presentation

Written communication skills and techniques can be acquired and will improve with practice.

Oral communication

The spoken word will take up a large proportion of any manager's time, whether it is in face-to-face situations or over the telephone. Oral skills will be used in the following situations:

interviews
briefing sessions
discussions
negotiations
meetings
lectures
seminars
presentations
conferences
introductions
speeches
votes of thanks
radio/television broadcasts
telephoning
teleconferencing
intercom use
public address systems

The nature of a manager's work will determine the extent to which the above are used or appropriate. Different situations will necessarily make different demands on the speaker, and will call upon a range of skills and resources if the communication is to be effective. Success will depend upon an awareness of the following essential elements:

sound preparation
thinking before speaking
clarity
audibility
pacing
sequencing
tone
level
choice of words
avoidance of technical terms and jargon

All these pointers will apply to virtually any form of oral communication but, additionally, where it is face to face, the speaker needs to:

- seek to establish eye contact with the recipient;
- look out for instantaneous reactions;
- maximize the opportunity to respond to feedback;
- avoid the use of distracting mannerisms;
- limit the amount of non-verbal signals used.

Telecommunications and Technology

All up-to-date organizations will wish to make good use of the wide range of sophisticated systems and techniques which are currently available, thanks to the advances in telecommunication and technology generally. However, it should be noted that the application of such techniques should be given careful consideration in terms of the following:

- suitability for the purpose;
- convenience for both sender and receiver;
- operational ease for the user;
- acceptability to the receiver;
- reliability in terms of speed and safety;
- security of information;
- validity in terms of the provision of a record;
- practicability for the organization.

How important is listening?

Given that communication is a two-way process, any discussion on communication would be incomplete without reference to listening. Listening is at least half of communication and its importance cannot be overstated. Listening is a skill the lack of which will be detrimental to successful management. Listening is not the same as hearing, nor is it simply 'not talking', although it is surprising how often people in all circumstances fall into such traps. Listening is an active process, something we can all learn and yet something which is rarely included in formal education and training.

There are certain situations when it is particularly important for a manager to listen, and these include:

- where a decision has to be reached based on verbal evidence;
- where instinct would suggest instant disagreement or rejection of an idea, proposal or problem;
- where level of comprehension is in question;

- where the subject matter is foreign to the listener;
- where there is a requirement to sum up;
- where there is a requirement to pass on the information;
- where a written report is required afterwards.

The charactistics of a good listener

- willingness to be interested;
- open-mindedness;
- a good filter system, able to extract and hold the main points;
- ability to resist pre-judging issues;
- good powers of concentration;
- enjoyment of the mental exercise;
- ability to balance an argument;
- ability to critically evaluate the content of what has been said;
- ability to establish eye contact with the speaker;
- ability to make brief notes.

The characteristics of a poor listener

- a desire to be entertained;
- critical of the delivery rather than of the content;
- tendency to 'switch off';
- pre-judging of issues;
- easily distracted;
- collecting personal thoughts in preparation for an opportunity to speak;
- attempting to memorize great detail;
- making little effort to be interested;
- paying undue attention to the speaker's appearance;
- fidgeting;
- making copious notes.

These points can be compared with those mentioned in connection with barriers to effective communication, from which it can be seen that there are decided links worthy of note.

A high degree of communication skills is fundamental to effective and efficient management at all levels. Communication is central to everything a manager or supervisor does, and consequently it is vital that appropriate techniques and strategies are recognized and applied.

9
Interviewing

'There was a little shuffling and throat-clearing and then Sir Rufus took him gently through a formal application check – full name, age, degree, and so on until David began to wonder whether the whole thing was rigged . . . and that his presence here was no more than a polite ritual.'

R. F. Delderfield
To Serve Them All My Days

Interviews intimidate. Interviews investigate. Interviews discriminate. They are used by organizations every day, for one reason or another. There are four principal types of formal interview situation which managers or supervisors are likely to be involved in at some time:

- the selection interview;
- the appraisal interview;
- the disciplinary interview;
- the leaving interview.

Interviews will also be held for grievances, counselling and problem solving.

The quality of interviewing varies enormously between organizations and even within the same organization. With the possible exception of the Personnel Department, few managers undergo formal training in the art of interviewing. In any event, the fact that it is an art makes it difficult to learn the subtleties and nuances which combine to produce the effective interviewer.

Irrespective of the situation, there are certain general guidelines in respect of good interview practice which can be applied to produce successful results. Points for consideration by the interviewer prior to and during the interview are:

- the objectives of the interview;
- the information required from the interviewee;
- the homework required prior to interview;
- the way in which the interviewee should be advised of the interview;

- the structure of the interview;
- the location and environment for the interview;
- the need for quietness and freedom from interruption;
- the interview style to be adopted;
- the sorts of questions to be asked;
- the sequence of the questions;
- whether the answers received are sufficient to enable a judgement to be made or a decision reached;
- whether listening skills are effective;
- whether he (the interviewer) is talking too much;
- whether the interview is succeeding in getting the best out of the interviewee;
- the non-verbal signals which are being received;
- the need to note points raised by the interviewee which must be followed up after the interview;
- whether the interviewee is being given a fair hearing;
- the need to summarize as the interview progresses;
- the need to make notes during and, more importantly, immediately after the interview.

In addition, all personnel involved in interviews must be aware of current employment legislation.

Where the interviewer keeps to these guidelines, the chances are that the interview will be carried out with a sense of purpose and will achieve its intended outcomes.

Useful Qualities in an Interviewer

The following characteristics are likely to prove useful in someone conducting interviews:

- courtesy;
- tact;
- open-mindedness;
- inventiveness – ability to cope with difficult or unanticipated situations;
- capacity to 'read between the lines';
- powers of judgement – e.g. ability to discriminate and to evaluate the level of interviewee performance 'on the day' against potential;
- quickness and presence of mind;
- flexibility;
- persuasive powers;
- decisiveness;
- ability to operate as a member of a team (where panel interviews are used).

Interview panels

Sometimes the interview will be undertaken by an interview panel or board. In such circumstances it is important that the members of the panel decide in advance the areas on which they will question and, if necessary, who will chair the proceedings. This is important because co-ordination and structure are vital in panel interviews, otherwise the interviewee will tend to feel bombarded from all directions. Such situations are also likely to make the interviewee more tense and may sometimes confuse the candidate, who has to decide to whom the answers to general questions should be addressed. Nevertheless, panel interviews are often used in selection interviews to provide a cross-section of opinion, a variety of questioning styles, the opportunity for closer scrutiny of candidates and joint decision making.

The Selection Interview

The term 'interview' is frequently associated with job interviews, and indeed selection interviewing is an important area of activity for both the organization and the individual concerned. Appropriate and reliable selection techniques are essential if costly errors are to be avoided. The following statement, taken from the Trade Union and Labour Relations Act 1974, indicates the serious consequences for management which can arise as a result of making an error of judgement when selecting employees:

'Each employee shall have the right not to be unfairly dismissed by his employer and the remedy of an employee so dismissed . . . shall be by way of complaint to an industrial tribunal.'

Purpose of Selection Interviews

The intention is to provide a forum for the exchange of information between interviewer (organization) and interviewee (candidate for a vacancy). It is a two-way process whereby both parties should be enabled to 'fill in the gaps' between the application form or curriculum vitae (CV) and the job description.

Selection interviews will range from short, relatively informal chats about pay and working conditions to lengthy, highly structured formal selection board interviews where, for example, the candidate's motivation, expectations and career aspirations are explored in detail. The nature of the job will largely determine the format the interview takes. Usually the former type will apply to unskilled jobs, whereas the latter would be appropriate to more senior positions. The more experienced and higher the level of the candidate, the higher the position sought and consequently the more thorough the interview.

From the point of view of the employer, the interview will serve to:

- find out what sort of person the applicant is;
- check the details already held;
- obtain further information relevant to the position to be filled;
- clarify any points;
- provide an opportunity to expand on information about the job;
- determine the suitability of the applicant for the job;
- assess how the interviewee acts, reacts and interacts.

At the same time, the interviewee will have an opportunity to:

- 'sell' himself to the interview panel;
- ask questions about the job;
- determine whether or not the job seems 'right' for him.

The procedure also enables both parties to discuss conditions of employment, salary scales and promotional prospects and generally to form the basis of a mutually acceptable contract of employment.

Once the necessary interview preliminaries have been taken care of (see Chapter 15), attention can be focused on the interview itself. This concerns the way in which the interview is opened, the extent to which it is structured, the sorts of questions to be asked, the sequencing of questions and the way in which it is drawn to a close.

In selection interviews the interviewer(s) will attempt to establish a rapport with the interviewee so that the candidate will relax as quickly as possible and feel sufficiently at ease to talk freely. The early stages will also be used to set the scene for the interview by introducing, where necessary, the members of the panel, ensuring that the broad details of the job are understood by the candidate and explaining the general purpose and format of the interview.

Selection interviews tend to be highly structured; once the introductory matters are dealt with, questioning proceeds along a logical pre-determined pattern. It is usual to go through the educational/career profile of the candidate, providing him an opportunity to talk and elaborate on the information provided in the application form or CV. Interviewers may ask questions in a variety of ways, but must not pose questions which contravene the Equal Opportunities legislation.

Types of questions

Direct questions provide limited scope on the part of the candidate to be selective in the response but are essential where the interviewer wishes factual information or a very specific reply. The interviewer may even, on occasion, wish to limit the response even further, in which case the question will call for a straight Yes/No answer. This sort of questioning technique is used where a definite answer is wanted quickly, but it will seriously inhibit the candidate who lacks confidence and consequently finds it impossible to expand.

Leading questions are those where the candidate is likely to provide the sort of answer the interviewer expects, and as such are of very limited use in a selection interview situation. For example, a question may be prefaced by the words 'Would you agree that . . .?'

Loaded questions may be used where an interviewer wants to ascertain whether the interviewee can resist being led and how strongly his views and opinions are held. Such questions may also be posed deliberately to test the degree of assertiveness or aggression of the interviewee. For example, assertiveness may be an essential ingredient required of the successful applicant, and asking the candidate a loaded question can be one way of finding out whether he possesses this quality.

Open-ended questions are those which permit maximum freedom on the part of interviewees. Such questions can be revealing and will also help demonstrate how well the candidate is able to gather his thoughts and generally articulate his point of view. However, on the negative side they can be extremely time consuming and may even, with the practised interviewee, succeed in turning the direction of the interview away from that originally intended.

Hypothetical questions can be useful where it is considered important to gauge how a prospective employee might react in a particular situation. This is the 'What would you do if . . .?' type of question. This provides the interviewee with an opportunity to demonstrate problem-solving ability and imagination, whilst for the interviewer it can reveal a number of factors, particularly about the character of the individual and his attitudes and opinions.

Prompting questions may need to be asked where an interviewee is struggling to respond or is apparently having difficulty in seeing the purpose of the original question.

Probing questions will be used when the initial response does not fully answer the initial question or where the interviewer wishes a more detailed reply.

Multiple questions are those which necessitate more than one answer in that they cover several points. Politicians are possibly the most skilled at handling this type of question! In the interview situation the best that might be expected is that the interviewee will ask for the question to be repeated, whilst at worst there will be total confusion all round.

Questions from the interviewee

An interview should allow for questions from the interviewee. Usually these will tend to be of a fairly predictable nature and the interviewer should endeavour to provide full and satisfactory responses. The interviewee will normally ask questions towards the latter stages of the interview and it is important that all matters appertaining to the job, the salary and the conditions of employment have been adequately covered in the course of the interview. Where an interview has gone according to plan, all avenues should have been explored, all questions posed and answered, and all objectives met.

Bringing the interview to a close

At this point it will be the interviewer's responsibility to draw the interview to a close by telling the candidate what the next stage of the procedure will be – e.g. whether he should return to the waiting area and await the result or whether the decision will be conveyed in due course. Sometimes it can be difficult to draw an interview tactfully to a close; two tips for interviewers are either to glance at a watch or, where glasses have been worn, to remove them and put them in a pocket. At the end of an interview it is important to be positive by standing up, shaking hands and, possibly, accompanying the candidate to the door.

The Appraisal Interview

Appraisal is dealt with in Part III, but frequently the process includes an interview which should be managed in an appropriate manner if it is to achieve its objectives and if the whole appraisal scheme is to have credibility. Like any other form of interviewing, it is a skilled activity and the individual conducting the appraisal should be well prepared.

For many employees the appraisal interview is the most dreaded event of the year, whilst for many managers the event may be equally unpopular and smacks of 'going through the motions'. Such attitudes should be discouraged wherever possible, with positive steps taken to counteract the negative connotations which often accompany appraisal procedures.

To be successful from the perspectives of both the employer and the employee, the appraisal interview must be meaningful and have a sense of purpose. Otherwise, the whole exercise is in danger of being construed as a waste of time. How far the staff appraisal interview is seen as being critical by employees is likely to rest on the extent to which it is instrumental in determining promotion or career development generally.

A Checklist for positive appraisal interviewing

(a) *Before the Interview*
1. Ensure that all employees are familiar with the scheme and its aims, and that they are given sufficient notice of the forthcoming interview and of their role.
2. Make sure that all the necessary paperwork is to hand – viz. job descriptions, employee records, reports by superiors, previous appraisal forms, rating scales and any self-appraisal that may have been conducted by the employee. (This may be anything from the completion of a pro forma to an ad hoc note of points, questions, topics for discussion at the interview.)
3. Ensure that the location of the interview is made known to the employees and that the room is suitably arranged – viz. comfort and privacy ensured.

(b) *During the Interview*
1. Establish a comfortable, easy atmosphere – e.g. sit side by side rather than at opposite sides of the table.
2. Set the scene by laying the necessary ground rules and establish the tone of the interview.
3. Begin with general questions and move to the more specific and perhaps problem-related areas. It is important to reach critical areas reasonably quickly; otherwise the time allocation may run out or the interview will over-run if these issues are to be fully explained.
4. Examine both strengths and weaknesses – encouraging the employee to identify them personally and discuss ways in which the weaknesses might be overcome.
5. Offer praise as well as constructive criticism.
6. Provide the employee with sufficient opportunity to talk and put his point of view across.
7. Jointly identify problems and possible solutions.
8. Provide the employee with the opportunity to put his side of the story or 'put the record straight'.
9. Determine and agree the future course of action – e.g. training of some kind, further education, a sideways move.
10. Try to establish the employee's future aspirations.
11. Summarize joint decisions and agreements.
12. Finish on a friendly, positive note.

(c) *After the Interview*
1. Provide a written record of the interview, the decisions reached and the reasons for them.

2. Initiate necessary follow-up procedures – e.g. ensure that supervisors are briefed to monitor weaknesses identified, arrange necessary on-the-job training and report back on the employee's progress.
3. Follow up the process and check for successful implementation.

The Disciplinary Interview

Of all interview situations the disciplinary one is the one which most managers and supervisors find most stressful and difficult to handle. However, to avoid taking the necessary action is to shirk responsibility and enable misconduct to continue unchecked. The need to conduct a disciplinary interview may arise for a variety of reasons, including

- stealing;
- drunkenness or drug abuse;
- poor timekeeping;
- excessive absences;
- unsafe working practices;
- insubordination;
- fighting or violent behaviour likely to endanger the safety of others;
- wilful damage or destruction to property or equipment.

Proper procedures must, however, be followed where the matter reaches the stage of a disciplinary interview; otherwise, employees may have grounds to appeal against any decision reached or be in a position to seek compensation. Employees who do consider that their treatment has been unfair may take their cases to industrial tribunals under one of a number of Acts, such as:

Trade Unions and Labour Relations Act 1974
Sex Discrimination Act 1975
Race Relations Act 1976
Employment Protection (Consolidation) Act 1978

Management is required to ensure that any measures taken are within the scope of the personal authority of the individual conducting the interview, and that proceedings are in line with company policy and within the legislative framework. A useful framework of reference is given in the *Code of Practice on Disciplinary Practice and Procedures in Employment* published by the Advisory, Conciliation and Arbitration Service (ACAS).

In the UK, regulations for disciplinary problems are based on principles of natural justice and are strongly influenced by case law already on the statute book – i.e. precedent. Briefly, the fundamental points for consideration are:

- that the individual should be aware of the standards of performance expected of him and of the rules to which he is expected to conform (organizations can help ensure this by making these an integral part of a written Contract of Employment and requiring that all new employees issued with contracts sign and return a copy of the document, indicating that they have understood the conditions when they accept the offer of employment;
- that faults/misconduct should be clearly indicated;
- that, where at all possible, opportunity should be provided to improve conduct or rectify matters before disciplinary action is taken (sometimes formal disciplinary action may be inappropriate and unnecessary, and, wherever possible, efforts should be made to resolve matters before they reach this stage – disciplinary interviews, like all others, are costly in terms of both time and money, and often all parties concerned would be much better off engaged in productive work);
- that employees should be informed of the nature of the complaint or accusation;
- that employees should have the opportunity to state their cases;
- that thorough investigations should have been carried out prior to disciplinary action;
- that the employee should have the right to be accompanied at the interview by a friend or trade union representative;
- that the employee should have the right to appeal against any disciplinary action taken.

Before actual disciplinary proceedings are undertaken, three stages will have been gone through:

- Oral warnings of an informal nature.
- Oral warnings of a formal nature, often accompanied by a warning in writing. Such warnings point out the issue concerned and the likely consequences of continued or further offences of that nature.
- A formal and final written warning, setting out the next stage of events – e.g. suspension, disciplinary proceeding, dismissal – should the offence recur.

Where an offence does result in a disciplinary interview, the following checklist should be applied:

(a) *Before the Interview*
- Ascertain the full facts.
- Secure written reports and records of allegations.
- Review any similar previous issues.
- Clarify the legal position.
- Find out whether the employee is to be accompanied.

(b) *During the Interview*
- Establish the appropriate tone at the outset.
- Inform the employee of the allegations.
- Explain the management position.
- Provide the employee with opportunity to comment.
- Strive to discover any extenuating circumstances which require to be taken into account.
- Reach a joint solution if possible – e.g. the problem may be such that counselling rather than disciplining is required.
- Where insufficient evidence is available, the interview may have to be adjourned.
- Where misconduct is admitted, determine the next steps according to the severity of the offence – e.g. were there mitigating circumstances, is the employee desirous of making amends? (In either of these instances a time limit may be set, during which the employee can demonstrate that he has heeded the outcome of the interview, has moderated his behaviour and improved the situation.) Alternatively, an employee may refuse to make amends, be suspended and have the matter referred to a higher authority.
- The interviewer needs, above all, to stay calm, retain objectivity and endeavour, where possible, to persuade the interviewee to modify his behaviour in his own interests.
- Where the interviewer is unable to persuade or convince the interviewee that amends need to be made, he must indicate his disapproval and take steps to implement appropriate penalties and further action.
- Once the facts are established, the interviewer must ensure that the employee understands the course of action open to him should he disagree with the decision. (This will involve supplying a copy of the grievance procedure and notifying the employee of the time within which any appeal must be lodged.)

(c) *After the Interview*
- A written record of the interview should be prepared, indicating results and action agreed, and two copies should be sent to the employee – one copy to be kept by him, the other signed and returned for management's records.
- Those present at the interview should also receive copies.
- Any agreed action should be initiated.
- Progress should be monitored and results evaluated.
- Where an offence is of a minor nature and there is due effort to make amends, any mention of it should be removed from the file of an employee as an incentive to keep his record clean in future.
- Preparations should be made, if necessary, for any further disciplinary activity.

The Leaving Interview

Many organizations choose to interview all employees who resign. Such 'exit' interviews, as they are often called, can serve several useful purposes. As well as providing the organization with an opportunity to thank employees for their services and wish them well for the future, leaving interviews may be conducted for the following reasons:

- to help monitor staff turnover;
- to ascertain the reason for leaving (this may not always be what it appears on the surface);
- to identify supervisory problems which may exist;
- to evaluate morale;
- to gather material for updating job specifications;
- to gain insight into competitors to whom the leavers may be turning;
- to compare salaries elsewhere;
- to learn of working conditions and opportunities elsewhere;
- to project a favourable image of a caring, fair, open-minded organization in the eyes of those leaving.

In theory such an idea is sound, but in practice it may present problems and fail to produce the desired result in that employees:

- may be reluctant to participate openly and honestly in such an exercise;
- may be nervous of yet another interview;
- may fear that any criticism on their part may adversely affect their future requests for references;
- may or may not wish to bring personalities into the forefront of discussion, so clouding the issues;
- may feel resentful at lack of promotion or poor pay;
- may not wish to reveal the true reason for their departure and throw in a red herring to defuse the real situation.

Leaving interviews should not be left till the last day of employment, as other events will be likely to take precedence over the interview. Ideally they should be conducted as soon as possible after a resignation is received (or sometimes, where an organization is desirous of retaining an employee, prior to the acceptance of the resignation). In some instances, organizations may succeed in securing the withdrawal of a resignation where they are able to ascertain the cause and rectify the situation before it is too late!

Individuals who are leaving should be advised in advance that such an interview is to take place, in order that they may have an opportunity to collect their thoughts and weigh up what they wish to say. This type of interview will be much less of a two-way process than any of the others mentioned because the aim is to encourage employees to talk about their jobs and their reasons for leaving.

The atmosphere should be friendly and diplomatic in that constructive criticism by the leavers can be helpful in avoiding future errors. Here the interviewer will act rather as a sounding board on which the employee may voice his opinions and views. Where the interviewee is made to feel relaxed and when he knows that the interviewer is listening to what he has to say, he will often feel encouraged to talk at length and get problems off his chest, so revealing a lot of valuable information.

Reports on leaving interviews should be completed as soon afterwards as possible, preferably using a standard pro forma. As well as factual data, a record should be made of all criticisms and complaints made by the leaver, together with any positive suggestions. Such reports will prove useful in collating turnover statistics but may also form the basis of future action – e.g. improving supervisory skills, up-dating job descriptions, giving more attention to recruitment and selection procedures, introducing incentive schemes and improving training and staff development opportunities.

10
Meetings and Committees

'The room fills up; the sociologist and social psychologists, sophisticates of meetings, readers of Goffman who all know intimately the difference between a group and an encounter, who are expert in the dynamics of interaction, come in and pick their places with care, examining existing relationships, angles of vision, even the cast of the light. Finally the elaborate social construct is ready. Marvin sits at the head of the table, in that curious state of suspended animation appropriate to the moment before the start of a meeting.'

Malcolm Bradbury
The History Man

Meetings

How often have you read or heard comments such as: 'A meeting is a body of people who keep minutes but waste hours' or 'A camel is a horse designed by a committee'?

Meetings and committees are targets for criticism within organizations, and often there will tend to be very negative reactions about attending 'yet another meeting' where not a lot may be achieved set against the time spent and the input involved. Meetings have the reputation of being classic time-wasters when, in fact, they should be viewed as essential tools to effective management.

Why have meetings?

Meetings are held for many reasons, which include:

statutory requirement
providing information
'floating' ideas
solving problems
reporting back

collective decision making
dispelling rumour
creative thinking (brainstorming)
co-ordinating
fact finding
rubber stamping

Whatever the reason, it is vital that the purpose is clearly understood by all those attending in order that business may proceed efficiently and progress be made. Much of the responsibility for this must rest with the leader (chairman); indeed, a poor chairman will often be to blame for an ineffective meeting.

There may be sound reasons for holding meetings but what are the advantages of this form of activity over others?

- shared decision making;
- the benefit of different opinions;
- the benefit of different strengths and specialisms;
- the pooling of talents and ideas;
- the breadth of knowledge and experience introduced;
- one idea acting as a catalyst for others;
- the willingness of subordinates to support decisions in which they have been directly involved;
- the building of a high sense of group commitment;
- the persuasive qualities of group discussion;
- a vehicle for staff development.

Formal or Informal Meetings?

This will depend on the nature of the meeting and its purpose, but, generally speaking, the factors which determine the degree of formality are:

- the rules and regulations governing procedure (e.g. Articles of Association or Standing Orders – see Glossary of Terms at the end of this section);
- the order of proceedings;
- the need for official documentation – notice, agenda, minutes;
- the presence of a chairman.

Other significant factors are:

- the venue selected;
- the numbers attending;
- the duration;
- the frequency of meetings.

To categorize according to formal or informal is to provide a very broad framework of reference, but the types of meetings which normally fall into these categories in the strict business sense are indicated in the examples given in Figs. 32 and 33.

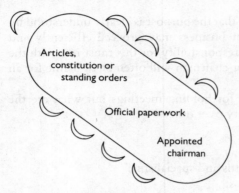

Chairman

Articles, constitution or standing orders

Official paperwork

Appointed chairman

Fig. 32   Formal meetings
1. Annual general meeting
2. Extraordinary general meeting
3. Board meetings
4. Executive committees
5. Advisory committees
6. Standing committees
7. Joint committees
8. Sub-committees
9. Ad hoc committees

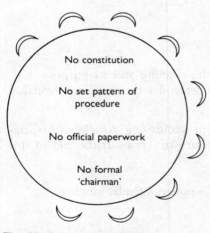

No constitution

No set pattern of procedure

No official paperwork

No formal 'chairman'

Fig. 33   Informal meetings
1. Intradepartmental meetings
2. Briefing meetings
3. Progress meetings
4. Working parties
5. Task groups
6. Brainstorming
7. Planning
8. Problem solving
9. T-groups

Other types of formal meeting include:

tribunals
public inquiries
company winding-up meetings
Royal commissions
council meetings of a local authority

Common features of meetings

Irrespective of whether meetings are formal or informal, they will follow certain common conventions in terms of preparation and conduct, including:

advance preparation
initiating discussion (someone will have to start the ball rolling)
exchanging ideas
giving opinions
testing feelings
clarifying
summarizing
recording decisions
making notes
requesting action

What goes wrong at meetings?

If we accept that many meetings are considered a waste of time, what goes wrong?

- notice is too short (where there is no minimum requirement);
- preparation is inadequate (both by the chairman and by those attending);
- the agenda is too long;
- the agenda order is wrong;
- agenda items are badly timed;
- too much conflict;
- no team spirit and sense of common purpose;
- participants are unclear of the terms of references;
- there is a hidden agenda (see below);
- chairmanship is weak (see below);
- inappropriate leadership style (see also Chapter 5).

The 'Hidden Agenda'

This is a term often given to explain underlying personal objectives and emotions which will exist within individuals and sometimes groups of individuals when they attend meetings. They are likely to include:

- defensive behaviour in order to protect interests;
- camouflage techniques to cover up some previous error or omission;
- pairing with other committee members to strengthen a case;
- aiming to impress a colleague or superior;
- using the meeting as a forum to play out some personal vendetta;
- indulging in some form of 'ego trip';
- ganging up to obstruct a proposal;
- playing out some personal interest.

Where a hidden agenda is present, it requires the skill of the chairman to keep the meeting from degenerating to a personalities level and thus losing sight of the original purpose. Emotional reactions must be recognized and dealt with accordingly. Also, it is the responsibility of the committee members to determine the extent to which they are prepared to allow personal or minority views to influence the effective operation and cohesion of the group as a whole.

What is the chairman's role?

Many of the observations already made place considerable responsibility on the chairman, whose role is vital to the success or failure of a meeting. All managers need to acquire skill in chairmanship, and it requires more consideration than simply studying a list of do's and don'ts.

The key qualities will be flexibility and the ability to think on one's feet, given that any manager, in the course of a week, may be expected to chair several meetings on a range of subjects, all requiring different treatment and the adoption of different styles of leadership (see Chapter 5). Sometimes the task will be to inform, sometimes to gauge opinion, sometimes to negotiate, sometimes to placate and sometimes to persuade, whilst at other times it will be to solve problems or reach decisions. Whatever the purpose of a particular meeting the chairman must adopt the appropriate style.

The style (Fig. 34) adopted will vary considerably and may range from a highly controlled standpoint as in A to a much more free-ranging discussion as in B, dependent upon the outcome to be reached coupled with the experience of the chairman.

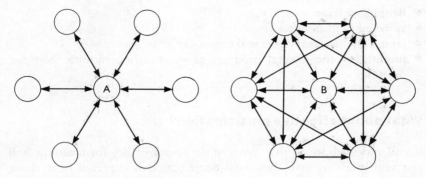

Fig. 34   Chairmanship styles

Duties and responsibilities

The chairman must fulfil various duties and responsibilities before, during and after a meeting, and these include:

- agreeing a draft agenda;   *BEFore*
- delegating necessary organizational tasks;
- starting promptly;
- introducing any new committee members;
- dealing with procedural matters – e.g. signing previous minutes, ensuring a quorum;
- initiating discussion;
- guiding the meeting through the agenda;
- taking chairman's action if/when necessary;
- dealing with the 'hidden agenda' if there is one;
- controlling discussion;
- ensuring relevance;
- encouraging free discussion;
- resisting the temptation to talk too much himself;   *During*
- restricting the over-talkative;
- encouraging the reticent;
- clarifying points as required;
- summarizing discussion;
- helping the meeting reach a decision;
- putting matters to the vote;
- declaring results;
- giving rulings on points of order;
- being mindful of time constraints;
- sustaining objectivity and impartiality;
- closing or adjourning the meeting;

- liaising with the secretary;
- agreeing draft minutes;
- taking any necessary personal follow-up action promised;
- monitoring the general progress of other action minutes between meetings.

What about effective participation?

It's all very well to say that much of the responsibility for meetings will rest with the chairman, but what contribution is expected from those individuals who attend meetings – many of whom will be managers in their own right? Meetings allow for two-way communication, and as such it is essential that all those attending make an effective contribution and feel that their presence has been beneficial. It is worth remembering that most managers will need to operate through some form of committee network to achieve many of their own objectives and that skill in committees can be a valuable attribute to any practising manager. What, then, are the guidelines for effective participation at meetings?

- be prepared (do the necessary homework, study the advance paper-work, highlight and make notes);
- lobby committee colleagues as appropriate;
- be positive in attitude to attendance at meetings;
- be prepared to put points of view in a logical way;
- be willing to support the ideas of others;
- be ready to help reduce conflict wherever possible;
- be prepared to disagree if appropriate;
- listen carefully to what is said by others;
- be well versed in committee procedure;
- try to develop a sense of timing;
- be familiar with the composition of the committee and the different personalities and interests involved;
- be prepared to take any follow-up action required.

Committees

Committees are groups of people specifically designated to perform some administrative activity. They function only as groups, and membership is typically a part-time activity.

Types of Committees

Many organizations operate on a complex committee structure (Fig. 35) in which several types of committee will be represented:

Executive committee	Sub-committee
Standing committee	Ad hoc committee
Advisory committee	Joint committee

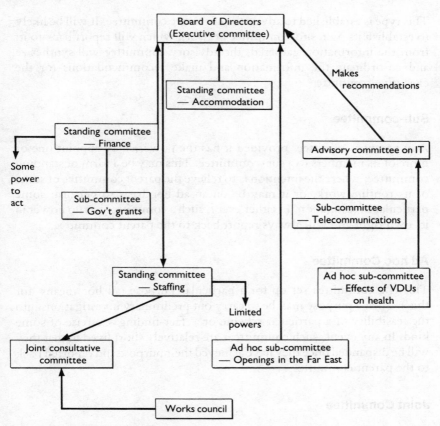

Fig. 35   A committee structure

Executive Committee

This committee will carry out the actual administration of the organization and will have the authority vested in it to act on its own and to take decisions. An example of such a committee is, in fact, the Board of Directors.

Standing Committee

This type of committee is formed to deal with specific matters delegated to it and its role is to attend to routine business within the particular remit – e.g. Finance. Such committees are permanent in tenure.

Advisory Committee

This type is established to advise the executive committee. It will be likely to establish its own sub-committee network which will report back to it; from the information gathered, the advisory committee will synthesize and co-ordinate the information and make recommendations for the executive committee.

Sub-committee

Any parent committee, provided it has the power, may appoint one or more of its members to a sub-committee. This may be a form of standing committee, where the intention is to relieve the parent committee of some of its routine work, or it may be on an ad hoc basis to perform some particular investigation. In either event, such a committee has no power in its own right and will always report back to the parent committee.

Ad hoc Committee

This is a committee set up for a particular purpose (ad hoc means 'for this'). Such a purpose may be to carry out preliminary investigations into the feasibility of a particular scheme or a 'fact-finding' exercise of some kind. In any event, such committees are relatively short lived in that they will be disbanded once they have achieved their purpose and reported back to the parent committee.

Joint Committee

This is formed for the purpose of co-ordinating the activities of two or more committees, usually with the express desire of improving communications and informing the workforce of management decisions. Therefore the two committees represented may be a Management Committee and a Works Council Committee. Joint committees may be permanent or ad hoc in nature.

Conditions favouring the use of committees

It may be advantageous to use committees or working parties in the following circumstances:

- when a wide divergence of information is needed to reach a sound conclusion – e.g. an issue which calls upon information from several departments (here, committee representation will ensure that the range of individuals is well versed in the necessary detail and is thus able to give good advice and assist in the co-ordination of whatever action is agreed by the committee);
- when the decision is so vital that it will be desirable to call upon the judgement of several suitably qualified persons – the 'safety in numbers' idea;
- when successful execution of decisions depends upon full understanding of the ramifications – e.g. when introducing office automation within a company (here it will be essential that the committee help in the planning stages and are involved in the selection process, the implementation, the training and follow-up routines);
- when the activities of several divisions, departments or sections of an organization need to be co-ordinated (this may be the result of a split-site operation where one site's activities are crucial to the scheduling of activities of another).

All such committees or working parties need not be given authority to make decisions. Their brief may be to give advice to management on key issues affecting the organization.

The misuse of committees

Committees are often subject to misuse for the following reasons:

- they are overused and costly to operate and service;
- they spend too much time on trivia at the expense of important matters;
- they are sometimes used to evade personal responsibility on the part of an executive;
- issues are often dealt with by committees which could and should have been dealt with on an individual basis;
- there is the danger of compromise decision.

How to achieve effective committee operation

Where an organization wishes to achieve effective committee operation the following criteria must be applied:

- it must operate within the framework of a well-conceived committee structure;
- terms of reference must be clearly defined for all committees;
- the extent of power and authority must be spelled out;
- membership should be restricted in terms of numbers;
- membership composition must be carefully considered;
- procedures must be established and adhered to;
- chairmanship must be competent;
- committees must be serviced by committee secretaries or clerks who discharge their duties efficiently and effectively.

Glossary of meeting terminology

Ab initio From the beginning.

Abstention Where a member refrains from casting a vote either in favour or against a motion.

Action minutes These minutes, in addition to providing an account of events, specify the action to be taken, and by whom, following any recommendation made, course of action demanded or decision reached at a meeting.

Addendum An amendment which **adds** words to a motion.

Address the Chair Where a member wishes to speak he must first address the chairman – i.e. 'Mr Chairman . . .' or 'Madam Chairman . . .'.

Ad hoc From the Latin, meaning 'for the purpose of'. For example, an ad hoc committee, sometimes referred to as a 'special committee', is one set up for a special purpose and when that purpose is fulfilled the committee is disbanded.

Adjournment The chairman, with the consent of those present, may adjourn a meeting and reconvene it at a later date to complete unfinished items on the agenda.

Advisory Offering advice or suggestion and making recommendations, but taking no direct action.

Agenda Schedule of items drawn up for discussion at a meeting.

Amendment An alteration to a motion by the addition, deletion or modification of words.

Annual general meeting (AGM) A statutory meeting held once a year which the organization's entire membership is eligible to attend.

Apologies for absence. Excuses given in advance for inability to attend a meeting.

Articles of Association The rules, required by law, which govern a company's internal organization and activities.

Ballot A written secret vote conducted in accordance with the organization's constitution.

By-laws Rules governing an organization's activities.

Casting vote In accordance with the rules and regulations, a chairman may be granted a vote, or a second vote, when there is an equal number of votes for and against a motion.

Chairman The person given authority to conduct a meeting.

Chairman's action The right of the chairman to make a decision within his terms of reference without consulting the committee.

Chairman's agenda An elaborated form of the basic agenda, with space left on the right for the chairman to make notes.

Collective responsibility A convention whereby all members agree to abide by a majority decision.

Consensus Agreement by general consent without a formal vote being taken.

Convene To call a meeting.

Co-opt To invite an individual to serve on a committee as a result of a majority vote. A person is normally co-opted because of some specialist knowledge or expertise he can provide.

Ex officio One invited to attend 'by virtue of his office' but without voting rights.

In attendance Present on invitation to give expert help, advice or information but with no voting rights.

In camera In private.

Lie on the table Something is said to 'lie on the table' when the meeting decides that no action should be taken on it at the present time.

Lobbying The term given to the practice of seeking the support of others prior to a meeting.

Majority vote One where the greater number of members voting were either for or against a motion. Articles or rules will set out whether a majority of a certain proportion is necessary for a motion to be carried or defeated.

Memorandum of Association The statutory requirements which govern a company's objects and general relationship with the outside world.

Motion A formal proposal moved by a member that a certain topic be discussed at a meeting and certain action be taken upon it.

Nem con No one contradicting – i.e. no votes against the motion, but some members may have abstained.

Nem dis No one dissenting, as 'nem com' above.

No confidence A vote of 'no confidence' may be passed by members of a meeting if they are at variance with the chairman.

Opposer One who speaks against a motion.

Out of order The chairman can rule a member 'out of order' where the member is not keeping to the point under discussion or is speaking improperly.

Point of order A query raised in respect of procedure or a possible infringement of the standing orders or constitution.

Postponement The action taken to transfer the holding of a meeting to a later date.

Proposer The member putting forward a motion for discussion at a meeting.

Proxy A member may be appointed to vote by proxy – i.e. on behalf of another member who is unable to attend a meeting, subject to the articles, standing orders or constitution.

Quorum The minimum number of persons who must be present at a meeting to make it valid.

Resolution Once passed, a motion becomes a resolution.

Rider This is an addition to a resolution after it has been passed. It adds to a resolution rather than altering it. It must be proposed, seconded and put to the meeting in the usual way.

Right of reply The proposer of a motion has the right of reply once the motion has been fully discussed but before it is put to the vote.

Seconder One who supports the proposer of a motion.

Sine die For an indefinite period.

Standing orders The rules compiled by an organization in respect of the way in which business must be transacted.

Status quo As things stand at present.

Statutory meeting A meeting (usually of the shareholders of a public company) which **must** be held in order to comply with the law.

Sub-committee A group of members from the main/parent committee, appointed to deal with a specific aspect of the main committee's work. The funtions will be delegated by the main committee, to whom reports and recommendations will be submitted.

Tabled The description applied to a document to be presented to a committee 'on the table' – one which has not been included with the agenda and supporting papers.

Terms of reference A statement of the work to be carried out by a group or committee, providing guidelines as to how it should be done and expressing any limitations in respect of methods.

Ultra vires Outside the legal power of authority of the organization or committee.

Unanimous All being in favour.

Verbatim Word for word.

11
Decision Making

'An administrator often feels more confident when "flying by the seat of his pants" than when following the advice of theorists.'

Charles E Lindblom
The Science of Muddling Through

Decision making is about making choices from options available, and is an integral part of the activity of management. It is a dynamic process which has no beginning and no end. Today's decisions will affect tomorrow's just as yesterday's will condition today's.

Who makes decisions?

Decisions are made by everyone but decision making in organizations tends to be seen as the prerogative of top executives and those occupying the higher echelons of the organization. Classical theorists, however, suggest that decisions should be assigned to the lowest competent level of the organization. In other words, decision making should be entrusted as far down the organization as possible, and the further down it goes the greater will be the extent of decentralization.

The decision-making process would be speeded up if problems were resolved at the point where they occurred, by those directly involved and affected by them. Not only should this be efficient but it would also remove frustration by providing individuals lower down the hierarchy with opportunities to exercise initiative. Northcote Parkinson recognized the value of this view when he wrote:

'The man who is denied the opportunity of taking decisions of importance begins to regard as important the decisions he is allowed to take. He becomes fussy about filing, keen on seeing that pencils are sharpened, eager to see that windows are open (or shut) and apt to use two or three different-coloured inks.'

(*Parkinson's Law*, 1958)

The problem arises in establishing whether or not an individual is competent to decide. Position and status, for example, may not in themselves be sufficient to enable the individual to reach decisions on certain issues which require specialist knowledge of some kind, whether it be technical, legal, financial, local or global.

Rational Decision making?

Decisions are thought to be rational when they take account of:

reaching defined goals
alternative solutions available
consequences of particular courses of action

but it will depend on the context in which the decision is to be made and on the personality(ies) of the person(s) making the decision. Also, there are few issues which are so clear cut that there will be only one rational decision.

Economic theories of decision making presuppose that rational decisions are reached by Simon's 'economic man' who will decide on the basis of the option which will produce the maximum economic return. However, this fails to take account of man's emotions and total behaviour, and Simon suggests that, in practice, decisions are more usually reached by his 'administrative man' who 'satisfices' by looking for the satisfactory solution, the adequate profit and the fair price, rather than the highest profit of all.

Whether decisions are rational or not they will be taken at three main levels within the organization:

- policy decisions made by top management;
- administrative decisions made by heads of department;
- operational decisions made by managers and supervisors.

What kinds of decisions are there?

Decisions will fall mainly into two categories – programmed and unprogrammed.

Programmed decisions are those which are made in response to routine incidents and are usually made at supervisory level. They are likely to arise out of events or problems which can be dealt with at the point of contact. Where their existence is known higher up the organizational pyramid it will be normal practice to refer the matter elsewhere in the organization to wherever and whoever possesses the necessary competence to make the decision. It will be more usual to pass problems down through the organization (decentralization), provided the resources are there to respond, than it will to refer problems requiring programmed decisions to a higher authority (centralization).

Unprogrammed decisions will include those which arise out of problems, crises or unexpected opportunities, and as such will require higher level managerial judgement than routine decisions. They may even be reached following consultation with and advice from management colleagues within the organization or from contact with external consultants. Alternatively, where time permits, a working party may be established.

Additionally, decisions may be **intuitive** – based on the 'gut reactions' of individuals. There tends to be an element of this sort of instinctive flavour in all decision making but it is important that decisions arrived at via this process are capable of being supported in fact. There will also be those decisions which are made **based on experience**, where the solution proferred takes its rationale from the fact that a similar situation may have arisen previously and been satisfactorily resolved in a particular way. Whilst it can be useful to apply tested solutions to problems based on the premise that 'history repeats itself', it can also be flawed in that it is vital to recognize that nothing is ever exactly the same and that modifications should therefore be incorporated as necessary.

How are decisions reached?

Decisions are reached via decision-making **processes**, and these are hedged by a number of constraints which affect the capacity to make logical, sequential and rational decisions. Decisions may be arrived at by individuals, by groups (or committees) or collectively as a result of a joint-consultative process. The processes will be affected by a variety of factors both internal and external.

Internal factors affecting decision-making processes

- the importance of the decision;
- the number of people involved;
- the degree of autonomy of the decision makers;
- the rules and procedures which govern the process;
- the quality and extent of the information available;
- the time available;
- the consequences of reaching the wrong decision;
- the personalities involved;

- the rationale underpinning the composition of the group – e.g. ex officio, democratic or statutory;
- the technical competence or expertise required to reach a decision;
- the nature of the organization;
- the length of the chain of command – e.g. the shorter the chain, the faster the decision and the swifter the problem is solved.

External factors affecting decision-making processes

- the economic climate – boom or slump;
- the political dimension – ideologies and preferences;
- legislative controls;
- social and moral pressures;
- national and international opinion;
- the number of interested parties;
- the extent of opposition;
- the extent with which compliance is required in response to demands by external agencies;
- the degree of interdependence which exists – e.g. the reliance on external suppliers;
- the turbulence in the market place or in the field of competition;
- image – e.g. the desire to be non-controversial, overtly supportive or disassociated with an issue.

Autonomy of decision makers

The scope of decision makers to actually make decisions will vary from one organizational context to another, which makes it difficult to be precise as to the capacity of any one group to take decisions. Autonomy to take decisions will be conditioned by a variety of factors – e.g. the nature of the goals of the organization, and its production process. Of significant importance, however, is the nature of the relationship between the organization and its environment. Where environment is taken to represent a range of external interests which will exercise varying degrees of control, it will possibly inhibit the autonomy of the decision makers. David Hickson and his colleagues at the University of Bradford Management Centre viewed organizational environment as a political network or coalition, capable of exerting varying degrees of control or influence. At one extreme, where an organization is set in a coalition producing a series of restrictive controls, the effect is to produce, for the decision takers 'paralysis' – i.e. little or no room for manoeuvre. One example quoted is an electricity board which finds its hands tied on such important decision areas as pricing and the siting and laying of cables. At the other extreme, an organization located in a coalition, but with fewer controls exerted, may have considerable autonomy in the decision-making process. For example, a university will have control over student selection and the range of courses it provides.

What makes decision making difficult?

Decision making is difficult in that it is concerned with:

risk
conflict
change
choice
differing opinions
ensuring adequate consultation
creativity
imagination
self-discipline
heightened perception
awareness of the feelings of others

Aids to decision making

Various techniques and aids may be called upon to assist in decision making. For example, mathematical techniques are frequently applied to financial aspects of decision making, and include:

cost/benefit analysis
linear programming
critical path analysis
break even analysis
discounted cash flow

   Other useful aids are:

decision trees (Vroom and Yetton, 1973)
brainstorming
T-groups
management 'think tanks'
lateral thinking (Edward de Bono, 1982)

Sources of information in decision making

Good decisions are largely dependent on the quality and extent of the information available to the decision maker(s), and it is important that no stone be left unturned. Information comes in a wide variety of forms and will be available from many different sources. The following are some of the types and sources of information which will prove useful in arriving at decisions:

office files
company files
personnel records
company handbooks
data bases (internal and external)
company reports
minutes of meetings
trade union agreements
viewdata systems
reference books
the media
libraries
specialist agencies
government departments
Advisory, Conciliation and Arbitration Service (ACAS)
professional and trade associations
Industrial Training Boards (ITBs)
Manpower Services Committee (MSC)
tax offices (Inland Revenue)
local council offices
published reports (HMSO)

The decision-making process

The decision-making process will vary according to the nature and complexity of the decision and the manner in which it is being dealt with – i.e. either by an individual or by a group. Irrespective of these differences, however, it can usefully be illustrated in the form of a flow chart, as in Fig. 36.

Implementation problems

Given that decisions taken in a dynamic business environment will increasingly rest on more variables and contain greater levels of uncertainty, more attention has to be given by management to the process by which decisions are reached. Wrong decisions or indecision can be costly and damaging to an organization.

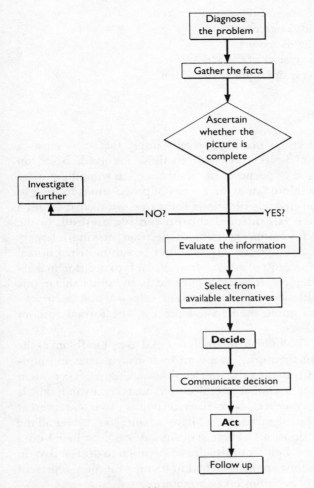

Fig. 36 The decision-making process

Identifying problems is one thing, but deciding what to do and putting the decision into action can be a very different proposition. Implementation problems include:

- deciding who will do what;
- deciding when it should be done;
- letting those involved know what's happening;
- overcoming employee barriers and resistance;
- bridging the gap between the forum at which the decision was taken and the level within the organization at which it is to be activated;
- assessing the likely ramifications of the decision;

- monitoring the progress of the action(s) taken;
- producing unintended outcomes;
- misinterpreting what is required;
- communicating the results of the action;
- evaluating the success or failure of the action.

Muddling Through

Whilst accounts of decision making typically imply that there exists a well-considered logical process available to those involved, based on information and a sense of purpose, the reality is often something quite different. Charles Lindblom* drew up a series of propositions relating to the reality of decision-making situations compared with what is often assumed to be the case. His **rational comprehensive method**, or the 'root' method (i.e. the formal account of decision making), largely comprises a series of assumptions which cannot be substantiated in real life. For example, the amount of information available to decision makers is nearly always incomplete, frequently out of date and unreliable in one way or another. Although appropriate – i.e. relevant and accurate – research is needed to guide the decision process, the formal account ignores such inadequacies.

On the other hand, the 'branch' method, referred to by Lindblom as the **science of muddling through**, accepts all such inadequacies and limitations at the outset. Consequently, the decision-making process is often taken to be illogical and irrational since decisions are taken by individuals who work to their own beliefs, have different points of view, represent different factions of the organization and have no time to consider all the implications of their decisions. These will, in any case, be based on a number of inadequacies. Lindblom also draws attention to the fact that, in any event, most decisions are incremental in nature – i.e. they represent minor modifications of decisions taken previously.

*Lindblom, CE (1959). The Science of Muddling Through. *Public Administration Review*, **19**: 79–88

12
Delegating

'A managerial role is one from which work is delegated to subordinate roles, the manager remaining accountable for the results.'

Wilfred Brown

Delegation is the principle of passing authority from one level to another and effective delegation is a key factor in making organizations work. At organizational level it is the essence of decentralization (see page 33) whereas at individual level it is the transfer of personal performance of duties to another.

Delegation is an art and a valuable, if not *the* most valuable time-management tool, available to a manager. It is also the root of successful leadership and motivation (see also Chapters 5 and 6) in that it is central to the concept of getting work done through other people.

Despite its apparent simplicity, it is a concept that is frequently misunderstood and abused. At worst, it will represent total abdication where one individual simply 'off-loads' to another in order to free himself of work. It is not intended to promote idleness on the part of managers and no manager can relieve himself of ultimate responsibility by delegating. A former American President, Harry Truman, summed this up rather nicely with a notice on his presidential desk which read, 'The buck stops here'; this is something many managers would do well to remember.

A common management failure is to abdicate rather than delegate authority. What often goes wrong in the delegation process is the failure on the part of the delegator (the manager) to ensure that the subordinate has the authority to match the responsibility he has been given. One cannot be delegated without the other, and it must also be remembered that once authority is delegated it can no longer be **used** by the manager although he will still retain the responsibility for its use. This is the crucial distinction which exists between authority and responsibility.

The key to retaining control over the authority delegated is accountability (see Chapter 2). The manager must explain clearly to the subordinate and agree with him on the way in which accountability will work. The subordinate needs to know the extent to which he is expected to account to the manager. This will apply in exactly the same way as the manager needing to know the way in which he is expected to account to his superior for the authority which has been delegated to him.

Why delegate?

The reasons for delegating are basically twofold – to help the manager and to develop subordinates – with the intention of strengthening the organization and improving its efficiency and performance at the same time. Individually these reasons will stand closer examination.

Helping the manager

Managers are appointed and paid not simply for their administrative capabilities but also for their potential, their creative talents and their ability to influence events. They will be expected to handle routine matters as a matter of course, but their value to the organization will be in the other attributes which they can bring to the job. To explore these avenues demands time and energy, and the manager can devote these only when he is successful in delegating.

Another factor contributing to the need to delegate may be the additional burden and pressure introduced by the increasing complexity of rules and regulations and administrative paperwork which managers have to contend with, together with the specialist techniques and skills which are often required. Such elements become part of the routine but this will often be routine which could be competently handled by others.

A manager should aim to have more time to himself so that he can think and plan for the future. He will achieve such 'thinking time' only when he convinces his subordinates that they can manage without him and convinces himself that he does not always need to see that every 'i' is dotted and every 't' crossed. Subordinates need to be encouraged to find their own solutions rather than relying on the manager all the time. This will also have a bearing on the 'people' skills of the manager – how good he is at communicating, how well he is able to inspire confidence and how much he is able to demonstrate that he trusts his subordinates.

Also, only by delegating and thus making some 'free' time can a manager demonstrate his own capacity for doing more than he was appointed to do – e.g. come up with new projects and ideas, improve existing systems and procedures, familiarize himself with new technology and introduce new training programmes for his staff. Promotion will tend to come more rapidly to the sort of manager who demonstrates that he is a 'winner' and can handle everything and anything that is placed before him.

Developing the subordinates

Individuals need to be given opportunities to develop and prove themselves. People have a remarkable capacity to 'rise to the occasion' when someone has confidence enough to give them the chance in the first instance. People learn from their mistakes and, provided the nature of the work is not such that mistakes could prove catastrophic, individuals welcome the opportunity to use their own initiative and be given responsibility for a particular aspect of work. Motivationally this is good and subordinates rate it highly. They respond positively to the recognition that they are fit to undertake the task and will develop a sense of commitment to their work and to the objectives of the organization.

Delegation is also a valuable way of training for managerial succession in that it should broaden skills and experience whilst ensuring adequate cover during any temporary absence by the manager. No manager should see himself as indispensable, difficult as this may sometimes be. The time will always come to move on or to make way for someone else, and it is part of the manager's role to ensure that subordinates are being prepared to take over.

Symptoms of poor or insufficient delegation

These are many and varied, but include:

- working longer hours than others;
- having no lunch/coffee breaks;
- taking work home;
- spending time on mundane tasks;
- 'helping' others who could do without the help;
- repeated interruptions from subordinates seeking advice or asking for decisions on something which, strictly speaking, the manager does not need to decide;
- the 'perfectionist syndrome' – an obsession with trivia;
- unfinished tasks;
- no time for pleasure or recreation.

Reluctance to delegate

Managers may be reluctant to delegate for a variety of reasons:

- the 'I can do it better myself' fallacy;
- lack of confidence in subordinates (see below);
- inability to direct (including poor communication skills);

- fear of Murphy's law – i.e. 'If it can go wrong, it will';
- temperamentally unsuited to taking a chance;
- fear of competition should the subordinate prove highly successful and place own position at risk;
- fear of expressing favouritism amongst subordinates;
- no contingency plans to cope with unanticipated problems;
- unwilling to let subordinates make mistakes;
- fear of repercussions and personal judgement being called into question;
- a desire to cling to simple tasks out of personal interest.

Lack of confidence in subordinates

This is always an interesting reason for any manager's reluctance to delegate, as it unearths a range of problems and poses a number of questions. It may, for example, be due to any of the following reasons:

- the age profile of the subordinates – either too young and therefore inexperienced and perhaps incapable of commanding the respect of others or too near retirement and so lacking the motivation and interest necessary;
- the lack of necessary training – this questions the adequacy or even existence of appropriate training;
- the inadequacy of the staff to undertake the work – this begs the question of selection procedures, although it could be that the staff have been inherited with the job (they may be good candidates for staff development or they may not).

In addition, lack of confidence may be subjective and almost unconscious on the part of the manager who may give lip-service to decentralization but in the actual working relationship refuses to let go.

Reluctance to accept delegated duties

Delegation is a two-sided relationship, and even when a manager is ready to turn over authority the subordinate may shrink from accepting it. There are several possible reasons for such reluctance:

- it may be easier to ask the boss what to do than decide for himself;
- lack of confidence in his own abilities;
- already too much work to do;
- the 'What's in it for me?' syndrome (often present when there are inadequate positive incentives – e.g. no extra pay, no chance of promotion and no enhanced status);
- fear of criticism, particularly of the destructive variety should things go wrong;

- fear of adverse reactions from colleagues – e.g. passing remarks such as 'Who's the blue-eyed boy then?';
- lack of adquate information about the task – e.g. unaware of the background to the subject and the personalities involved and their unwillingness to co-operate, but aware that there is 'something' about the task;
- insufficient resources to do the job well – e.g. when asked to draw up a report there is no secretarial assistance available.

What to delegate

Deciding on what to delegate can often be difficult, and will be based on whether the aim of the delegation is to reduce personal pressure, develop subordinates or a combination of the two. The sorts of questions a manager needs to ask when determining what to delegate are:

- What keeps coming up again and again in my job?
- What are the minor decisions I make most frequently?
- What detail takes up most of my time?
- Where will least damage occur should a mistake be made?
- Which tasks are my subordinates as well equipped or even better equipped to deal with than I?
- Which tasks do I enjoy doing just because I've always done them?
- What jobs could be delegated that would provide more variety and challenge to subordinates?
- What aspects of my work are directly related to something a subordinate does already?
- What kind of experience would be directly beneficial to subordinates in developing their skills and experience?
- What duties can be delegated which will have clearly specified directions and will require minimal control?

What not to delegate

In *The Practice of Management*, Peter Drucker identifies areas of what he terms 'executive action' which he views as management responsibilities which should not be delegated:

- setting policy objectives;
- organizing employees into an efficient team;
- motivating and communicating;
- checking and analysing results;
- setting training objectives.

These would all come within the exclusive domain of the executive manager.

Drucker's suggestions provide helpful guidelines. Additional aspects of his role and function which a manager should also retain will be disciplinary and human relations matters.

Planning for delegation

Successful delegation must be planned carefully and systematically if it is to free the manager and enable him to become involved in other management priorities whilst still developing the skills and abilities of subordinates. Attention needs to be given to:

- delegating gradually;
- talking to subordinates and listening to what they have to say;
- assessing capabilities and identifying weaknesses;
- soliciting ideas from subordinates;
- identifying potential problems so that the risk is minimized;
- improving the organization of his section or department.

These are general points to which a manager should give attention but he should also set up a procedure for delegating.

Procedure for delegation

(a) Phase I
- Critically examine own job.
- List **all** tasks currently undertaken.
- Add to the list any tasks which are currently omitted through lack of time.
- Extract tasks which cannot/should not be delegated.
- Rearrange the remaining items in descending order of importance.
- Note the estimated time required to perform each task.
- Start at the top of the list and work down to a point at which there are sufficient tasks to cope with, bearing in mind the time allocations made.
- Draw a line across the list – all remaining tasks are possible candidates for delegation. (Even if some big tasks still remain – no matter. People have to learn and they have a knack of growing into the job.)

(b) Phase II
- Critically assess the capabilities of subordinates (allowing for development).
- Match the tasks to the subordinates.

- Brief each subordinate on the task (time spent on this will pay dividends).
- Ensure that the parameters are understood.
- Indicate the level of support you will provide.
- Indicate the feedback you will expect to receive.
- Delegate the necessary authority.
- Inform all those who need to know of that authority.

(c) Phase III
- Monitor progress by checking periodically.
- Check the progress of the job, not the ability of the subordinate to do the job.
- Keep your eyes and ears open but don't look for trouble.

Why can delegation fail?

Basically this will be the result of insufficient knowledge, experience, authority, information or control, and will occur when:

- managers don't delegate enough to know the pitfalls;
- managers fail to treat each situation as unique;
- there is a communication breakdown of some kind;
- the delegated areas are not defined clearly enough;
- no allowance is made for inevitable errors;
- insufficient checks and control mechanisms are built into the project to prevent disaster whilst still allowing freedom and encouraging the initiative of the subordinate;
- the extent of the authority afforded the subordinate results in upsetting the equilibrium of the department or section;
- true delegation does not take place – i.e. the delegator fails to let go of the reins.

In short, the manager or supervisor who recognizes the value of effective delegation and takes time to consider how best it may be used in particular situations cannot help but see the benefits. Not only is there the welcome reduction of personal workload and the resultant time to think, but also there are the opportunities which increased authority and responsibility afford to subordinates to develop and realize their true potential.

13
Managing Time

'Most of us can do three or four times as much as we ordinarily do without lengthening working hours or even driving ourselves to exhaustion by the day's end. Even if we have apparently reached our highest level of effectiveness it is usually possible to improve by a little effort.'

F W Taylor
Principles of Scientific Management

The idea of effective time management is not new, but considerably more attention has been paid to it in recent years, perhaps because it is one thing, even in a sophisticated technological society, over which we have no real control. Time is a scarce and limited commodity in any organization and a very real enemy for most managers who, daily, have to contend with its shortage. They are also faced with the dilemma of achieving more and better results in less time.

There is a limit to what any individual can pack into a day, irrespective of level of commitment and need for sleep. What is important is that the time he has available is used to effect, and this will depend on a number of factors:

- the type of person he is;
- his ability to identify things which waste time;
- his ability to delegate successfully;
- his ability to prioritize;
- the way in which fellow workers handle their time;
- how well organized he is;
- how assertive he is;
- how inclined he is to procrastinate.

Additionally, the nature of the work itself will be highly significant in terms of determining the way in which time can be applied. Henry Mintzberg and Rosemary Stewart have looked at what managers actually do, and the latter also studied the value of diary keeping as a training tool for managers in order to help analyse their use of time. An understanding of what is involved in the work situation is fundamental to beginning to give consideration to the management of time. Certain sorts of jobs, by their very nature, will contribute to more wasted time. For example, the vast amount of travelling which many managers need to do as part of their daily life or the number of meetings which the job necessitates will both be highly significant.

What are the likely time-wasters?

If you were to ask managers to list their 'time-wasting' activities, their answers would vary according to the nature of the job, the personality of the individual and his personal preferences in terms of the way time is used. However, the following are those which many are likely to identify:

- attending too many meetings;
- telephone calls that don't produce results;
- paper chasing;
- travelling and generally being away from the desk;
- performing unnecessary work;
- doing other people's work;
- checking up on other people's work;
- interruptions – unwanted telephone calls and visitors;
- not planning ahead;
- being indecisive;
- procrastinating;
- slow reading;
- poor filing systems;
- slow or late information;
- idle chit-chat.

Six practical pointers to successful time management

1. Make the best use of secretarial support

Where a manager is fortunate enough to have a personal secretary or the support of a highly skilled 'professional', he needs to recognize that he has in this individual his most valuable time management asset. By a 'professional' is meant someone who is able to provide the full range of secretarial support in addition to the technical skills of shorthand, typing and word processing. Such a person will possess organizational ability and administrative flair, be well versed in communication and human relations skills and have a sound business management awareness. She will be able to assume responsibility, use her initiative, exercise judgement and make decisions within the bounds of her authority. Secretaries can greatly enhance a manager's worth within an organization, and it is unfortunate that negative connotations frequently tend to be associated with the word 'secretary' and the secretarial role.

2.　Organize the work area and the desk

Some rooms or work areas are more conducive to efficiency than others, and it is worth while considering whether a few minor adjustments in terms of layout or the changing of actual furniture might improve matters. Different jobs require different facilities, and it is important that sufficient attention is paid to matching the environment to the job (see also Part III).

Basically, things should be arranged to facilitate work flow and eliminate unnecessary movement, whilst lighting and decor should be appropriate to the tasks performed. In terms of furniture, some researchers would go as far as to suggest that many managers could and should do without a desk in that any reading they do could just as easily be done from a comfortable chair whilst such writing as was needed could be done at a small table. However, perhaps this is taking the issue a little too far!

What is important is that an appropriate desk be selected from the wide range available and that it should be organized to ensure that proper use is made of it. This will mean:

- removing all clutter;
- making sufficient working surface available;
- ensuring that all working materials are to hand;
- keeping all materials in the same place or drawer;
- placing the desk to avoid unnecessary distractions and to aid concentration.

3.　Motivate staff

Just as good secretarial support is invaluable in terms of saving time, so too are well-motivated staff. Managers need to recognize that staff will make the best contribution to the work of the department, section or unit:

- when they feel that their contribution is worthwhile;
- when the work offers sufficient stimulation and challenge;
- when their abilities and talents are recognized;
- when they are given opportunities to develop and to use their initiative;
- where their efforts are afforded due appreciation;
- where they are consulted and share in the decision-making process.

It is important that managers take time to explain things to subordinates. Doing so provides the sort of positive and interested leadership which subordinates will appreciate and be only too eager to follow. Also, it will be time well spent in that it will pay dividends in the long term by improving morale and increasing motivation. Clear explanations build confidence all round and help dilute the 'indispensability factor' in a manager which can be seriously detrimental to his effective management of time.

4. Control Paperwork

Managers can control paperwork in different ways, although the most obvious thing is to eliminate all unnecessary paperwork entirely. This can be done by:

- limiting the mail which is dealt with personally (the secretary should do the preliminary sort of the mail, passing on only that which the boss needs to see and deal with personally);
- writing fewer letters – e.g. sometimes a compliments slip will suffice rather than a covering letter;
- telephoning rather than writing;
- briefing the secretary to highlight key points in lengthy letters and reports prior to passing them to the boss;
- encouraging subordinates to reduce the amount of material they refer 'for information';
- removing the manager's name from circulation lists of inessential material;
- trying to get things right first time – e.g. avoiding the tendency to alter something just because it has been prepared on the word processor and can, therefore, be easily changed;
- limiting the amount of photocopying that goes on within the department, section or unit;
- adopting pro formas and house styles as appropriate (as well as possibly saving paper, the familiar layouts will tend to facilitate faster reading);
- ensuring that paperwork is not allowed to accumulate (establishing sound filing procedures and filing daily).

5. Polish up Personal Performance

Most people can improve their personal performance on at least one dimension. It may be that reading speed could be improved or listening skills sharpened, or it may be that the job necessitates a technique (e.g. report writing) which has previously been absent or has not featured strongly in the career to date. Where this is the case, it will be important to recognize the need for self-development in order to acquire new skills or to improve on existing ones. A wide variety of short courses is available and managers should take advantage of them as appropriate (see page 294).

6. Develop Personal Systems and Techniques

Everyone has his own way of doing things, and what works for one person may be totally useless for someone else. What matters is that areas of weakness – e.g. those things which tend to be forgotten or overlooked or which take an inordinate length of time and effort – should be identified and some device set up or technique adopted to improve matters. For example:

- making a list of 'Things to do today';
- introducing colour coding within filing and indexing systems;
- developing a personal card index system;
- using priority/urgent/routine folders for day-to-day work;
- introducing a follow-up system/'tickler file' of some kind;
- investing in a pocket dictating machine and learning to use it;
- employing a personal 'bleep' when absent from the desk;
- building a library of useful reference books;
- keeping a scrap book of press cuttings and magazine articles;
- adopting abbreviations for use in note-taking and at meetings;
- devising a system of flagging or highlighting when reading.

Twenty more ways in which time management can be improved

- Clarify objectives.
- Plan.
- Organize.
- Improve systems and procedures.
- Delegate.
- Establish priorities.
- Communicate effectively.
- Schedule work.
- Harness technology.
- Adopt visual planning devices.
- Develop routines.
- Break tasks into manageable units.
- Make contingency plans.
- Be proactive rather than reactive.
- Set at least one target for every day and achieve it.
- Pay more attention to diet.
- Pay more attention to health matters and physical fitness.
- Learn to say 'No'.
- Set aside time – a 'quiet hour' – every day for personal reflection and relaxation.
- Don't put off till tomorrow what can be done today.

In a nutshell, a lot of this has to do with recognizing the difference between efficiency and effectiveness. Efficiency is doing the job right whereas effectiveness is doing the right job.

Diaries

The normal use for a diary is to note and schedule appointments and to plan ahead – an activity which should be synchronized and performed in close liaison with the secretary. However, managers can also usefully employ a diary-keeping exercise to monitor their work patterns and accurately evaluate the content of their own jobs.

Such an exercise requires a disciplined approach and will be facilitated by the preparation of specially designed activity sheets for each day of the predetermined period during which the exercise is carried out. The sheets, which should be drawn up to reflect the duties and responsibilities of the individual manager, might take the form of a matrix into which a tick or a code letter would be placed in accordance with the task/activity performed. Provision should also be made within the design of the exercise to record the time spent on the various activities. A specimen activity sheet is provided as Fig. 37.

TIME MANAGEMENT										
Name					Designation					
Monday (time)	Time spent	Activity code:							Nature: R/N–R	Degree of importance
		A	B	C	D	E	F	G		

Fig. 37   Activity sheet
Notes: *Activity codes* represented as A–G allocated according to principal activities identified in advance – e.g. telephone, meeting, dictating, reading, delegating, problem solving.
Nature: R=routine; N-R=non-routine
Degree of importance: rated 1–5 in descending order; CI if considered a critical incident

At the conclusion of the exercise it will be possible to analyse the types of activities undertaken together with the times involved, the level of contact with other people, the amount of time spent away from the office, the routine tasks and the unusual activities.

Critical Incident Logs

Another useful technique in helping managers evaluate how they use and manage their time is the maintenance of a critical incident log in which all unusual or crisis items are recorded. This sort of exercise is useful in helping determine the level of non-routine matters which a manager has to deal with in the course of his day-to-day work. A critical incident could be defined as any out-of-the-ordinary event which necessitated judgement and decision-making capacities over and above those normally associated with the job. Critical incident logs are also referred to in Chapter 15 under 'Appraisal'.

Self-knowledge

Much of successful time management will ultimately come back to the individual and how well he knows himself. Self-knowledge is a valuable asset in the effective management of time, but it is far from easy in that it involves analysing one's habits and recognizing personal strengths and weaknesses. Robert Burns put it rather succinctly when he wrote,

'O wad some Pow'r the giftie gie us
To see oursels as others see us!'

Some aspects of behaviour will be relatively easy to isolate – e.g. working practices and long-standing routines. However, aspects related to habits and personality traits are more difficult to recognize in oneself and, even when identified, may not be readily accepted and modified. Nevertheless, in terms of getting to grips with time management so that the best can be got out of every working day, it is a nettle which is well worth grasping.

14
Innovating and Changing

'Successful industry is about change. If it isn't changing, it's dying.'
Sir John Harvey-Jones
Chairman of ICI

Characteristics

Innovation and change are here to stay! Few organizations will escape the necessity to innovate or respond to change. They will need to review their existing practices, their organizational structures or the adequacy of their workforce. The capacity to innovate or change quickly is emerging as the criterion for survival in the future; consequently, strategies capable of sustaining flexibility and adaptability will, more than ever before, assume a greater significance and consume a greater amount of management time.

Innovation may be defined as something representing **newness**, either in product processes or individual behaviour within the organization, whereas change represents **something different**. Innovation is the implementation of new ideas or novel applications of new systems and procedures. However, what may be innovative for one organization may already be typical in another.

This suggests that organizations are at different stages in the innovative process, and such differences will tend to be produced by the extent of dynamism or turbulence within the organization's environment. Demand for innovation and change is produced by the environment which will itself be in a continuous state of flux.

Different kinds of innovation and change

Despite the fact that most organizations tend towards being bureaucratic, they show a remarkable capacity for innovation and change; otherwise they would not have survived this far. Indeed, the imperative of 'survival' will often be the primary factor initiating innovation or change – which may suggest an element of crisis management, as compared with a management oriented towards, for example, capturing more of the market share for its products. There is this qualitative difference between organizations which innovate in response to crisis as distinct from those wishing to secure and sustain their position as front-runners in a particular activity.

Reasons for Innovation and Change

There are many reasons for innovation and change. The goals of the organization and the extent to which these are being fulfilled are important and often produce the desire to introduce innovation or change in order to achieve greater levels of efficiency and effectiveness. This in turn means that the reasons given are often expressions of dissatisfaction with things as they currently exist – e.g. a significant area of weakness which requires improvement. Organizations often experience problems or run up against faults which may lead to innovation or change in the following areas:

- the organization system – especially communication and delegation;
- the quality of the product or service;
- the established working practices and procedures;
- the quality of interpersonal relationships; particularly between the worker and the supervisor;
- the capacity to meet increased demand for products or services.

The list is not exhaustive, as the reasons are endless and difficult to categorize. Any area which is considered to be inadequate is ripe for innovation or change, and failure to respond appropriately may be disastrous for an organization.

Innovation and organizational goals

Innovation is often used in an attempt to reduce the gap between an organization's goals and the actual levels of performance being reached. Consequently, innovation, in one form or another, will be tried as a result of forecasts and plans made by management (see Chapter 4).

When applied to products or services, innovation may be used to overcome a limited range of products or a weak portfolio of services. Such a situation can lead to over-reliance on a specific set of customers or clients; merely their failure to renew orders as quickly as they did previously will create problems – financial and otherwise – giving cause for concern as to the survival of the company.

To innovate (i.e. diversify product/service range) whilst performing well with existing lines does, on the other hand, make for effective forward planning and for enhanced levels of profitability. Whatever the situation, diversification will require modification of the organization's goals in order to reflect the new trends. This supports the view already put forward in Part I – viz. that goals are not meant to be fixed for all time, but rather to be open to review and amendment as required – say, every three or four years.

Innovations in Management

Given the rate and pace of innovation and change generally, organizations have been required to introduce innovative management to reflect both the magnitude of the problem and the expectations of employees in the contemporary work situation.

One of the most significant changes to have taken place within organizations in post-war Britain has been in the field of human relations. This has been partly as a result of government initiatives (e.g. in relation to employee participation in decision making and changes in trade union legislation) and partly as a result of a changing social climate. These factors have tended to blur distinctions between different groups or classes of workers (e.g. blue collar and white collar), and have brought about changes in individual attitudes towards authority and discipline.

Increasing worker participation in decision making is a favourite topic amongst writers on organizations and management, and indeed most practising managers would today agree with the validity of this approach. The problem, however, is how to achieve effective participation. Individuals involved need to feel that they have made a worthwhile contribution which is fully appreciated by management, whilst simultaneously enhancing their commitment to the organization. Two relatively new approaches aimed at solving this problem are Team Building and Quality Circles, discussed below.

Overcoming barriers to innovation

The introduction of innovation within any organizational setting relies to a considerable extent on employees seeing the validity or even the common sense behind the proposals. Barriers to innovation and change can be greatly reduced where there is a consensus that change is necessary and desirable to resolve widely accepted problems. Obscure or badly presented arguments for change are, on the other hand, likely to be met by resistance, as will be those plans which are hurried through.

Finding ways of encouraging participation by **everyone** in at least certain aspects of decision making is one highly effective means of harnessing the commitment of employees to the organization and subsequently enhancing their levels of performance at work. Improving participation, however, does not provide a guarantee for successful implementation of innovation or change. For example, there is little value in management joining discussion with employees about what needs to be done on a piece-meal basis and without strategies for subsequent development. One possible solution to this dilemma lies in the introduction of an Organization Development (OD) plan.

Organization Development

Whilst not a new idea – OD has been around since the early 1970s – more and more organizations are beginning to see the need for a systematic development plan. Organization development (OD) is aimed at providing a coherent – and organization-wide – plan, rather than simply taking a fragmented approach. It is based on individuals taking responsibility for their own actions through group discussion and interaction. It takes the working group or team approach, rather than the individual worker, to be the means of introducing and implementing innovation and change in the workplace.

The role of management is to provide the appropriate conditions – i.e. organizational climate (see page 101) – within which subsequent innovation may flourish. Much will also depend on the leadership style adopted, as this will be a significant factor likely to inhibit or enhance successful organization development. The need for OD plans will be particularly significant in situations such as:

- where a merger or take-over between two or more organizations takes place;
- where the design of the organizational structure is to be revised;
- where new communications systems are required;
- where new skills are needed in response to diversification programmes;
- where external pressure calls for change in processes, products or services.

Any organization may be confronted by one, or indeed all, of the above difficulties; OD plans would seek to resolve such issues by:

- establishing a corporate plan for the organization;
- identifying working groups with responsibilities for particular aspects of work;
- establishing procedures to enable collaboration to take place;
- introducing new systems to deal with problems;
- developing new organizational goals and devising an appropriate structure to achieve them;

- securing effective means of co-operation between different units or departments;
- providing training and re-training opportunities;
- evaluating the performance of the whole organization and making adjustments as required.

Changes in working procedures or in patterns of work represent the type of situation in which OD is likely to be beneficial. The approach taken is based on the human relations dimension discussed earlier, where no contradiction is seen between demonstrating concern for the welfare of the individual in the workplace and the attainment of the organization's goals. Indeed, a more positive view would be that the latter depends on the former. Training and/or re-training is also an essential element of any sustained OD plan, where self-renewal is a critical factor in the pursuit of goals which are constantly being modified. For it to be effective, it is the staff themselves who will identify their own training needs in the light of developments taking place within the organization both now and in the foreseeable future.

Team Building

As organizations become increasingly complex, so there has developed the need to introduce team building. In a sense, the very existence of teams is recognition of the fact that no one individual can do everything! Team building is an ideal vehicle for achieving several important organizational factors all at the one time:

- it provides an opportunity for participation in decision making;
- it provides members of the team with a feeling of belonging – even importance;
- it provides an effective forum for representation from different areas within the organization;
- it enhances communication throughout the organization;
- it helps establish and maintain a corporate identity;
- it provides for increased awareness of mutual dependence;
- it is not based, necessarily, on rank or hierarchy;
- it is specific to one area or aspect of work.

As with any team, success will depend on the goals to be achieved, knowledge of the rules and the quality of the team members. Any team will only be as good as its weakest member. The goals of the team will need to be consistent with those of the organization, and membership of the team should, initially at least, be based on the contributions individuals can make towards goal accomplishment. Other criteria for success of the

team will be found under the discussion on managing meetings in Chapter
10.

The actual team-building process, however, will necessitate careful
consideration of the following questions:

- Who, if anyone, is to be the leader?
- Who is to decide the composition of the team?
- What is to be the basis of representation – selected, elected, nominated or status?
- What size of team is required?
- What is the specific remit of the team?
- Is membership of the team to be permanent or for a set period?

Other questions may be added to this list, but usually it is a particular
area of work or organizational activity which will finally determine both
the composition of the team and its purpose. For example, if functional
elements of the organization are team building then the production
function will require quite a different kind of team from that required by,
say, the marketing function. Function, together with the occupational
roles held by individuals – rather than just status – will help determine
membership. To get the best team possible will require satisfactory
answers to the following questions:

- What is the team for?
- What are the limits within which it must work?
- How much freedom does the team have?
- How much authority does the team have?
- Why is the team important?
- What special skills, experience or expertise are needed?
- Might there be personality problems?
- Are team meetings to be open or closed?
- How are decisions to be communicated outside the team, especially to management?

It is particularly important that as many members of the organization as
possible be involved in one way or another. This will help ensure that
there is no feeling of exclusion, elitism or decisions being taken behind
closed doors.

Quality Circles

Originating in the USA but applied effectively in Japan, quality circles
(QC) comprise small groups of individuals. The basis for membership
will typically be the possession of appropriate skills and the support of
fellow workers. Unlike the team, which has an extensive range of topics

and issues to contend with, the QC is concerned with one small aspect of work and then from one perspective only – **quality**.

The intention is that QCs be small in composition, say no more than ten to a group, and that their remit be limited if not precise. They are expected to come up with solutions and make recommendations – suggestions – to management as to how improvements can be made. An example of the application of QC is provided by Jaguar, the famous and now independent Midlands motor manufacturer.

'Jaguar now has sixty circles each around a dozen members (meaning 10 per cent of the work force) . . . Since the circles were introduced, in 1980, the number of quality inspectors employed has dropped from 677 to 360.'

(*Management Today*; April 1984: p. 41)

The principle underlying the use of QCs is that members take on the responsibility for ensuring the quality of the work even if it means complaining to fellow workers in another part of the organization or to outside companies who fail to fulfil their obligations (e.g. in terms of the supply of parts). Although derived from working practices on the shop floor, the application of the QC is potentially without any obvious limitations and can easily be applied to all aspects of organizational activities where improvements in quality of product or service are sought.

Another important factor is that eventually the number of circles can not only be extended to cover all aspects of the organization's activities but can also offer the potential of including **every** single employee in one or more of the circles. There is the additional advantage in that circles are sufficiently flexible to allow appropriate overlap with one another, as Fig. 38 illustrates.

Another way of looking at QCs is to see them as part of an overall network approach to problem solving. Networking is likely to take over in the future from the hierarchical structures as a more appropriate means of problem solving, in that it is related much more closely to the nature of the job and those who have to do it. In his book *Megatrends*, John Naisbitt (1984) comments on this when he says 'The failures of hierarchies to solve society's problems forced people to talk to one another – and this was the beginning of networks.' Eventually, groups of practitioners will, through the network of quality circles, determine the nature of their problems, associated with their functional tasks, thereby displacing the hierarchically based individual.

Problems of Implementation

The implementation of quality circles is likely to be neither easy nor instantly successful. This is hardly surprising, given that the traditional hierarchical structures have established a firm hold on the way in which

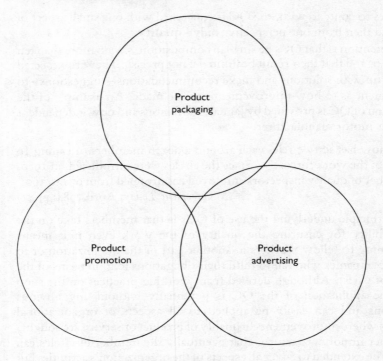

The marketing function

Fig. 38   Quality circles

organizations operate. This tradition, firmly rooted in a 'top down' style of management, does not easily translate into a 'bottom up' approach, which would, for some organizations, represent a revolutionary concept.

It has already been suggested that management simply does not have the monopoly on good ideas, and consequently collective approaches to problem solving are often, although not always, fruitful. Nor are all organizational structures appropriate for the introduction of QCs – or team building – and this is especially so where there is a strong hierarchy based on rank (e.g. the armed forces, the police, the Civil Service).

Flexible structures, then, together with appropriate organizational climate and leadership styles are essential prerequisites for the introduction of effective vehicles of worker participation. Given these provisos, commitment by both managers and supervisors will be secured, leading to the likely success of the implementation of QCs. These are all exciting trends but they are not likely to happen overnight.

Questions

(a) What are the main characteristics of a well–designed selection interview?

(b) How can an interviewer improve the effectiveness of the interview?

(ICSA, Summer 1985)

(a) Outline the main methods of communication which exist in a large organization.

(b) Compare and contrast two of these methods.

(ICSA, Summer 1985)

(a) Why is an understanding of motivation important to a supervisor or junior manager?

(b) What do you understand by the following:
(1) motivating factors?
(2) hygiene factors?

(IAM, Summer 1984)

You have been asked to give a lecture at your organization's staff training centre on effective delegation. The audience will consist of junior administrative officers. Outline and justify the content of your lecture.

(IAM, Summer 1985)

Discuss fully the relationship between motivation and performance.

(IAM, Winter 1985)

You have a responsibility for servicing executive meetings. Prepare a checklist which you will use yourself for ensuring that any meeting is efficiently prepared and serviced.

(IAM, Summer 1984)

What do you consider to be the main reasons why organizations set up and use committees to make decisions more than in the past?

(IAM, Summer 1985)

Discuss the concept of leadership in organizations. How important is it to look for qualities of 'leadership' in those considered for promotion to senior administrative posts in public sector organizations?

(ICSA, Summer 1985)

'In a business environment which has become increasingly unpredictable, we could well question the necessity for long range planning.' Comment on this statement.

(IAM, Winter 1985)

What are the reasons for management considering the introduction of an incentive scheme?

(LCCI, 1982)

What are the main conclusions that can be drawn from the Hawthorne Experiments?

(LCCI, 1982)

There are many different forms of communication and different ways would be used in different circumstances. State eight factors to be considered before deciding on the method to be used. Briefly justify your choice in each case, giving examples where necessary.

(PEI)

How would you minimize the problems of communication which might exist as a result of the Technical Division being about five miles distant from the main office?

(LCCI, 1983)

Sound decision making depends in the first place on the manager having a clear picture of what he is trying to achieve. How can the private secretary help him in this task?

(LCCI, 1983)

Comment on the contribution to management knowledge of any well-known management theorist with whose work you are familiar.

(LCCI, 1984)

Explain clearly the difference between planning and forecasting, quoting examples.

(LCCI, 1984)

How can one try to ensure that any sub-committees do achieve the purpose for which they were established?

(PEI)

Outline the importance of delegation to effective office organization, and the factors to be considered when delegating duties to a junior.

(PEI)

Recent management decisions have created staff unrest. You consider adequate communication beforehand could have avoided this. Provide a written statement for management, indicating how such communications could be improved.

(PEI)

(a) Explain the importance of 'feedback' in relation to the field of communication studies.
(b) Give an example showing how communication may fail in each case due to faults in:
(1) the communicator;
(2) the transmission of the message;
(3) the receiver.

(IAM, Summer 1985)

Leadership style is influenced by factors relating to the individual leader, the situation in which leadership is exercised and the subordinates for whom the leader is responsible.
(a) Define what you understand by 'leadership style' and mention any classifications of leadership style known to you.
(b) Select and explain in each case not more than four variables which will influence leadership style relating to:
(1) the individual leader;
(2) the situation;
(3) the subordinates.

(IAM, Summer 1985)

(a) 'Effective delegation begins with a manager's philosophy about people.' Explain what you think is meant by this statement.
(b) Suggest and exemplify four matters to which a superior should give attention when delegating responsibility to a subordinate for the performance of a task or function.
(c) Give two reasons why a person may be unwilling to accept delegation and suggest how such objections may be overcome.

(IAM, Winter, 1985)

(a) Identify and comment on four factors you would consider when deciding to use either oral or written methods of communication.
(b) The development of so-called 'quality circles' is a recent phenomenon. What is a quality circle? What are its aims, and how are these achieved?

(IAM, Winter 1985)

Decision making has often been categorized under the terms 'strategic', 'tactical' and 'operational'. Analyse and compare the information require-ments of each of these three categories.

(IAM, Summer 1984)

(a) 'Overcoming resistance to change is but a special case of attitude change.' What is an 'attitude'?
(b) How may you seek to change negative attitudes to innovation into more positive ones?

(IAM, Summer 1984)

The administrative manager is frequently faced with the task of introduc-ing change into the office environment. Outline the problems associated with organizational change and show how their worst effects can be reduced.

(IAM, Winter 1985)

We are going through a period of great technological change which is obviously a great challenge to management. What steps can be taken to minimize any problems that may occur as a result of this?

(LCCI, 1982)

(a) Why, in current management theory, is so much stress placed on the importance of employee motivation?
(b) Show, with examples, how:
    (1) the Managing Director of a multi-establishment company and
    (2) the Supervisor of an Accounts Office
    might foster employee motivation.

(RSA, 1983)

Computext Limited, a computer software company established in Amer-sham, Buckinghamshire, approximately five years ago, has been remark-ably successful. It provides a range of software services to a clientele that is still growing in numbers, although there have been some signs in the past year of a falling off in the rate of growth of market demand in some sectors of activity. The company employs 120 persons, a high proportion of whom are under 30 years of age. Most of the staff are highly trained in their respective skills, and salary levels are well above the national median for the given category of employee. Miles Frensham, the Managing Director, has, since the inception of the company, pursued the practice of informal consultation amongst the staff, although he admits that, with the growing workforce, this has become more difficult recently.

Beaufors p.l.c. is a medium-sized engineering company with a single factory at Coventry. This long-established company has been in decline for many years and has been heavily hit by the recession. There is, as yet, no sign of any improvement in its markets. The average age of the workforce of 8,500 persons is 48. The company has for several years been dealing with a problem of over-manning by a process of 'natural wastage' but this is proving a very protracted process. The only newcomers to the payroll in recent years have been a few maintenance staff and some younger specialist engineers; enquiry has revealed that they would have preferred employment in another company but for the limited job opportunities in the area. Charles Hatton, the Managing Director, has run the company autocratically for the past twenty years and is opposed to modern participative systems of management.

Compare the two companies in terms of management problems and effectiveness, and assess the likely differences of motivation of employees between the two companies. In the light of your comparison, do you consider that the management of Beaufors has anything to learn from Computext in improving the level of employee motivation?

(RSA, 1985)

The main planning period of a certain industrial company with its headquarters located at Derby is one year from January to December. It is established practice for the Managing Director to call, early in October each year, a meeting of the heads (and their deputies) of the different functions together with the five branch factory managers. The aim of the meeting is to enable him to summarize the performance to date within the current year, to specify the parameters to company operations in the forthcoming year, to indicate any adjustments necessary to strategy, to suggest the basis of next year's development and to invite comments and proposals from the participants. This meeting, which is expected to reach some initial conclusions, will be followed by a series of meetings for dealing with more specific matters, sometimes with smaller membership, until the provisional plans are completed early in December.

To provide a sense of occasion and to foster a co-operative spirit, the initial meeting in October is held at a country hotel near Matlock in Derbyshire. As personal assistant to the Managing Director:
(a) Suggest what arrangements you would need to make in preparation for the meeting.
(b) Draft a brief agenda and notice of the meeting to send to intended participants.
(c) Suggest how you might be involved during the course of the meeting.

(RSA, 1985)

Caravone Limited is a single-establishment company which constructs and markets caravans and equips mobile homes. The company, although still comparatively small, has grown rapidly since its establishment seven years ago and already employs 160 persons. The company comprises six departments: Design and Technical Development; Production; Marketing; Purchasing and Stores Control; Personnel; Accounting and Administration.

In the past months there has been some discord within the management of the company and this has been reflected in a falling off in both sales and profits performance.

A proposal has now been made by a major shareholder within the Board of Directors that a system of formal planning based on consultation throughout the organization be introduced. Jack Brymar, the Managing Director, has undertaken to look into the matter and report back to his fellow directors. As founder of the business, and being exclusively a design engineer by trade and previous experience, he has managed the business in a somewhat casual manner and strongly believes that 'the boss should decide'. Indeed, he has been known to express contempt for 'professional management'. Nevertheless, at times and especially when in difficulties, he turns to you, his Personal Assistant, for advice. What would you say to him as to:

(a) the significance, and possible benefits, that the introduction of a system of consultation and formal planning might have for the company and for Jack Brymar in particular;

(b) the problems which might be encountered in its introduction, and how these might be overcome?

You should make, and state, whatever assumptions you consider to be reasonable.

(RSA, 1984)

PART III

Management in Context

'The context of the firm had become one in which decisions were so numerous, and so diffuse in character, that for it to survive effectively required each person to surrender a large part of his autonomy, and to exchange information and ally himself in decisions with extensive groups of people.'

T Burns and G M Stalker
The Management of Innovation

The context in which management activities operate is wide and varied, and it is impossible for every manager to be an expert in every aspect. Consequently, areas of management have been hived off whilst new specialist areas have developed to keep pace with change. This Part seeks to illustrate four such areas.

The first – personnel – is a specialist functional area of management concerned with the human dimension of organizations. Effective personnel management can make a significant contribution to the smooth running of the organization by the influential role it plays in key areas – e.g. manpower planning, recruitment and selection, training and appraisal.

The second area – accommodation and facilities – concentrates on the management of the physical setting and on the nature of the various courses of action available to management. There seems little doubt that a well-designed workplace has a significant bearing on the behaviour of individuals and their attitude to work. This applies to both managers and staff. Consequently, the working environment has been receiving increased attention. Accommodation, furniture, fittings and equipment call for major capital expenditure by any organization whilst power, heat and light will represent considerable overheads. Nothing, therefore, should be left to chance – hence the need to gain a degree of expertise and to know when to ask for expert advice and guidance.

Conference management is the third area and is taken to include all events from meetings, product launches, seminars and training programmes to full-scale exhibitions and conventions. This is a relatively new dimension for management but, nevertheless, has stimulated interest based on an increasing awareness of the value to be gained from holding successful events.

The final area is office automation. Changes over the last decade have effectively revolutionized many of the standard office functions as well as providing management with information on a scale previously unimagined. Many organizations have been quick to respond to the benefits to be gained – especially in terms of efficiency – from integrating office functions, whilst others have been reluctant to 'take the plunge'. Nevertheless, office automation continues to make inroads into all forms of organization and is rapidly becoming part of the everyday office scene.

15
Human Resources

'Personnel must develop long-term policies and strategies and it must also be in there pitching when day-to-day problems arise, when tough negotiations are being faced, . . . In a sense there is the creative philosophical role, the preventive role and the day to day role.'

Sir Peter Parker
'How I see the personnel function'
(*Personnel Management*, January 1983)

The human resource is the most valuable one which any organization has. All enterprises rely on an efficient and effective workforce to achieve results and keep them competitive. Consequently, it is reasonable that time and care are taken by management to ensure that it secures and retains the right staff.

Personnel is, in its own right, a branch of management and is described by the Institute of Personnel Management as forming 'part of every manager's job' but being 'the special concern of those employed as specialists on the management team'. In larger organizations the personnel function is handled by a separate department whose duties and responsibilities correspond with those outlined briefly in Part I (page 10). However, given the significance of this function and the fact that it is present in all types of organization, some elaboration is given here.

Manpower Planning

The Department of Employment (1971), in its guide entitled *Company Manpower Planning*, describes this as 'a strategy for the acquisition, utilisation, improvement and preservation of an enterprise's human resources' – which, in simple terms, is to do with ensuring that the right people are in the right place at the right time.

Manpower planning is about matching supply and demand. It recognizes the fact that there may often be a gap which personnel specialists will need to help fill by sharpening up recruitment procedures, enhancing and accelerating training and staff development programmes, and improving industrial relations.

What factors influence supply?

- company policy in respect of recruitment;
- company policy in respect of promotion;
- company policy in respect of retirement;
- company policy in respect of redundancy;
- pay and working conditions;
- availability of skilled labour from outside the organization;
- employment legislation.

What factors influence demand?

- the organization's aims, objectives and policies;
- future expansion or contraction in existing activities;
- the introduction of new activities;
- changes in technology and working procedures;
- organizational changes – e.g. decentralization, alternative structures;
- financial ceilings in respect of personnel appointments;
- moves to new locations or premises.

How is supply assessed?

Supply forecasting is an essential element of manpower planning used to measure the quantity of manpower available to the organization, both from within and from outside. Forecasts are tackled in various ways, but take account of:

- existing resources via a staff audit which will analyse manpower figures and classify according to department, function, age distribution or other appropriate criteria;
- the turnover of staff, bearing in mind the reasons for leaving;
- the promotion and transfer of staff within the organization;
- the level of absenteeism;
- local patterns of employment/unemployment;
- competition from other organizations;
- the pool of skilled labour;
- the availability of part-time workers;
- the desirability of the area in terms of location, housing, education, transport and amenities;
- national trends – e.g. the demand for particular categories of workers;
- the output from educational institutions on to the labour market;
- the take-up of government-sponsored training programmes;
- the impact of employment legislation.

How is demand assessed?

The process of forecasting or estimating the demand for manpower will be dependent upon the future plans of the organization in respect of the quantity and quality of products and services it intends to provide. The actual techniques will be dependent largely on the size of the organization and the nature of its activities, but are likely to include:

- the judgement of management based on departmental estimates and proposals for future staff requirements;
- statistical techniques such as ratio–trend analysis, whereby excess staff demand would be calculated on the basis of the number of staff required to do the current workload and taking into account the projected additional work;
- work study and O & M techniques (see Part I, page 23).

Manpower planning needs to be an iterative process whereby supply and demand forecasting is monitored and evaluated in respect of matching and mismatching and where shortfalls or surpluses may be identified and remedied as quickly as possible. The process of manpower planning is shown in Fig. 39.

Job Analysis

Just as manpower planning is concerned with the long-term matching of supply and demand, job analysis is concerned with matching people and jobs on a day-to-day basis. It is a means towards effective working practices, sound recruitment and selection procedures, relevant appraisal techniques and appropriate training and staff development.

The term itself is a generic one used to describe the systematic study and analysis of jobs via a variety of possible techniques which include:

observation
interview
questionnaire
diary-keeping exercises

and are likely to result in the production of job descriptions, job specifications and person specifications. Considerable confusion arises out of these three terms but, briefly, the distinctions are as follows.

Job descriptions are detailed statements giving information in respect of:

- job title;
- job grade (if applicable);

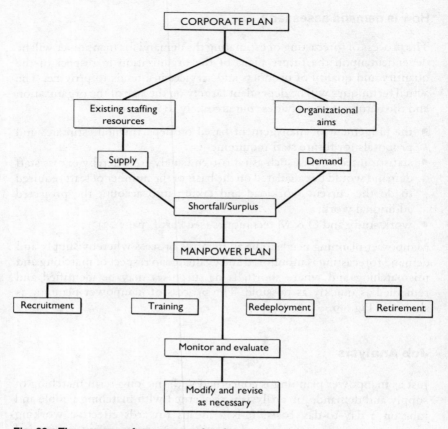

Fig. 39 The process of manpower planning

- job location(s) (if relevant);
- purpose of the job;
- main duties and responsibilities;
- specific duties;
- position in the organization structure – i.e. to whom responsible, and for whom responsible (if relevant);
- working environment;
- training opportunities;
- conditions of employment.

Job specifications identify the particular knowledge, skills and attitudes which are required in order that the job may be performed effectively, and they are often expressed in behavioural terms. In a detailed job specification each task associated with the job is analysed separately in respect of the knowledge required. It may specify certain minimum qualifications and the level of skill sought, and give an indication of any previous experience which would be desirable. Additional prerequisites may be a high level of interpersonal and communication skills, together with an indication of the attitudes required to satisfactorily fulfil the particular post. These attitudes may include personal qualities such as tact, diplomacy and discretion.

Person specifications are really extensions of job specifications in that they seek to interpret the job specification in terms of the sort of person who could best fulfil the job, and as such are used basically in selection interviewing. Different models have been applied to this activity but one which is particularly well known and often quoted is the 'Seven Point Plan' put forward by Professor Alex Rodger (1968) of the National Institute of Industrial Psychology. He considered that the attributes which an interviewer needed to consider in selecting the successful applicant for a job were:

- physique;
- attainments;
- general intelligence;
- special aptitude;
- interests;
- disposition;
- circumstances.

Job Evaluation

Job analysis forms the foundation of job evaluation, which enables jobs to be placed in a hierarchical order following a comparative exercise whereby all jobs are measured, analysed, compared on common criteria, graded and placed in a structure for pay purposes. Grading values are affected by a variety of factors, including:

- relative values of similar jobs within the organization;
- any negotiated pay scales which are in operation;
- equality factors of different jobs and the desirability of 'equal pay for equal work';
- market rates prevailing at any time.

Job evaluation techniques

Two principal general techniques are used – non-analytical and analytical. The former examines jobs as a whole, the latter breaking jobs down into constituent parts and assessing from there. Two examples of non-analytical techniques are job ranking and job classification or grading, whilst points rating is probably the best known and most frequently applied analytical method.

Job Ranking

This is the simplest method of job evaluation and is approached by comparing one job with another and then arranging the jobs in order of importance. Jobs may be compared on one criterion or factor or on a number of criteria. What are termed 'benchmark' jobs are identified in the process and these operate as yardsticks against which all other jobs may be compared. New jobs introduced into an organization will also be compared against the 'benchmark' jobs and placed in the ranking order accordingly. The main advantage of this technique is that it is readily understood and easily applied but has the disadvantages of being ill-defined in terms of standards and having no real way of gauging differences between jobs, so it can be difficult to achieve agreement between those carrying out the evaluations. In general, it is more likely to be appropriate in smaller organizations where the number of jobs is relatively few.

Job Classification

This approach is really semi-analytical in that it begins by defining the grades into which jobs will be classified, according to a range of predetermined characteristics. At its simplest, this type of scheme requires job descriptions to be prepared; from these, jobs can be placed into grades. The number of grades will be dependent upon the shape and size of the organization, the levels of hierarchy and the ranges of responsibility. Here again benchmark jobs are pinpointed and this greatly facilitates the grading of new jobs when they are created. The system is easy to operate and better in that standards are pre-set by grade definitions at the outset. However, classification of complex jobs presents problems as their characteristics are unlikely to fit neatly into established grades. The Institute of Administrative Management has published a classification scheme for clerical workers and this can be used to ensure objectivity and to help guarantee inter-organizational comparison.

Points Rating

This is based on the analysis and comparison of defined characteristics (factors) which are considered to be common in all jobs being evaluated. Factors are allocated a number of points, the number being dependent on the degree of each factor present in the job – i.e. factors are weighted according to their importance in the particular job. For example, in some jobs the experience factor may be considered more important than the skill, so experience would be weighted accordingly. As a technique, being a numerical system, points rating has the advantage of being more objective than non-analytical methods and of being consistent, whilst also being flexible enough to cover a wide range of jobs and accommodate technological change. However, it is complex to set up and maintain and no standardized points system is available to organizations, so many will actually employ more than one system.

Factors to consider when introducing job evaluation

Where an organization is setting up a job evaluation scheme, due consideration needs to be given to:

- the way in which staff should be informed;
- the nature and extent of staff involvement – e.g. the establishment of a job evaluation committee;
- the attitude of trade unions, if applicable;
- the range of jobs to be evaluated and the identification of 'benchmark' jobs;
- the method(s) to be used;
- the identity of the evaluators – i.e. will outside consultants be used or internal staff;
- the training issues involved;
- the time factor;
- the implications in respect of the need to publish pay scales;
- the implications for job alterations and changes;
- the Equal Pay Act 1970;
- appeals procedures when individuals question their job grading;
- the review procedures to be introduced to monitor and evaluate the scheme.

Recruitment and Selection

The recruitment and selection process is the area of activity which is possibly most readily associated with the personnel management function. It involves four basic steps:

- identifying requirements and preparing the necessary job descriptions and specifications;
- making the vacancies known to appropriate candidates;
- the selection process;
- the follow-up procedures on making appointments.

Identifying requirements

Requirements should be readily identifiable from the manpower plan coupled with the usual staff changes which are part and parcel of any organization. Some vacancies will arise out of the natural wastage, whilst others will be the result of requests for posts to fill newly created jobs. Whatever the situation, a job description/specification should be produced. This may mean reviewing and up-dating an existing one or carrying out a job analysis and producing a job description/specification for a new position.

Advertising vacancies

Once the identification stage has been completed the Personnel Department is then in a position to consider how it should set about attracting likely applicants. Numerous options are open to organizations, and these include:

- advertising internally;
- advertising externally via the national and/or local press;
- advertising in specialist journals;
- 'sifting' through files of unsolicited enquiries;
- using private personnel agencies;
- using MSC's Job Centres;
- using MSC's Professional and Executive Recruitment (PER);
- direct recruitment from educational institutions;
- executive search organizations ('head hunters').

It is important to weigh up the different options and consider which source will be most likely to produce the desired results. This will tend to depend on:

- the category of appointment;
- the time scale available to make an appointment;
- the cost factor.

Where it is decided to advertise – and advertising should always be capable of justification – care must be taken in preparing the advert or selecting the advertising agency to be used, choosing the best media for the particular requirement and selecting suitable times/days for advertising in order to ensure a good response.

What makes for a good advertisement?

Different styles of advertisement will serve different purposes but all advertisements should aim to attract attention, stimulate interest and provoke a response, and so too with job advertisements. They should give all essential information under a suitable heading which will normally be the job title or an arresting caption appropriate to the job. The advertising copy should include:

- details of the job;
- the requirements of the person sought;
- the name of the organization (a consultancy may be used in order to retain anonymity);
- the nature of the company's business;
- the location;
- grade and/or salary details, where known;
- details of how prospective candidates should apply;
- a closing date for applications (where applicable).

In the preparation of advertisements it is important to take account of the Sex Discrimination Act 1975 and the Race Relations Act 1976, which make it unlawful to discriminate in terms of sex or race.

Leading up to the interview

Good advertisements should produce good responses, although it has been suggested that the perfect advertisement should produce only the ideal candidate for the job! Dependent upon the wording of the advertisement, prospective candidates will have telephoned for more information (a popular technique of many organizations, particularly where they may wish to assess the telephone technique of applicants), written in for more details and an application form or applied directly submitting a curriculum vitae. The Personnel Department will log progress, keeping an accurate record of all details sent out and monitoring all applications returned. Some organizations acknowledge all applications, but where the volume is high it has become increasingly less common to do so and the next thing a prospective candidate is likely to hear is that he has been shortlisted and called for interview.

A Checklist of Interview preliminaries

Interviewing is concerned with more than conducting the actual interviews. These will be the culmination of a range of related preparatory activities, which will involve:

- determining the vacancy;
- preparing the job description;
- drawing up the necessary job specification;
- advertising the position;
- sending out further details and application forms;

- shortlisting the candidates;
- taking up references (where this is done prior to interview);
- notifying the candidates to be interviewed;
- drawing up the interview schedule;
- arranging for the reception of candidates;
- appointing an interview panel (where appropriate);
- ensuring that they have copies of all the necessary documentation;
- arranging for any tests to be conducted;
- organizing the environment – waiting area and interview room;
- arranging guided tours (if appropriate);
- arranging for informal 'interviews' with members of staff (where applicable);
- arranging hospitality;
- determining selection criteria;
- designing interview assessment forms;
- briefing interview panel (as required).

Appointment interviews take many different forms, ranging from relatively informal, person-to-person interviews to formal selection boards. Interview procedures and techniques also vary considerably although guidelines were suggested in Chapter 9. Whatever the circumstances, it is the responsibility of the Personnel Department to ensure that all the necessary preparations have been made.

Making and confirming offers

Once the interview process has been completed and the selection of candidate(s) made, a provisional offer may be made – usually 'subject to satisfactory references' and/or perhaps 'subject to a satisfactory medical'. In such circumstances the candidate(s) would normally indicate a willingness to accept the post, but nothing is binding on either side until the offer is confirmed and accepted. It is at this stage that the Contract of Employment would be prepared.

What is an employment contract?

A contract is made when an offer of employment is made and accepted. Contracts do not need to be in writing to be legally binding – a verbal agreement will suffice. However, where it is provided in writing this can reduce the likelihood of difficulties or misunderstandings arising later.

What is required by the Employment Protection (Consolidation) Act 1978 is that full-time employees should receive, within thirteen weeks of starting work, **written details** of the major terms of the contract. However, where confusion may arise is that not everything needs to be in writing to become part of the contract. Where terms are agreed in writing they become 'express' terms but there may also be 'implied' terms – e.g. those established by custom and practice or by conduct. However, where a full written Contract of Employment is provided it will be likely to include:

- job title;
- outline duties;
- commencement date;
- rate of pay;
- hours of work;
- holiday arrangements;
- sickness allowances and notification requirements;
- periods of notice, either side;
- grievance procedures;
- disciplinary procedures;
- union membership arrangements;
- rules appertaining to the work;
- arrangements for terminating employment;
- any special rights or conditions prevailing;
- any rights to vary the contract.

The Induction Process

This is where the organization welcomes new employees and provides them with the basic information they need to help them settle down quickly and comfortably in the new organization. From the point of view of management, the aim of an induction programme is threefold:

- to help pave the way quickly and smoothly for new employees;
- to establish the organization in a favourable light and so create a good and lasting impression with new staff;
- to help secure an effective contribution from new employees at the earliest opportunity.

Induction programmes vary from company to company in terms of both duration and content. They may range from as little as half a day to a matter of weeks, and may be organized on a company basis and/or departmentally. They will often be supplemented by a staff handbook, which should provide information on the following:

- company background and development;
- organizational structure;
- health and safety information;
- holiday arrangements;

- procedure for requesting leave of absence;
- sickness notification requirements and procedures;
- pay scales;
- pension scheme information;
- works rules;
- incentive schemes;
- promotion procedures;
- disciplinary procedures;
- grievance procedures;
- union agreements;
- joint consultative agreements;
- education and training facilities and provision;
- medical services;
- first aid facilities;
- restaurant and canteen facilities;
- the operation of any centralized services;
- rules for filing and indexing systems used;
- procedures in respect of the receipt of personal telephone calls and correspondence;
- travel and subsistence allowances and how to claim them;
- social and sports facilities;
- welfare arrangements;
- transfers;
- employee profit-sharing schemes;
- disturbance allowances;
- appraisal schemes.

Many of these issues will warrant special treatment during the induction programme but such times may be stressful for new employees and there will be a lot of information to absorb, so it is useful to have it clearly set out, with specimen forms and worked examples (where appropriate) and issued to staff in the form of a handbook. This will usually be loose-leafed so that additions and amendments may be easily incorporated.

Part of all such programmes should include introductions to immediate supervisors; it is useful for the manager and/or supervisor to have a brief chat with each newcomer so that any feelings of isolation and remoteness are quickly dispelled, making the new employee feel at ease and able to approach his superior in the certain knowledge that they have met at least once before.

Training

The induction process may include some very preliminary training of a general nature. However, where organizations wish to improve the performance of their employees in order that the company will benefit from increased productivity and efficiency, whilst employees themselves will have enhanced job satisfaction through working to their potential, a training plan needs to be drawn up. Training should not be a haphazard occurrence organized on an ad hoc basis to fulfil a one-time need, but a systematic activity where training needs are clearly defined, appropriate programmes devised and the results of training continually evaluated with methods modified and/or improved as considered necessary.

What kinds of training are there?

Training falls into numerous categories, ranging from half-day training courses on, for example, basic machine operation to three-day courses on first aid, to apprenticeship schemes, to part-time day and evening courses at educational establishments, to full-time postgraduate programmes of study.

Education and training of all kinds are available for all categories of the workforce, from those of the shop floor to those in the upper echelons of management. It may be carried out on or off the job and within the organization or outside. It may be general in nature and thus applicable to a variety of organizations, or organization/industry specific and hence designed to meet particular needs or requests.

Whatever the training and for whomsoever it is required, a training need will have been identified. That need may be one of the company as a whole, a need linked to a function or department or a group of workers, or to an individual, but it will have been brought to light by careful analysis.

How are training needs identified?

At organizational level, training needs should be highlighted in a manpower plan and should reflect the corporate policy of the organization. It should be readily possible to identify strengths and weaknesses and to recognize gaps in the knowledge and skills which need to be filled if the organization is going to achieve its objectives.

At departmental and individual levels, training needs are more likely to be identified by conducting surveys and interviewing staff in relation to the work of the department and their personal contribution to that work. Renewed consideration of job descriptions will also prove invaluable when taken in conjunction with future plans and commitments.

Such analyses will often produce a training gap between the skills, knowledge and expertise currently available and that required to realize future goals and targets.

What form should training take?

Since numerous options and combinations exist, it will be a matter of selecting the most appropriate in given sets of circumstances. Some of the points which will require consideration are:

- the availability of courses;
- the nature of the training;
- the content of the programme;
- whether it would be preferable on-site or away;
- whether the trainers should be company personnel or outsiders;
- whether the programme should be tailor-made for the organization or available to other organizations;
- the time scale involved;
- the techniques to be used;
- the level of motivation of the individual(s) receiving the training;
- the standards of performance expected of the training;
- the implications for other staff whilst training is taking place;
- how training is to be evaluated.

A word about management training

It is widely believed that formal management training – off the job – is no substitute for on-the-job experience. Many managers question the value of external management training courses unless they provide lots of opportunity to practise existing skills, exchange ideas and solve problems via group activity and discussion. Appendix 1 provides a sample list of short courses arranged by the British Institute of Management (BIM), the Industrial Society (IS) and Guardian Business Services (GBS), to name but three providers, and will give some indication of the types of courses which are obviously popular with managers.

Many of the titles are really concerned with 'development' as opposed to training *per se*; whilst management training will often be considered as an unlikely activity for practising managers, developmental activities have a different connotation, satisfying different criteria. As such they are welcomed by those holding management positions in that they not only provide an opportunity for self-development by introducing new areas of interest but also offer situations in which to practise and improve existing skills while benefiting from interaction with other managers occupying similar roles in other organizations.

Such programmes are not inexpensive but, like any other staff development activity, it needs to be appreciated that individuals do not stand still. They move on and they move out, and it is the responsibility of organizations to ensure that they have adequately prepared for management succession by effectively developing staff throughout the hierarchy. People with promise must be identified and given the guidance and encouragement to progress and fulfil their potential both in their own career interests and in the interests of the organization.

Transactional Analysis

One technique which has been successfully used for management development is transactional analysis (TA), devised by Eric Berne. It is a way of looking at human behaviour which provides insight into personal relationships and offers some practical techniques for change. The central idea is that people interact with each other on three levels, which Berne referred to as Parent, Adult and Child. The Parent part manifests itself when individuals express attitudes and opinions based on entrenched values and beliefs conferred by parents, whilst the Adult makes a mature, objective appraisal of a situation, processing data, estimating probability and determining the action to take. The Child, on the other hand, is evidenced by the adoption of spontaneous and emotional standards of behaviour that would be accepted and expected from a child (e.g. the need for immediate gratification) but which would be unacceptable and totally unexpected from an adult.

All three 'ego states' are necessary for healthy functioning of individuals but malfunctioning occurs when any of the three states is repressed or allowed to predominate disproportionately. It is perfectly normal and largely acceptable to switch from one state to another in given circumstances, but the switching must be controlled.

As a training model, TA has the goal of helping people recognize personal chronic behaviour patterns and those of others. Identifying any which may be hyperactive and repressing them accordingly may enable individuals to moderate their behaviour and increase their potential. Transactional analysis is used successfully in many management development situations.

Appraisal

Some form of appraisal is likely to exist in most organizations, whether it be an informal chat once a year with the boss to see how the staff are 'getting along' or a highly systemized exercise involving the completion of assessment forms and formal interviews with all staff, sometimes even on a six-monthly basis.

Whatever form staff appraisal takes, it has the following main purposes:

- it operates as a means of collecting information to improve the running of the organization;

- it identifies training needs;
- it enables assessments to be made of the present and future potential of staff;
- it identifies staff for promotion purposes;
- it motivates staff to improve personal performance;
- it provides a forum at which individuals may seek guidance or advice, may be offered constructive criticism, praised or warned about shortcomings;
- it provides a basis on which pay awards may be considered;
- it operates as a check on the effectiveness of personnel selection and training procedures.

Appraisal exercises can generally be divided into three elements:

- performance review;
- potential review;
- reward review.

Performance reviews are conducted to assess past performance, clarify any issues relating to work and determine plans for the future. Such a review should identify strengths and weaknesses, provide a forum for discussion between employee and manager, and give counselling for the future.

Potential reviews are carried out with the specific objective of identifying the way in which an individual's career should develop and the time scale envisaged. Assessing potential is a difficult task for any manager in that it is highly speculative for an immediate superior to contemplate how an individual may react in circumstances different from those in which he is currently readily observable. Some organizations attempt to secure greater objectivity by involving a manager other than the immediate superior in conducting the review.

Reward reviews are appraisal exercises which usually take place in conjunction with the award of annual increments or bonuses. Rewards may be given or withheld on the basis of performance throughout the assessment period. Clearly such activities may be detrimental to staff morale and motivation, as all other issues will tend to be clouded by cash implications.

Appraisal Techniques

Various techniques are available to managers in carrying out reviews, including the following.

Overall assessment is where the manager is called upon to prepare a written statement in narrative form, commenting generally on the employee, sometimes having been given a checklist for guidance. The approach is simple but highly subjective and reliant on the manager's ability to express himself well.

Guideline assessment is where specific questions are posed of the manager and answers sought. Although results should have greater precision the guidelines may be too vague, resulting in relatively unhelpful comments.

Grading scheme is where managers are required to select the statement which most closely answers the question in respect of the individual employee. Here there is at least some degree of uniformity but the difficulty still exists in determining how good is 'good' and how poor is 'poor'.

Merit rating is where number allocations rather than descriptive words are used to grade performance. This has the advantage that results are readily quantifiable, which can be helpful in determining pay scales or indicating training needs, but in terms of staff motivation or providing a basis for assessing actual performance on a job it is unlikely to be either systematic or objective.

Critical incident method is where a manager has to adopt a more open-ended approach by observing a range of activities illustrative of an employee's behaviour in the job. Such a technique will examine successful and unsuccessful or less successful aspects of the job performance, so providing a balanced picture over the period of the appraisal. It is, however, extremely time consuming and requires that the manager be well versed on the actual job observed in order that his critical incident report is informed and objective.

One technique which can help here is the adoption of a **critical incident log** where the individual to be appraised is required to keep a log each day over a predetermined period. (The nature of the work appraised will determine what would be a realistic period. For example, for a senior manager it may be appropriate to allocate a few months, whereas for a worker whose job is routine in nature a few weeks would be adequate.) In the log he will need to identify the one incident which caused him to experience the greatest difficulty. This is a particularly useful technique, where a major objective of the appraisal is to identify training needs. Here the training activity could be restricted to 'training by exception', attention being concentrated on the aspect(s) of the job which caused most difficulty as revealed by the critical incident log.

Appraisal interviews as such were dealt with in Chapter 9.

Welfare

The word 'welfare' tends to have connotations of Victorian paternalism and 'do-gooding', which is rather unfortunate in that it tends to colour the view held of employee welfare services in today's personnel management. Indeed, there are varying opinions as to whether or not welfare as such should still be part of the personnel function.

Originally, welfare services were introduced into industrial organizations at a time when there was no Welfare State and when working conditions were often appalling. Such days, fortunately, are long gone. The nature of workers' problems has changed and legislation has been introduced to ensure employee protection, health and safety in the work place.

Why are welfare services needed?

Possibly the most convincing argument in support of welfare services is the social one. Given that people spend at least half their waking hours in the context of work, it is reasonable to suppose that a large proportion of their problems and worries will be work-related or involve relationships they have at work. Therefore, there is an onus of responsibility on employers to treat employees as human beings by giving time and consideration to their hopes, fears, worries and anxieties. Additionally, although there is no guarantee that the provision of welfare services by an organization will improve morale and increase motivation, it is, none the less, likely that an organization which enjoys a good reputation in this respect will have low staff turnover and experience little difficulty in recruiting new staff. Therefore, there can be an economic benefit, even if it is not the direct one of increased productivity.

What sort of welfare services exist?

Services will be likely to fall into two categories – those provided on an individual basis and those set up for groups.

Individual services tend to be of an advisory or counselling nature, and may be directly work related or concerned with personal and domestic problems which can affect performance or attendance at work. The types of service offered by organizations vary but may cover:

- sickness;
- bereavement;
- domestic problems – e.g. family worries;
- legal advice;
- housing difficulties;
- career development;
- redundancy;
- retirement;
- working relationships.

People handling such issues need to possess counselling skills and maintain complete confidentiality in respect of the employees concerned. Dependent upon the size of the organization, there may be scope and need for several trained Welfare Officers, each of whom will handle a caseload. Where such a provision does exist, departmental managers and supervisors will be relieved of many employee problems in that the subordinate will often be more likely to take them direct to the Welfare Section.

Group services, on the other hand, will tend to fall more within a social or mutual aid context, as they are likely to include:

- the provision of sport and leisure facilities;
- the establishment of a social club;
- savings schemes;
- mutual–aid benevolent schemes for the sick and bereaved;
- long–service award schemes.

The involvement of the Welfare Section in these instances will be more supportive than anything else in that it will tend to be the workforce themselves who will be instrumental in stimulating support and interest.

The significance of some of these services, particularly those of a social nature, will be very dependent upon the location of the organization and the availability and cost of similar services outside the work environment. However, where provision exists for clubs and societies to generate their own funds and extend membership to outsiders, organizational facilities will tend to be well used in that the standard of provision is often high and the subsidies offered too tempting to ignore.

The future of welfare services within organizations

With more leisure time and the increased interest in leisure pursuits, sports and recreational activities by society generally, it is difficult to speculate on the direction in which organizational welfare could and should go.

Some level of welfare and counselling service within organizations will still be useful, particularly where there are trained specialist staff to offer help and advice. Stress is fast becoming the phenomenon of the 1980s and is likely to remain, given the pace of change and the pressures of modern life. In smaller organizations where specially designated staff do not exist, advice and counselling will come from the general staff of the Personnel Department.

This does not preclude individual managers or supervisors from offering advice, of course, although employees are often reluctant to reveal problems of a personal nature for fear of jeopardizing future chances of promotion and showing themselves in a less than favourable light with their superiors. Also, the old maxim 'a little knowledge can be dangerous' is significant where the problem may be of a kind that requires specialist advice. Training courses for personnel and supervisory staff can help but where a problem is of a very delicate nature or where sufficient experience is unavailable within the organization, help should be sought outside – perhaps via the trade union.

Industrial Relations

Over half the working population in the UK belong to a trade union, and, wherever there are trade unions, personnel management will be seriously involved in industrial relations. No precise definition exists for industrial relations (IR) but it is concerned with the complex web of systems, rules and procedures devised by trade unions and management in the interests of workers.

These involve pay structures, working conditions, interests and rights of employees in the work situation. They are concerned with things such as worker participation and collective bargaining, and are an integral part of the industrial pattern of Britain.

This is a complex area of study and much of it is value-laden opinion rather than hard fact. However, a few of the principal factors are discussed here to provide a perspective of industrial relations.

What rules are involved?

The rules involved in IR fall into several categories:

- those passed by Parliament – i.e. statute;
- those laid down by management – e.g. working procedures;
- those made jointly by management and employee – e.g. in the contract of employment;
- those made collectively by management and trade unions;
- those – often unwritten – which have grown out of 'custom and practice'.

Government legislation

Rules resulting out of legislation (i.e. Acts of Parliament or Statutory Instruments conferred on bodies such as ACAS or Industrial Tribunals) provide the legal framework in which industrial relations operate. For many years there was relatively little employment legislation but in the last twenty years there has been a marked increase, and the following legislation has had considerable impact on industrial relations:

Redundancy Payments Act 1965
Equal Pay Act 1970
Industrial Relations Act 1971
Industry Act 1972
Employment and Training Act 1973
Health and Safety at Work etc. Act 1974
Trade Union and Labour Relations Act 1974
Sex Discrimination Act 1975
Employment Protection Act 1975
Race Relations Act 1976
Trade Union and Labour Relations (Amendment) Act 1976
Employment Protection (Consolidation) Act 1978
Employment Act 1980
Employment and Training Act 1981
Employment Act 1982
Employment Act 1984
Trade Union Act 1984

Industrial Tribunals

Where a dispute arises over the rights of an individual employee the case normally goes before an Industrial Tribunal. Industrial Tribunals have jurisdiction over claims across a wide area of legislation from unfair dismissal, to equal pay and sex discrimination, to suspension on medical grounds.

Advisory, Conciliation and Arbitration Service (ACAS)

In addition to carrying out the activities apparent from its title, ACAS has authority conferred upon it by Act of Parliament to issue Codes of Practice on such topics as disciplinary matters (see also Chapter 9, 'Interviewing'), picketing and the closed shop. These codes offer practical guidelines to employees and may be used as evidence in court although they are not legally enforceable. Their principal advantage is that they are concise and written in straightforward language as compared to many Acts of Parliament which are often long and difficult to unravel.

Collective Bargaining

Collective bargaining is a joint regulatory process whereby management and unions can negotiate and discuss matters of mutual concern. Agreements reached will apply to particular groups of workers and will be unlikely to affect members of other unions, who will need to come independently to their own agreements. Collective bargaining has both a political and an economic dimension in that agreements will be concerned both with changes in the conditions of employment and with pay structures. The accelerating pace of technological change within the economy has brought with it many changes in working practices, and these have led to an increased number of revisions in collective agreements reached previously.

Parties involved in IR

A range of interested parties is involved and all have unique roles to play:

- the Government;
- management;
- employers' associations;
- personnel specialists;
- trade unions;
- union representatives or shop stewards.

Government's role is to create the necessary legal framework in which industrial relations will operate. It does this by passing Acts of Parliament on employment legislation and conferring powers on institutions such as ACAS (see above) in order to encourage good working practices and to set up the necessary mechanisms for joint consultation.

Management's role is to steer the organization to the achievement of organizational goals. This will necessitate planning, directing, organizing, controlling, communicating, motivating, negotiating and all the other functions associated with the total management activity. It is management's responsibility to lead the workforce, to encourage teamwork and a sense of common purpose and commitment via the establishment and maintenance of good working practices, conditions and employee relations.

Historically, management has frequently received a 'bad press' in the field of industrial relations. Much depends on the leadership style of the organization and how the workforce is treated. Industrial relations will vary according to economic conditions and the state of employment. Currently, for example, concern is more with protecting jobs given the technological advances which many industries are experiencing, rather than pressing for improvements in general working and living standards, which was very much the call of the 1970s. Major issues remain the remit of senior management but IR issues on more specific matters relating to working practices and procedures tend to become the responsibility of middle management and supervisory levels.

Employers' associations arise out of the formation of groups of employers just as trade unions are the result of groups of employees joining together. The intention is to join forces, share problems, pool resources, provide an advisory service and secure assistance with trade union negotiations. However, in recent years there has been a decrease in the tendency of groups of employers to band together and form associations, largely as a result of the decline in national industrial bargaining with most bargaining now taking place at company level.

Personnel specialists used to be at the very heart of all IR matters, often taking the 'middle' position between management and the unions. Very few agreements, however, actually specify a role for the personnel specialist and consequently it will be rather one of offering advice to management in the handling of industrial disputes. On the other hand, the personnel specialist may be directly involved in any negotiations and bargaining which takes place between management and union. It is, none the less, the establishment of sound personnel practices and procedures *per se* (e.g. job evaluation, staff appraisal schemes and training programmes) which will contribute greatly to the overall effectiveness of an organization in establishing and sustaining good industrial relations.

Trade Unions

The Trade Unions and Labour Relations Act 1974 defines a trade union as an organization which 'consists wholly or mainly of workers of one or more descriptions and is an organization whose principal purposes include the regulation of relations between workers of that description or those descriptions and employers or employers' associations'. This is rather confusing. In simpler terms, a trade union is an organized group of people in employment who join together to improve their working lives with the intention of:

- enhancing their bargaining capacity via collectivism;
- securing better pay and working conditions;
- increasing job security;
- improving the status of workers;
- seeking greater democracy and increased worker participation in decision making.

Trade unions exist in all sections of working life and serve a wide variety of interests. They have a complex structure operating at national, regional, local and organizational levels and many are affiliated to the Trades Union Congress (TUC).

The Trades Union Congress

The TUC attempts to draw together the various factions of the trade union movement with a view to securing solidarity and achieving objectives via a collective approach. It provides a forum, with main headquarters in London, whereby policy may be determined collectively, whilst offering a full range of advice on economic, social, legal and industrial matters. It produces a variety of publications and is represented on a wide range of external agencies such as ACAS, the Manpower Services Commission (MSC) and the National Economic Development Council (NEDC). It provides assistance in the handling of industrial disputes and liaises closely with ACAS.

Shop Stewards

A shop steward is a trade union member elected by the workforce to represent them in all issues affecting them. Frequently cast as the aggressive 'villain of the piece', out to cause trouble at any price, the shop steward can be valuable to both management and fellow workers. He can help by providing an interface between shop floor and management, and, by doing so, ensure not only that members' interests are represented to management but that unreasonable requests or complaints from the shop floor are squashed before they reach dispute proportions. His job is not an easy one as there may be conflicting ideals when, for example, he has to deal with the grievance of an individual member, whilst, at the same time, protecting the interests of **all** union members.

The effective shop steward has to be able to operate in a variety of situations and it is important that those elected are capable of performing the necessary duties. The election process and accompanying procedures are important, as is the eligibility of individuals to stand for election. For example, candidates need to be suitably qualified in terms of duration of service and fully aware of the nature of the duties they will be required to undertake. There should also be a certain number of shop stewards to represent a given number of union members and elections should be appropriately conducted – preferably on company premises in order to ensure optimum participation. These are issues which need to be discussed openly by management and unions.

On appointment, a shop steward should receive a written statement of his rights and responsibilities as jointly agreed by management and union, and his appointment should be acknowledged throughout the organization via appropriate publicity and an interview with a member of senior management. An individual appointed as a shop steward will be released, on pay, from his normal duties in order to perform union business. This will include attending meetings with management and being present at negotiations which may affect the union membership. Additionally, he may represent the membership interest on a wider committee network by attending meetings outside the organization and providing feedback to the members he represents on issues of general interest and concern.

Training for IR

Effective industrial relations depend on the quality of training given to all levels of personnel involved. This will include training of managers, supervisors and shop stewards.

Every member of an organization is affected directly or indirectly by industrial relations and it is essential that those operating at the forefront should be appropriately trained. For managers and supervisors this will mean providing them with sufficient background information on IR generally and on their own organization in particular, together with knowledge of roles and functions of individuals, communicating strategies, pay structures and negotiating and bargaining procedures. Where individuals have considerable direct involvement, it may be necessary for them to attend refresher courses periodically in order to develop essential skills and to keep up to date.

Similarly, formal training should be provided for shop stewards who need to be *au fait* with their own union and with the industrial relations issues of their particular organization, as well as their personal functions and responsibilities. Additionally, they need to be able to participate effectively in joint concerns of union and management (e.g. joint consultative committees) and to possess adequate negotiating skills in order that they may represent their union membership effectively. Training should not be a once and for all event but rather a continuous process providing the maximum opportunity to develop new skills and discuss relevant issues.

Influential factors in determining the state of IR

Healthy industrial relations are essential to any successful enterprise, and the achievement of a satisfactory condition will be dependent upon:

- the economic climate of the country;
- the turbulence of the particular industry;
- employment and industrial relations legislation;
- the attitude of management to unions;
- the attitude of unions to management;
- the relationship with other unions;
- the relationship with the TUC;
- the ability of management and workforce to resolve differences and difficulties amicably;
- the strength of the unions;
- the effectiveness of shop stewards;
- the extent of union membership;
- the extent of grievances and disputes;

- the level of joint participation;
- the success of collective bargaining.

In short, almost ten years on, the words of the Bullock Report (1977, *The Report of the Committee of Inquiry on Industrial Democracy*) still ring out loud and clear:

'There must in the future be a new legitimacy for the exercise of the management function within a policy framework agreed jointly by the representatives of capital and labour . . . In our view it is unreasonable to expect employee representatives to accept equal responsibility, unless, through equal representation on the board, they are able to have equal influence on the decision-making process.'

Human resource management will directly or indirectly affect all those involved in the management or supervision or staff. Whilst many aspects will come primarily within the remit of the personnel function, an awareness of the principal areas is important and useful for all practising and aspiring managers.

16
Accommodation and Facilities

'Companies may relocate in search of economies or to cope with expansion: in either case relocation is a complex business . . .'

Peter Fearfield and Chris Ling
(*Management Today*, July 1985)

Something like one in three workers in Great Britain are employed in what might be termed office jobs (in the USA it's around 50 per cent), so in recent years considerably more attention has been given to office accommodation and facilities.

The growth in offices and office work has been going on for the last 200 years or so, following the change from an agrarian to an industrial economy and taking into account the increase in paperwork that such a change has necessitated. Never before has there been a greater demand for information and for the maintenance of records and the filing of returns to a growing number of external agencies.

Consequently there is a need for a high level of office productivity, and one of the factors which governs this is the accommodation and environment in which office staff do their work. Efficiency and effectiveness are more likely to be achieved when there are good offices. But what constitutes a good office? Offices are, by and large, designed with structural, technical and economic considerations in mind rather than what the individuals working there need to fulfil their duties and responsibilities effectively.

Management's role

Organizations need to give consideration to the choice, planning and management of space, along with the many other aspects which, together, help contribute to successful business management generally. Space is an increasingly expensive and precious commodity, so decisions about its utilization form an important part of management's remit.

In an economy which is becoming more and more information and service based – as opposed to manufacturing oriented – the selection and management of office accommodation take on more significance and receive more attention. The importance of space management and all that it entails – viz. the running, maintenance and adaptation of an organization's premises in terms of its overall costs – is, therefore, gaining more recognition.

The accelerating pace of office automation is a major contributory factor in the changes which are currently taking place in office design. Changes have emerged as a direct response to management's recognition that sophisticated office systems and appropriate facilities represent significant keys to improved performance. As efficiency is the password to profit, it is vital that sufficient attention be given by management to office accommodation and the working environment. Besides, even high level executives will still spend the major part of their working lives in the office!

Selecting a suitable location

Location is largely dependent upon whether the business is new or whether an existing business is moving to new premises. Where the business is new the deciding factors for choosing a particular location is likely to include:

- the nature of the firm's activities;
- the extent of funds;
- the availability of suitable premises;
- the need for proximity to customers/clients and suppliers;
- the availability of essential services;
- the convenience of transport and parking facilities;
- the availability of suitably skilled staff;
- the proximity to amenities, such as banks, shops and eating establishments.

Additionally, where the firm is a small concern, the preferences and local contacts of the founder may be of major significance.

On the other hand, when a move is being contemplated, it is necessary to view the above factors within the context of a rationale for making the move, which includes:

- lack of sufficient space due to office expansion;
- too much space due to contraction of business, or reduction of staff following increased automation;
- expiry of a lease;
- excessive rent and/or rate increases;
- difficulty of access;

- compulsory purchase order by the local authority;
- the need to enhance company image and status by improving premises or site;
- the need to reduce overheads;
- the need to realize a capital asset for alternative investment purposes;
- the desire to acquire a capital asset through property purchase.

It is these kinds of issues and situations which combine to produce a demand for alternative premises.

What are the available options?

Basically, it will be a matter of choosing from:

- town or city centre;
- suburbs;
- industrial estate.

Town/city locations would be further refined to centre/main street, or specific district/area according to the locations of associates and competitors. Choice will be determined by a detailed consideration of the points mentioned above, by comparing and contrasting locations available and by highlighting the advantages and disadvantages of the alternatives.

The ultimate selection of site will depend on the particular company concerned. Certain organizations, by their very nature, will consider only town/city centre locations, as is evidenced by the clustering together of major retail outlets in the high streets of all our towns and cities. However, improved communications, in every sense of the term, have made it less essential for other enterprises to opt for centre sites, and suburban or industrial estate locations can provide the following **advantages**:

- lower building costs;
- lower rents and rates;
- less expensive for staff in terms of travel time and costs;
- easier parking;
- cleaner, healthier and quieter working environment;
- better, more spacious working conditions and facilities;
- greater potential for expansion;
- sometimes, the availability of government grants or incentives.

These need to be offset against possible **disadvantages**, such as:

- loss of direct contact with associates and clients;
- loss of prestige;
- more expensive service and maintenance costs;
- increased communication costs;

- public transport difficulties;
- limited local amenities in respect of banks, shops and restaurants;
- increased requirements to arrange visits and appointments away from the office site;
- possible recruitment difficulties.

Premises

Renting, leasing or buying

Once the location is selected, there are other factors to consider before final decisions are reached. These will largely be determined by the geographical location of the organization, the type and size of property required and the general availability at any given time.

Certain types of property may be available only for rent or lease and it will then be a matter of considering the terms of the rental or leasing agreement. It is important to secure sound legal advice on the interpretation of such agreements, with particular reference to the rights which the tenant or leaseholder has in respect of:

- the use to which the property may be put;
- the extent to which structural alterations may or may not be made and any special conditions which exist;
- the onus of responsibility in terms of maintenance, repairs and decoration;
- the potential to sub-let;
- the options available to renew the lease;
- the penalties incurred for terminating the lease;
- the duration of the agreement;
- the rights of the owner to vary the agreement and the conditions or terms which exist;
- periods of notice which apply on either side;
- any special exclusions, terms or conditions.

Where buying is being considered, it will be a choice between buying an existing property and buying a site and having a building custom designed.

Existing buildings

These will fall into several categories:

- complete buildings;
- parts of buildings;
- old buildings;

- new buildings;
- buildings currently used for similar purposes;
- buildings requiring conversion.

This sort of purchase represents a major capital investment and organizations will call upon expert opinion and advice on legal, structural, planning and insurance aspects to ensure that they are fully aware of the following:

- any future developments envisaged for the area generally – i.e. new construction, demolition, roads, changes of priority;
- ground rent agreements;
- options on future acquisition of shared accommodation;
- the suitability of the building for the purpose intended;
- the strength of load-bearing walls;
- the suitability for computer installations;
- availability of telephone lines;
- access for servicing and maintenance;
- fire, health and safety regulations;
- potential to alter existing layout;
- potential to extend;
- restrictions in operation;
- insurance and security requirements;
- amount of unusable or wasted space.

All such aspects would be thoroughly investigated before any commitment was made to buy. It is important that an organization consult specialists at this stage – i.e. before a decision is made to buy. What is crucial is that possible problems should be identified before they arise, so making it a matter of prevention rather than cure. Where wrong decisions are made and expert advice is called in afterwards, not only will remedies be costly but also they may only provide temporary relief, whereas initial consultation might have prevented the ensuing symptoms entirely.

Professional advice

Similarly, it is important to seek professional advice at a time when existing premises may appear inadequate. Often the trained eye can see a solution which would not have been obvious to the non-expert who may have felt that a move to larger premises was the only solution. Analysis of the allocation and planning of available space is crucial to any decision, and re-planning will often be better given the sympathetic treatment of the professional who can consider the problems objectively and bring to them the experience gained elsewhere on similar issues. Organizations often consult planners for remedies to problems when what they really need is a new diagnosis.

Advice secured at the right time in the decision-making process may save an organization vast sums of money. Sometimes a move will not prove to be the best answer. It may be better all round to consider a re-utilization of the space and facilities already available.

Custom Design

This can be secured in several ways, the following of which are four possibilities:

- the acquisition of a site and the building of premises to precise requirements;
- the acquisition of a site larger than required and the commissioning of a developer to build in excess of personal requirements with the intention of leasing the surplus;
- the acquisition of a 'shell' within a new building constructed by a developer (very popular in new towns and specially designated development areas);
- the demolition of existing building(s) and replacement by custom-designed accommodation.

Whatever the circumstances, the design of a new building or the planning and utilization of space within an existing building require vision and careful forward planning.

Office layout

Layout will depend on the nature of the business, its size, the organizational structure adopted and the space available. Basically, any organization needs to carry out a process of evaluation in an attempt to establish its office needs by:

- analysing the overall work carried out;
- appreciating the patterns of work flow involved;
- identifying and recording functional relationships which exist between workers and working groups;
- making a systematic record of all communications – written, transmitted (telephone, intercom) and face to face – which take place within the office;
- analysing the organization in terms of its accountability, responsibility, direction and supervision;
- assessing those areas of work requiring special consideration or facilities;
- examining those areas which necessitate a lot of contact with external sources;

- identifying those services which are used by all the staff;
- fulfilling statutory obligations in respect of health and safety;
- implementing essential building regulations;
- adopting design standards and recommendations.

Such an exercise will produce a company profile and ensure that data are gathered which will indicate how an organization operates, its goals and objectives, and the options it has available for the best utilization of available space. Having undertaken this exercise an organization will be in a position to arrange its departments, sections, working groups, personnel and work activities to best advantage. Where accommodation extends to more than one floor, consideration will also need to be given to which areas of work should be allocated to which floor levels.

The main alternatives in terms of actual design are variations of 'closed' or 'open' offices. The former has hard walls as dividers and tends to be the traditional approach and one which is still favoured by many companies today. However it has been replaced in many instances by the adoption of work areas in open or partially open offices where flexibility is the keyword.

Closed or cellular offices

These are the sorts of offices where work takes place 'behind closed doors' with entry from a corridor either centrally located or running along one side of the building or floor.

Advantages

- privacy is easily available;
- there are instantly recognizable indicators of status and position in the hierarchy;
- better security;
- fewer distractions;
- personal control of the environment in terms of heating, lighting and ventilation;
- noisy equipment can be more easily isolated;
- furniture and fittings may be provided to reflect the status and position of the occupant(s);
- occupants may 'personalize' their surroundings more easily.

Disadvantages

- single rooms may not be readily available for all who need or request them;
- sharing may be unpopular amongst staff;

- pressures of individual working relationships may be strong;
- positioning and room allocation tend to be based primarily on hierarchical criteria;
- communication is much less direct whilst informal communication is discouraged;
- supervision is hampered;
- structural changes will be disruptive, costly and often difficult;
- valuable space is wasted with corridors.

Basic Open Plan

The original concept of 'open plan' was simply to organize large numbers of workers in one large office rather than allocate either individual or shared rooms. Arrangements tended to be in formal lines of well ordered rows and such offices were usually associated with routine, lower grade activities. Typical early exponents were large insurance companies where many insurance clerks worked from the one huge office.

Advantages

- saving of space;
- better control and supervision;
- improved work flow;
- better organization of repetitive tasks;
- ease of adding an extra desk;
- more direct communication;
- more opportunity to share expensive facilities and resources.

Disadvantages

- classroom-like appearance;
- over-close supervision;
- lack of privacy;
- noise and distraction;
- the spread of infectious diseases;
- the inability to personalize and control immediate surroundings.

Most of the problems associated with the early open plan idea were human ones and the advantages tended to be very much from the point of view of management in that such arrangements improved control and were less expensive to set up and maintain.

Landscaped Offices

In the late 1950s studies were carried out to maximize the use of office space whilst bringing to it an understanding of the needs of the individuals interacting in the workplace. German consultants introduced the term 'Bürolandschaft' or 'office landscape' and applied it to the arrangement of groups of office workers involved in related activities occupying a vast area of office floor. Such large scale open plan layouts were sometimes referred to as 'panoramic office planning'. Whilst the arrangements may have looked random they were the result of careful planning and consideration of the work carried out in offices. It was also thought to be important that workers should be able to see daylight through a window irrespective of where they were situated on the open floor. An example of 1960s style open plan is given as Fig. 40.

Adapted Open Plan

Huge open plan offices were not entirely successful and now tend to be viewed somewhat as 'fossils' by architects and planners. However, rather than turn full circle and return to closed offices, modifications have been introduced to open layouts resulting in functional and attractive adaptations where the emphasis is on shared facilities and accommodation.

This has been largely due to the growth in office technology where actual work space is getting smaller while support space is growing. Also the introduction of technology brings with it electronic equipment and the resultant increase in wiring, noise and general disturbance. This is not conducive to the increased productivity which traditional open plan offices were designed to achieve.

The aim of adapted open plan is, therefore, to strike an effective balance between the agoraphobic conditions of the original German idea of having entire offices set out on an open floor as illustrated in Fig. 40 and the claustrophobic conditions produced by small cellular offices. The result is the provision of a working environment designed to support activities performed by different workers and tailor-made to suit their individual needs.

Examples of present-day adapted open plan are provided by plans of two floors of Sunlight House in Quay Street, Manchester, taken over by Building Design Partnership in June 1986 and shown as Figs 41 and 42.

Action Office®

Herman Miller, one of the largest manufacturers of systems furniture in the world, developed their Action Office system in the 1960s. This

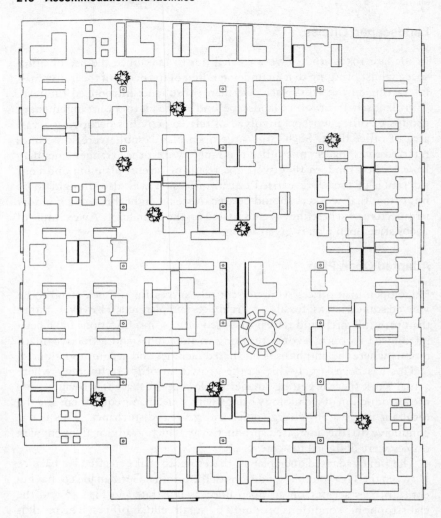

Fig. 40 Open plan 1960s style (*Reproduced by kind permission of BDP, Preston*)

followed years of intensive and detailed research into how people really work in offices, taking into account the nature of the work itself, physical and psychological needs and the general working environment. The concept of Action Office developed around the idea of movable, ergonomically designed panels which could support all manner of work surfaces, storage units and display areas (see Fig. 43).

The key to the system was versatility and flexibility in that any size of office could be adapted in this way and yet modified or altered as new

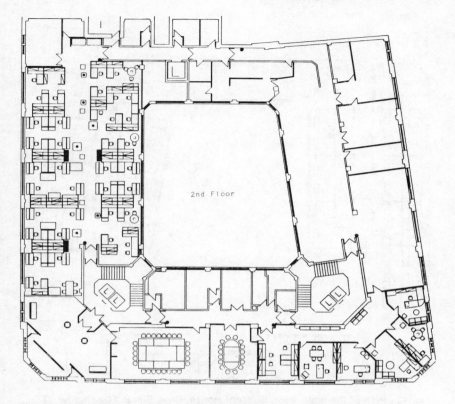

Fig. 41   Plan of the second floor, Sunlight House, Quay Street, Manchester

needs arose. Landscaped partitioning and multi-purpose, flexibly designed furniture could be incorporated to break up large areas of open space whilst maximizing the space available by doing away with formal corridors and providing a balance of individual and shared work areas. The idea was that people should determine their own requirements according to the sort of work they undertook and their resultant individual needs.

The principles of present office design

Modern office design is the result of a systematic examination of the space requirements of each worker, in terms of the job he does, the equipment and facilities he uses and the contact he has with others. From this information it is possible to determine individual requirements (for space and communications) and to translate these to an overall plan of the available area.

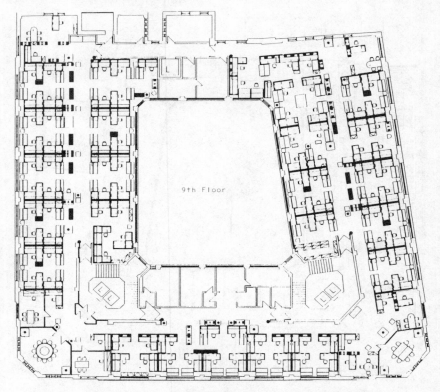

Fig. 42   Plan of the ninth floor, Sunlight House, Quay Street, Manchester

It is important to recognize that these principles may be applied to floor areas of varying shapes and sizes, accommodating different numbers of staff undertaking a wide range of activities. Two examples to illustrate smaller floor areas and planned to utilize different types of accommodation are given as Figs 44 and 45.

Irrespective of the scale of the project, the particular points which need to be considered are:

- communication networks in operation;
- type of heating, lighting and ventilation;
- provision of essential services – wiring, telephones;
- maximizing of acoustic materials;
- positioning of desks (work stations) to avoid constant eye to eye confrontation;
- design of work stations;
- access to work areas;
- extent of privacy required;

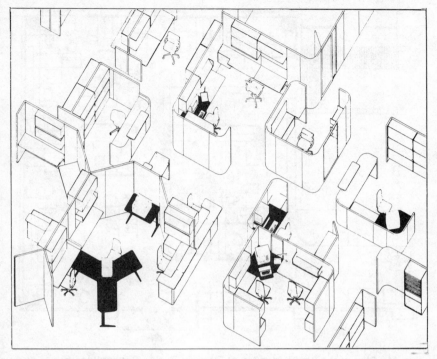

Fig. 43   Action Office®

- location of machines;
- servicing of facilities and equipment;
- location of partitioning or acoustic screens;
- design and positioning of reception area;
- inclusion of rest areas;
- refreshment facilities;
- siting of storage facilities;
- location of meeting areas;
- allocation of 'free' space;
- allocation of 'subjective' space, i.e. that associated with activities of particular individuals or groups;
- location of shared equipment.

Advantages

Basically this type of design will have all the main advantages of simple open plan but will also benefit in the following ways:

- maximum flexibility in that individuals, sections or departments may be easily moved around;

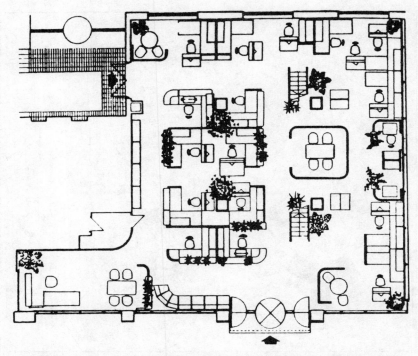

Fig. 44   Plan of the Sheffield office of Building Design Partnership, winner of the small office category of the Office of the Year Award 1983

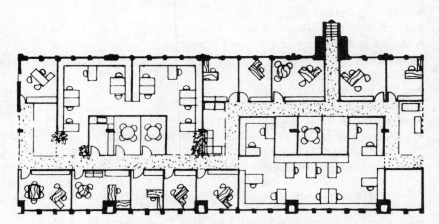

Fig. 45   Section plan of offices of the Electricity Supply Board in Dublin (Architects; Stevenson Associates, Space Planners – DEGW)

- layout is adaptable to changes in organizational structure or business emphasis;
- 'team spirit' is more easily achieved;
- accessibility of colleagues improves working relationships and promotes an understanding of the jobs of others;
- enables staff to benefit from the installation of expensive equipment and resources which they can share;
- promotes the reduction of a 'status race' by providing 'common ground' for everyone;
- encourages higher standards of behaviour and discipline in that there is pressure to conform with those around;
- furniture and fittings are of better quality in that there is a need to standardize and the standard tends to be high;
- purpose-built reception areas are essential to provide pleasant, relaxed conditions in which staff may greet guests, whilst creating a good first impression for the visitor.

Similarly, disadvantages will tend to be akin to those mentioned above in connection with open plan, although many of these factors can be minimized by imaginative design and good furnishings, coupled with the introduction of systems and techniques which help control things such as heating, lighting and ventilation in an acceptable way.

Why is modern office design different?

It is a 'total concept', carefully and thoughtfully planned from start to finish. There is nothing haphazard about it. It is an attempt to make office work as efficient as possible. It is designed with the interests of people in mind. It acknowledges what **actually** happens in offices not what people **think** happens and these are two very different things!

Office staff will tend to gain from such a layout as it will respect their need for privacy by providing adequate acoustic screening and foliage (even to the extent of real trees in some offices!) whilst preventing feelings of isolation and lack of involvement. It also enables workers whose job content is closely related to associate more easily. How much easier it is to turn round in a swivel chair or move to a neighbouring work station to speak with a colleague than to leave one office and go to another, perhaps only to find that the person is out or absent from work. Comfort is also maximized in that the size necessitates the provision of an artificial environment, where lighting, heating and ventilation are controlled automatically which will normally ensure conditions far superior to those found in conventional offices. Complete carpeting throughout will also enhance the feeling of comfort and luxury.

Flexibility

Management too will benefit from the flexibility which such a layout offers, together with the economic use of space. Such an environment will tend to provide a boost to morale for staff who will tend to respond positively to improved working conditions which enable careful regrouping of staff based on individual and work-related needs.

The provision of amenities is also a bonus in that they dispense with the rigidities of timed tea and coffee breaks, substituting the provision of rest areas which may be used as and when staff wish during the course of the working day. Time studies have indicated that such provision actually results in less time being taken up rather than more as would perhaps be envisaged with such an arrangement.

Responding to future needs

Office planning is more than a question of 'how many people can we squeeze into this office?' Such attitudes are far outmoded with attention being given to the future as well as the present. Things are changing and changing fast! Many organizations find themselves completely unprepared for the challenge which technology and office automation present in terms of accommodation. It is not merely a question of optimizing the use of available space but rather one of providing appropriate facilities for people, thus ensuring their well-being and enhancing the possibility of securing their commitment and increasing productivity.

What makes for good working conditions?

Having examined the factors determining the acquisition of accommodation and the design of layout, it is appropriate to turn to the working conditions which operate, whatever the property and whatever the layout used. Good working conditions will be found where attention is given to the safety, security and comfort of those who work there, together with attention to motivation, job satisfaction and morale as mentioned in Part II.

Following legislation in the form of the Offices, Shops and Railway Premises Act 1963 and the Health and Safety at Work etc. Act 1974, safety and environmental factors in offices have received attention. With regard to the former piece of legislation it should be noted that it contains very broad recommendations and lays down minimal acceptable standards in respect of things such as space allocation, heating and lighting, with which all organizations are expected to comply. The latter is an 'enabling' Act which, for the first time, places the onus of responsibility for matters of health and safety on employer and employee alike. It is, once again, fairly general in terms of the legislation laid down and makes frequent use of the phrase 'as far as is reasonably practicable', which is open to various interpretations. However, it does provide, within the general framework of the Act, for regulations and codes of safe working practice to be drawn up as considered necessary and desirable in the interests of health, safety and welfare, and this can be no bad thing.

Safety

All organizations now have a statutory obligation to produce a health and safety document for publication or issue to employees. Such a document will set out the company rules, regulations and procedures in respect of safety practices within the working environment and will be likely to include:

- a statement of intent by the organization, provided in the spirit of the Act – viz. the interests of health and safety will be paramount and always take precedence over working practices *per se*;
- indication that encouragement will be given to workers to co-operate with this endeavour;
- a statement acknowledging corporate responsibility but emphasizing the need for company-wide involvement and recognition of the importance of health and safety;
- a reporting mechanism for accidents and injuries;
- the location of the first aid box and accident book;
- a statement of procedures in respect of the provision of safety training;
- a code of safe working practices, broken down into different areas of work;
- where and from whom advice on safety matters can be sought;
- details of the roles and duties of official safety representatives;
- the name of the executive responsible for ensuring that the policy is fulfilled.

The Health and Safety at Work etc. Act can be enforced by local environmental health officers, who are at liberty to visit and inspect office premises at any time.

Office Safety – factors which should be given special attention

Offices, like any other work areas, have their own types of hazard and special attention would be given to the following:

- the actual building – its surroundings, layout and facilities;
- access and entry points;

- corridors and staircases;
- doors – with particular reference to fire doors and those of the swing-type variety or made of clear glass;
- partitions – in respect of their material from a fire-prevention point of view and glass ones in that they should have some sort of marking or pattern on them so that people can see that they are there;
- windows – care needs to be given to the means of opening and the height from the floor, particularly in tall buildings;
- lighting should be adequate throughout;
- gangways between desks should be adequate and free from obstruction;
- electrical fittings should be installed, serviced and checked by qualified personnel;
- sufficient training should be provided for staff in the use of all new equipment;
- furniture should be ergonomically designed and free from sharp edges;
- stepladders/stools should be made available for reaching any objects stored in high places;
- trolleys should be available for moving heavy equipment and supplies;
- warning notices should be placed on machines which are temporarily out of use;
- furniture should be arranged to facilitate work flow but minimize the dangers of collisions and obstruction;
- trailing wires should be avoided at all times;
- flammable liquids and materials should be stored appropriately in fireproof cabinets;
- fire extinguishers should be checked frequently and staff should be conversant with their use;
- all staff should be familiar with fire alarm and evacuation procedures;
- horseplay and other dangerous behaviour must be strictly forbidden in the interests of safety.

Security

It is impossible to achieve total security within an organization, but organizations which ignore its importance do so at their peril. Security is a two-way thing. It involves 'break-ins' and 'break-outs', or 'leaks' of information, and either way breaches in security take place. In the interests of both clients and staff, management has a duty to provide effective security measures and so minimize the dangers.

First of all it is a matter of determining what it is that needs to be protected and against what or whom. There are two principal areas of concern – physical security and security of information. The former is concerned with monitoring the access of visitors to the premises via stringent reception procedures, as well as restricting the movement of unauthorized personnel within an organization. The latter is to do with safeguarding confidentiality and minimizing the risk of theft, disclosure, modification or destruction of information which would be of value to a competitor.

Physical security therefore needs to take account of fire hazard, theft, criminal damage and the planting of bombs, whilst security of information covers all aspects of data protection, bugging devices and industrial espionage.

Security is a total concept which is applied throughout an organization and which has implications for all levels of personnel. Large organizations are likely to appoint a full-time Security Officer together with sufficient support staff, whilst a smaller organization – because of the high costs involved – may decide to rely on making someone, possibly the Personnel Manager or the Administration Manager, responsible for company security. This is an onerous task for anyone to undertake on a part-time basis and he will be well advised to seek consultations with relevant external agencies such as the police, the fire brigade and insurance assessors in order to obtain as much expert and professional advice as possible.

Issues at company level

The sorts of security issues which are considered at company level include:

- access to the site;
- the role of a gatehouse;
- emergency procedures – e.g. fire drills and evacuation procedures;
- security patrols;
- guard dogs;
- alarm systems;
- restricted access areas;
- the installation of closed circuit television (CCTV);
- the use of security agencies;
- the installation of fire and smoke detection systems;
- the installation of sprinkler systems;
- the acquisition of fire-proof filing cabinets;
- the vetting of security staff;
- the issue of keys, particularly master keys;
- the introduction of identification cards;
- the use of visitor's badges;
- car parking arrangements;
- the introduction of passwords for all computer users;
- the frequent change of computer passwords.

At a personal level

Individual staff within an organization will also be encouraged to be security conscious and vigilant and to introduce personal safeguards which may help maintain secure working conditions. Examples of what individual staff members can do are:

- be alert;
- be tidy;
- lock away all confidential papers;
- destroy, preferably by shredding, discarded confidential documents;
- destroy carbon papers and carbon ribbons;
- take care, when photocopying, not to leave originals in the flat bed of the copier;
- introduce coding systems to files and disks as necessary;
- note serial numbers of equipment and mark with indelible ink;
- escort visitors at all times;
- be careful when using the telephone;
- avoid idle gossip;
- mark confidential papers accordingly;
- use appropriate post office and messenger services.

Heating

A temperature of 60.8°F (16°C) after the first hour of work is considered reasonable in the Offices, Shops and Railway Premises Act 1963. However, most office workers would agree that this is rather on the low side and that a more acceptable temperature would be in the region of 70°F (21.1°C). It is important to bear in mind that much of office work is sedentary and that heating should be such as to enable workers to operate in comfort with the minimum degree of physical effort.

There will, however, always tend to be problems arising out of personal preferences in terms of heating and ventilation and, as ever, an acceptable compromise will be called upon to satisfy all parties.

What type of heating system?

Various possibilities exist, from central heating radiators fuelled by gas, oil or electricity, to convection heating, underfloor heating or a ducted warm air system of some kind. The system chosen is largely determined by the circumstances prevailing at a particular time and whether the building is geared to accept a preferred alternative. Different systems have different advantages and disadvantages, and different organizations will stipulate their own particular preference. However, in general terms, the sorts of points to be considered are:

- the size and type of building;
- whether the building is shared by others;
- the need for a backup facility;
- the need for a flexible system which can respond quickly to the need to raise temperatures quickly – e.g. as in the early mornings;
- the controllability factor;
- safety features;
- the ability to vary heating on a room-to-room basis;
- installation costs;
- running costs;
- maintenance costs;
- service support;
- availability of supplies – e.g. oil or gas;
- the ability to extend and/or update the facility;
- the appearance of the system;
- the space taken up by the system – boilers, radiators, pipes;
- the cleanliness of the system;
- the balance of cost effectiveness against convenience;
- the degree of sophistication of the system in keeping pace with other office developments.

One important factor to note in relation to current legislation is the absence of an upper limit for heating in offices. A temperature which becomes too warm can present problems and discomfort just as much as when it is too cold. Often, modern offices with a lot of glass can become virtual greenhouses in warm, sunny weather and yet there is no provision within legislation to take account of this.

Ventilation

To ensure maximum comfort, adequate ventilation is also important in offices. This can range from the adequacy of fresh air from opening windows to extractor fans, air-cleaning equipment or full-scale air conditioning. The last will be preferred in city centres where the noise from the traffic, together with pollution from dirt, fumes and smoke outside can make it virtually impossible to open windows. It is recommended that six air changes per hour take place if maximum comfort with high productivity are to be achieved. Good ventilation will also help to reduce the spread of disease.

Humidity

Humidity is concerned with the level of moisture in the air, and advances in heating and ventilation systems bring with them the need to consider humidity levels. In centrally heated, air-conditioned environments it is recommended that levels of relative humidity be in the region of 50–60 per cent. Where humidity levels are too low, problems will result from medical complaints such as breathing difficulties, throat infections and colds, and environmental hazards such as dust and build-up of static electricity, particularly where there is a lot of carpeting and other fabrics in use.

Lighting

The need for suitable and sufficient lighting is emphasized in the Offices, Shops and Railway Premises Act 1963. However, no precise recommendations are made and no indications given as to what would constitute 'suitable and sufficient', so organizations will need to seek advice from bodies such as the British Lighting Council in London.

Suffice it to say that careful consideration must be given to the quality and quantity (light is measured in lumens per square metre) of lighting installed within the working environment. Not every area will require the same degree of brightness, and certain types of work will be best undertaken in natural light, if at all feasible. When selecting the type(s) of lighting system(s) and fittings which should be installed, consideration must be given to the following:

- the type of building (number of storeys, depth, style and age);
- the level of natural light available;
- the nature of the work undertaken by different personnel;
- the level of accuracy required in some areas of work;
- the ages of workers;
- the use of equipment, including VDUs;
- the degree of reflection from furniture and equipment;
- the colour and texture of wall coverings;
- the existence of curtains or blinds;
- the amount of shadow caused by furniture and equipment;
- the level of maintenance and cleaning available.

Noise

Never before has society been bombarded, in fact some would say 'polluted', by so much extraneous noise. In an office environment noise will come from both outside and inside the building, and where noise levels become unacceptable comfort will decline and productivity levels will undoubtedly suffer. Noise reduction and control are, therefore, additional features which facilities managers must contend with in the interests of securing and maintaining a good working environment.

Noise is measured in decibels (the pressure of sound waves) or phons (sound output as it affects the human ear), and where severe problems are experienced in offices an acoustic engineer would normally be brought in to investigate. It is generally recognized that offices tend to be fairly noisy places, and acceptable levels are surpassed when it becomes impossible to conduct normal conversation.

Factors to consider in attempting to minimize noise are:

- the choice of location, if it is at this stage;
- the layout of departments;
- the size of windows;
- the installation of double or triple glazing;
- acoustic materials on ceilings and walls;
- sound-proofing for 'quiet' areas;
- the siting of noisy machinery – isolation areas;
- carpeting floors;
- sound-absorbent mats beneath equipment and the use of acoustic hoods for printers;
- non-slam door hinges;
- elimination of metal furniture in favour of wooden or synthetic;
- telephones with signal lamps rather than bells;
- the introduction of personal paging devices for staff who are frequently absent from their desks.

The Visible Features of the Environment

Physical factors such as heating, lighting, ventilation and humidity help determine the quality of the working conditions. They have an effect on morale and productivity levels but so, too, do the more visible things such as decor, furniture, fittings and equipment.

These are all areas of intense business competition and refurbishing or re-equipping can be a very expensive activity for any organization. As such it should not be left to junior staff or over-stretched middle management; it is a higher order decision which should be taken accordingly, following due consultation with users and others concerned. It is surprising, nevertheless, how often decisions on colour schemes, furniture and equipment are taken on an ad hoc basis rather than with an integrated approach which will be more likely to achieve the desired results and meet the specified objectives. Likewise, it is not uncommon for expensive decisions to be reached simply to satisfy an isolated short-term problem with little thought given to the ramifications for the future.

How important is Decor?

When we consider that half our waking lives are spent in the workplace, it is reasonable to expect a high standard of decoration at least comparable to that of a well-maintained home. Office decor has certainly improved over recent years, and there has been a rapid growth in the number of design specialists and consultants who give advice, often based on the results of studies carried out on the effect of surroundings on productivity levels and morale. Fashions and colour schemes come and go in offices just as in domestic properties, but basically what is sought is something which people will consider to be tasteful and appropriate, and which will promote comfortable and relaxed surroundings in which to work.

In many offices staff are given an opportunity to influence the decor by selecting elements of the colour scheme. Whilst this may be a good public relations exercise, it must be borne in mind that not everyone will have a flair for this sort of activity and such an exercise can seriously backfire on management, resulting in a hotch-potch of ideas and clashes of colour schemes. Possibly a good compromise would be to have experts consider a range of alternative total schemes which would be acceptable to management and serve to create the sort of impression which the company wishes to project whilst, at the same time, consulting staff as to their particular preferences. It is, after all, important to remember that the staff are the individuals who have to 'live' with the scheme; something which looks imaginative and striking on the drawing board may be very different in reality. This will tend to be true, for example, of highly patterned or geometrically designed wall coverings which may look good in a wallpaper book and be appropriate in theory but which may cause serious visual distraction or disturbance when used in a work area.

Colours should be easy on the eye, warm in tone, should blend together and complement the furniture and fittings. A colour scheme will be reflected in wall coverings, paintwork, screens, carpeting, curtains, and/or blinds as well as in pictures and ornaments. All should be selected with care as well as with a view to maintenance, tidiness and general overall appearance.

Floor covering is particularly important in an office. Carpet is maintained more easily and cheaply than any other form of floor covering and has the added benefits of safety, noise reduction, warmth and comfort as well as looking good to clients and visitors. Care does need to be taken in its selection, however, in that not only does it need to be hard wearing but also it should not attract build-up of static electricity which can be a hazard and inconvenience where a lot of electrical or electronic equipment is used.

What kind of furniture?

This will be largely dependent upon:

- the style of building;
- the design and layout of the office(s);
- the type of activity in which the organization is involved;
- finance available;
- ergonomic considerations (see below);
- suitability for the purpose;
- working efficiency;
- the space available – in total and in the immediate work area;
- durability;
- safety;
- appearance;
- mobility;
- weight;
- hygiene;
- flexibility of use;
- compatibility with other furniture and equipment;
- the status of the user;
- the range and selection available;
- the supply outlets.

The selection of furniture currently on the market is huge and competition is fierce between suppliers. It is an expensive commodity and represents a substantial capital investment, so care must be taken at the planning and selection stages.

What is Ergonomics?

The following are two dictionary definitions:

'the aspect of technology concerned with the application of biological and engineering data to problems relating to the mutual adjustment of man and machines'

Webster's International Dictionary

'the study of efficiency of persons in their working environment'

Concise Oxford Dictionary

The term was first used in about 1949, following a lot of investigation into industrial fatigue, and loosely it is often referred to as the science of 'fitting the job to the person'. Therefore, when reference is made to something being ergonomically designed it implies that the item has gone through some form of scientific testing to establish the correct sizing and shaping in order to prevent worker fatigue.

Fatigue comes in various forms – e.g.

- mental;
- physical;
- visual;
- nervous;
- chronic.

In the job situation, fatigue can be caused through poor working conditions as well as by lack of job interest and insufficiently demanding tasks. It is also brought about through excess pressure on the worker, and productivity will always suffer when pressure is great.

Scientific study of human needs in working situations utilizes various disciplines such as anatomy, physiology and psychology. In recent years considerable ergonomic research has resulted in the introduction of new concepts associated with reducing fatigue and improving working efficiency, especially in connection with developments in office automation and the use of VDUs (see also Chapter 18).

A great deal of research has now been done by ergonomists and office furniture manufacturers into the design of furniture and equipment to ensure that work postures, whether seated or standing, and whether engaged in clerical activities or machine operation, cause the minimum amount of discomfort and fatigue. Much of this sort of information has been published by the British Standards Institution.

Another technical term associated with this sort of work is **anthropometrics**, which is the study of human measurements and movements necessary for fitting furniture to the maximum number of users. This is obviously important in a flexible office environment where certain work stations may be used by a wide variety of people, all of whom have varied specifications.

Chairs

Given that much of office work is sedentary, a comfortable chair will be vital and each chair should be designed to suit the individual user. Obviously this is not feasible in practice but at least chairs should be adjustable, allowing for a variety of different users. The main points to consider in selecting a suitable chair are:

- the type of work;
- the height required;
- the depth of the seat;
- the stability;

- the durability;
- the type of covering;
- the safety aspects, including flame resistance;
- the degree of comfort it provides;
- whether or not it encourages good posture;
- whether or not it should have armrests;
- whether or not it should be adjustable;
- whether or not it should be on castors;
- whether or not it should swivel;
- the type of back support it should have.

Ultimately, any chair will receive approval or otherwise from the individual user and certain preferences will be stated, irrespective of ergonomic considerations. Where an employee has, for example, a history of back problems, he may prefer a firmer chair than would normally be considered appropriate. Also, wherever appropriate, staff should be given the opportunity to 'try' new chairs for themselves. No one would normally contemplate the purchase of a car without test driving it; no more would we buy a television without testing the quality of the picture – so why not with chairs?

Desks

Suitable desks are the next major area for consideration in offices. Arriving at an acceptable solution is not as simple as may at first appear, particularly when desks need to be highly functional and yet capable of being used in flexible office layouts. The main considerations in selecting a suitable desk are:

- the type of work;
- the size of working area required;
- the shape of the desk top;
- the height;
- the amount of knee clearance underneath;
- the drawer space available;
- the need for lockable drawers;
- whether single or double pedestal;
- if single pedestal, whether right- or left-handed drawers;
- the appearance;
- the finish – wood, plastic, metal, leather top?
- whether it should be free standing or part of a modular arrangement;
- weight;
- mobility;
- whether it should reflect status.

The importance of providing suitable desks cannot be over-stated, as a desk is the centre of productivity for each member of staff and is very much a tool of the trade, so any reference to 'work stations' is very appropriate.

System Furniture

Floor space is an extremely expensive commodity. Rates for office accommodation are calculated on the basis of square feet or metres, although total space is measured in cubic proportions. Consequently it can make good sense to give more attention to the utilization of at least some of the space above desk top height. Herman Miller, mentioned earlier, are major exponents of this technique, their system furniture making good use of vertical space. Their vertical panels, which are ergonomically designed and have round edges, have work surfaces and storage components attached, all of which are fully adjustable to suit any height of user or, where necessary, to accommodate a disabled user.

The term 'system' furniture came about with the need to accommodate today's sophisticated office equipment. System furniture is a bringing together of the different furniture components which have always been present in offices in a co-ordinated way. Therefore desks, tables, screens and storage units are designed to integrate in versatile, compact and compatible ways. It is designed to be adaptable yet stylish and attractive and manufacturers offer a number of ranges to suit all office needs and budgets.

Work Stations

In many modern offices individual desks are a thing of the past with the trend being towards multi-purpose work stations flexibly designed to enable workers to perform a range of activities seated within the one area. Work stations are arrangements of modular furniture designed to suit particular activities and job functions. Tasks are analysed for content in conjunction with the associated materials and equipment used and the furniture is then selected accordingly. For example, the user may write, make telephone calls, key information into a terminal or personal computer, call information up on to a screen from a company data base and store personal papers all from the same seat.

Desk and table tops may also be joined together in a variety of different configurations by using triangular linked tops. This idea not only saves space but can greatly facilitate work flow and communication whilst often enabling staff to share the facility of an expensive piece of office equipment.

Wire Management

Where there is a proliferation of computing hardware within offices there will be all the associated wire and power cables. Raised floors provide space for power, telephone and communications cabling whilst system furniture has been designed to accommodate this by packaging all the wires safely and neatly around the work stations via trunking or channels through which the wires and cables can travel unobtrusively and by countersinking all the sockets into a cradle arrangement which forms an integral part of the work station.

Such arrangements need to be well planned in order to accommodate the type and length of wires involved. Whilst the introduction of such system furniture can solve problems and look very effective it can also introduce rigidities in that new additions to equipment need to be carefully integrated into the existing scheme. Otherwise there will be a renewed problem of getting power to the new location.

Computer Aided Design (CAD)

Developments in 'facilities management', defined by the Institute of Administrative Management as 'how buildings are designed, maintained and managed to meet the objective of an organization, having regard to the comfort and efficiency of its occupants', have led to the increased application of computer aided design (CAD) techniques. These can help design offices, suggest possible layouts, solve problems and respond quickly to new situations. Their application can generally speed up the process of design from start to finish.

Concluding Remarks

The potential to design new layouts and introduce new furniture con-figurations grows all the time with the certainty that a large proportion of office workers will eventually find themselves equipped with electronic work stations which need to be installed within environments appropriate to the needs of both men and machines. Currently many offices are totally unprepared for this challenge and a lot of urgent re-thinking will have to take place if office workers are to have the facilities they need in the future.

So important is it to design and equip good offices that the Facilities Management Group (formerly 'Office Design Division') of the Institute of Administrative Management organizes a bi-annual competition for the 'Office of the Year Award'. Its principal assessment criterion in 1985 was 'to assess the quality and productivity of the office work place, both individually and collectively, in the context of the building as a whole', but the panel of assessors also considered:

- analysis of accommodation requirements;
- potential for flexibility;
- amenities and facilities;
- ergonomic aspects;
- value for money;
- the incorporation of information systems;
- energy conservation.

It is interest of this kind which helps place the importance of office accommodation and facilities in perspective. The nature of office work is changing and the environment must change with it.

17
Conferences

'A successful conference is probably one of the most cost-effective communication tools available to modern management.'

Paul Swan
(*Management Today*, April 1984)

Conferences of one kind or another occupy an increasingly significant role in successful business operations. Never before has information on so many subjects been so readily available and so much in demand. Receiving or imparting information in the participative environment of a conference has become a very popular technique and is used in a wide variety of circumstances.

Expenditure on conferences and meetings is growing annually and investment into the conference industry is now substantial. The money brought into the UK by those attending conferences and business meetings from overseas is estimated to be in excess of £100 million, although the true figure is difficult to assess.

Conference organizers

Professional conference organizers are to be found throughout the country and the **meetings industry** is certainly developing rapidly. In fact, it's big business. Their very existence is evidence of the skills and areas of expertise needed to organize successful events. Making effective arrangements is a challenging and extremely time-consuming task, and one which the majority of people probably learn 'on the job' – often as a result of their mistakes.

What is the role of the Conference Organizer?

A conference is a very demanding and complex area of activity and one which often requires the services of a professional organizer who has the expertise and time to devote to doing the job thoroughly. Ad hoc arrangements may end up as 'muddling through' and consequently it will be far better to engage the services of a professional conference organizer. However, this is not always appropriate or feasible in terms of the expense involved, and many conferences, meetings and seminars will be managed from the resources within an organization.

The appointment of the Conference Organizer is an important decision. It should be given neither to the most hard working and often already over-stretched manager nor to someone who may be under-employed but lacks the necessary drive and administrative ability to make a success of the arrangements. The person occupying the role of Conference Organizer must have appropriate skills and qualities, and these include:

- organizational ability;
- administrative flair;
- the ability to liaise with professionals;
- the skills of co-ordination;
- an eye for detail and presentation;
- a willingness to act in a consultancy capacity.

Additionally, the person appointed must be given the authority to take whatever action is necessary to ensure the success of the event and must be prepared to accept the responsibility and criticism when things do not work out according to plan. Some of the problems of conference organization are considered below, together with suggestions as to ways in which the task may be simplified and the end product improved.

Types of conference

Conferences can be full-blown events of several days or even a week's duration or they may be comparatively brief and quite small scale. They may be held annually, like party political or trades unions' conferences, or they may simply be company or trade conferences, commercial seminars, special events to launch a new product or brief a sales force, professional or technical training courses, summer schools or routine business events. In fact, any sort of occasion where a number of people are gathered together for a common purpose can, for planning and organizational purposes, realistically be described as a 'conference'. Therefore the numbers involved could be anything from 20 or less to something in the region of 3,000 delegates for a large international conference.

Preliminaries

How is the task approached?

For any event to be successful, whatever the scale and for whatever the purpose, it requires careful planning. Before it can be planned effectively, several basic questions must be answered by those wishing to hold a conference:

- **Why** do we need to have a conference?
- **What** do we want to achieve?
- **Who** should attend?
- **When** should it take place?
- **Where** should the event be held?

These may seem like fundamental questions but it is surprising how often they are insufficiently considered. It is important that they are answered satisfactorily because conferences are expensive events to mount, time consuming to arrange and attend, and certainly not occasions for indulging in whims which simply produce pleasant social gatherings.

Why have a conference?

In the first place, a conference should not be arranged where a less costly and equally cost-effective alternative is readily available. Nevertheless, conferences are frequently held as public relations exercises, often almost regardless of the expense. This may be to promote the image of an organization or to encourage group identity and corporate spirit and to attract external publicity and media interest.

What are the objectives?

Given that there is a sound reason for having a conference, determining the objectives should be relatively easy. They may be very specific to the event and can often be expressed in very precise terms – e.g. 'to train . . .'; 'to launch . . .'; 'to inform . . .' or 'to explain . . .'. In addition, it may well be that the event is scheduled with the express purpose of making a profit and, of course, this is the very reason why conference organizers are in business.

Who should attend?

The answer to this question will be a consequence of the previous two questions. The success of any event will be largely due to the appropriate representation of conference members, representatives or delegates. Consideration also must be given to the question of numbers (the minimum and maximum). Accurate assessment of numbers is important in terms of the costing of the exercise and the accommodation required.

When should the event take place?

The timing of a conference can be crucial to its success. Selecting the most appropriate time is not always easy and there will frequently be many intervening variables to contend with. Certain large-scale conferences take place according to tradition, and prospective delegates will know from one year to another to keep free a particular slot in their calenders. Apart from tradition, other things to consider include:

- the length of notice that is required;
- the volume of arrangements to be undertaken;
- the availability of venues;
- the availability of guest speakers;
- the proximity of holiday periods;
- the proximity of other competing events.

Where should the event take place?

This will have close links with the timing and will be dependent upon several of the other previous questions. The points to consider when selecting a suitable venue are:

- the location;
- the surrounding area;
- the time of year;
- the size;
- the facilities;
- the accommodation;
- the food;
- the service.

Venue

The Location

This can be anywhere from an organization's own premises to another part of the country or, for that matter, the world. Geographical location can be particularly important where delegates have busy schedules and where they may be attending the event from different corners of the country or the world. Where it is the former, it is possible that consideration would be given to using an outside venue which is reasonably equidistant for the wide range of delegates. Proximity to motorway and intercity rail networks might provide a starting point. Where delegates are travelling from overseas countries, proximity to international airports would also be appropriate.

The Surrounding Area

Dependent upon the nature and duration of the event the surrounding area may be important. Some conferences will favour a seaside location, whilst others may prefer the relative quiet of the countryside. Where conference attendance may encompass something of a social/vacational flavour with perhaps wives/husbands and/or families included, it may be appropriate to select somewhere which offers places and features of interest nearby.

The time of year

This is another factor which may well influence the choice of venue. For example, it would be unwise to select an inaccessible location during winter months when weather and road conditions might prove unpredictable. Similarly, it would be unwise to select a busy seaside place such as Blackpool or Brighton at the height of the summer season.

The size

The size of the venue chosen is important in that it must be adequate for the number of delegates expected to attend. This can be difficult to assess far in advance of making provisional arrangements and is one of the reasons for requiring a final date for applications to attend a conference. Predicting likely response is a notoriously difficult task and, of course, no conference organizer wishes to find himself cramped for space. On the other hand, it is unfortunate if the venue appears too big and perhaps impersonal for a small gathering or where your party may seem outflanked by other larger groups. Therefore a considerable degree of sound judgement, not to mention previous experience, is very helpful here.

The facilities

Facilities are an important consideration of any successful conference, and the organizer must establish well in advance the precise nature of the needs for the particular event. These might include display areas, exhibition halls, lecture theatres, syndicate rooms, rooms with blackout facilities for showing films and reception rooms.

It will be advisable for the organizer to actually visit the venue in advance of making a positive booking in order to establish that the facilities meet with the requirements of the particular event.

The accommodation

In addition to the general facilities for the conference programme itself, it will be necessary to arrange for suitable overnight accommodation where the event is arranged to take place over several days. The standard of accommodation can make or break such an event and it is essential to establish the availability of delegate accommodation well in advance. One important thing to consider is the number of single rooms available in hotels, as sharing accommodation is often unpopular. Also, the number of rooms with private facilities may be influential in arriving at an appropriate venue.

The food

Where an event is scheduled to run for several days the food is another important consideration. It is essential to specify at the outset of negotiations precisely what sorts of meals would be required, including catering for people with special diets. It may, for instance, be that a conference dinner forms a major part of the event; where it is intended that this be held at the same location it is important that the menus are decided upon well in advance. Similarly, where the full range of meals is required it is important to establish whether set meals or buffets or a combination of the two is wanted. Also, it is important to specify whether the event requires the services of a private bar or whether delegates will simply use the general facilities of the hotel or conference centre.

People are tending to become more diet conscious these days and heavy mid-day meals may not be well received by many delegates, particularly women. There is a call for lighter, more imaginative meals which will be less likely to lie heavily and send delegates to sleep during the afternoon sessions!

The service

The standard of service in hotels is also a very important factor, as this can greatly affect the timing of the programme. For example, where operating a tight schedule with predetermined slots for invited speakers, the last thing wanted is to have the programme knocked totally out of step by delays in the serving of meals or other refreshments during the conference. Also, some hotels may be rather too formal or simply not geared for the hyperactivity of many of today's conferences or training courses, where it is not unusual for the day's events to commence with an early breakfast and go on after dinner, sometimes well past midnight, with syndicate activities and simulations.

When relying on the use of special facilities it is also important that any special supplies and assistance are laid on and that help and support are on hand should they be required.

Specialist Venues

Given the complexities of finding suitable venues it is hardly surprising that many specialist providers have sprung up over recent years to cater specifically for the conference market. These range from hotel groups specializing in the provision of conference facilities to conference and exhibition centres, such as the National Exhibition Centre (NEC) in Birmingham, the recently opened GMEX centre in Manchester (built on a site previously occupied by a railway station) and the Harrogate International Centre which is a high technology building containing a 2,000 seat auditorium with every modern facility designed to cater for conferences, concerts, sports events, presentations and a multitude of other events. The centre is linked to six exhibition halls which contain over 120,000 square feet of space. Harrogate itself is situated in the heart of North Yorkshire and is equidistant from London and Edinburgh.

Recent entrants to the conference venue market have been university campuses and the in-house training headquarters of large private businesses. Initially these places opened their doors in an attempt to utilize accommodation throughout the year and recover overheads, but they are now becoming increasingly competitive with many hotels. What they do tend to have is the advantages of privacy and good technical facilities such as closed circuit television (CCTV), but offset against these may be limited availability due to vacation use only or pre-booking by the parent company, together with less prestigious accommodation which can reduce the enjoyment factor for delegates.

Unusual Places

These will include places catering for more unusual requests such as special food or sports facilities, but can also include out-of-the-ordinary locations. Stately homes would be in this category and there are an increasing number available. Their selection would be determined by the nature of the event, as, for example, where such a location would provide added motivation or special appeal for international delegates. Set against the novelty of exclusivity, however, are likely to be limited facilities and less polished service.

Floating conference facilities are also something of a novelty, with Sealink operating just such a service between Harwich and the Hook of

Holland. British Rail are also in on the act by offering a '125 mph Executive Boardroom' which is 'an exclusive conference, meeting and lounge/dining car with catering to your personal satisfaction'.

The careful selection of venue is extremely important, and wherever time permits an advance visit prior to confirming a booking is to be highly recommended. It pays to be painstaking, to ask to see everything, to try the food, judge the quality of the service, soak up the atmosphere and investigate the surroundings. Above all, organizers should resist the temptation to lower standards. Where they are not completely happy with what they find, they should try elsewhere. Perseverance usually pays dividends, and it is a good idea to devise a checklist so that nothing will be overlooked. A specimen checklist is given in Fig. 46.

Venue Checklist		
Event:	Date:	
Location:	Date of visit:	
Hotel/Centre		
Full postal address		
Tel. No.	Telex No.	
Contact	Answer back code	
Position	Ext No.	
Nearest railway station	Distance	
Nearest airport	Distance	
Distance by road from London/wherever?		
Accommodation		
No. of bedrooms	Double	Twin
	Suites	Single
Bathroom/shower facilities:	Private	Public
Dining/Lounge/Bar/Additional facilities		
Garaging/Car parking facilities		
Star rating		
Tariff details		

Fig. 46   Venue checklist

Other Facilities

Meeting room	Max. seating for
Acoustics?	Lighting?
Microphone?	Blackout?
Visual aids?	Cine projector
	Video — VHS/BETA/U-Matic/Philips
	OHP
	CCTV

Screens?	Fixed/Portable	Size?
Lighting?	Dimmable?	
Heating?	Ventilation?	
Air conditioning?	Noise factor?	
Syndicate rooms	No.	Size
Display area?		Size
Office support?	Audio/shorthand/typing/photocopying	
Technical support?	Projectionist/Technician/ Translator	

General comments/observations

Recommendation:

Details of preliminary reservations made

Final confirmation date

Special rates negotiated

Signed	Date
Conference Organizer	

Fig. 46   Venue checklist (contd)

The Programme

Programme content and design should be worked out as early as possible. It is particularly important that all participants have a copy of the programme and any subsequent alterations which may be made. All conferences aim to achieve their objectives, and whether they do so or not will be partly dependent upon the content and balance of the programme. Events will normally have a theme and the programme is designed to reflect that theme via a number of carefully selected contributions. These may well consist of a number of inputs from guest speakers, syndicate or task groups comprising conference delegates, workshops and plenary sessions. It will be important to strike the correct balance of activities and also to ensure that the time allocations and positioning within the overall framework of the programme produce the optimum result.

Scheduling the programme

First it will be necessary to decide on the number of sessions – i.e. how many slots in the morning, how many in the afternoon and how many (if any) into the evening, allowing for suitable breaks for meals and refreshments.

The next thing will be to determine the order of the sessions and this is normally best done by attempting to answer a few fundamental questions:

- What has to come first?
- Is there something which must follow or precede something else?
- How new is the material likely to be to the audience?
- How difficult is the material?
- How serious or how light-hearted is the material/speaker?
- Will the speaker use audio-visual aids?
- Will audience participation be wanted or required?
- Do other commitments restrict speakers to certain slots?

Briefing Participants

The success of any programme will also be greatly dependent upon the quality of the briefing given to all participants.

Speakers

Speakers will all require to be carefully briefed in every aspect of the conference's planning and specifically on the content of the programme and what is expected of them in terms of their contribution. They must know for how long they are expected to speak and whether they should allow time for questions at the end. They must also know at what point in the programme they are involved. This can greatly influence the style of presentation adopted – e.g. after lunch can be a difficult slot with delegates replete after a good meal.

It is essential that they provide a synopsis of their presentation well in advance and all synopses of presentations should be circulated throughout the group of speakers. Otherwise, where a thematic approach is taken, it is more than likely that there will be the inevitable overlap of what different speakers say and this is unfortunate all round. It can be difficult for later speakers in that earlier speakers may well have 'stolen their thunder', and a major criticism from the audience will be that they heard the same views expressed over and sometimes over again.

Where papers are presented formally for subsequent publication at the end of the conference it is important that speakers know the format required. Equally, it is important that speakers are alerted to the likely presence of the press or other media, as they may wish to modify their contribution or even refuse to participate.

Sometimes it is advisable to get speakers together in advance of the actual event in an attempt to co-ordinate inputs. However, this is a very time-consuming exercise and few busy speakers will be able to afford the added commitment.

The selection of speakers

Audiences will welcome the opportunity of listening to a well-informed, good speaker and, of course, good speakers are always in demand. It will be important, therefore, to approach the speakers you would like in good time as many are heavily committed throughout a year. It is worth remembering that people may be experts in their own field and yet poor at putting their knowledge across. The problem is often to find someone who is competent in both areas, and there is then the added risk of over-exposure which may mean that your audience has heard the person many times before. Finding good speakers is not easy and it is often worth attending other conferences to hear prospective speakers for yourself. It will also be important to aim for speakers who will complement one another, and it is always advisable to have reserves on stand-by in case a speaker has to pull out at the last minute. When operating on a tight budget, fees and expenses will also have to be considered, as some good speakers can command high amounts.

Chairing the Sessions

Often sessions are chaired and it falls to the chairman to introduce the speaker(s). Once again, adequate briefing is essential, and it will often be necessary for the speaker(s) to supply brief biographical details for use by the chairman. It will also be the chairman's duty to conduct any question session which may follow and ensure that delegates have a good opportunity to put their questions and that a fair time is allowed to each. It is vital also that the chairman does not permit a session to over-run.

Support staff

Support personnel will include technical support staff, such as projectionists and sound technicians, and chauffeurs whose responsibility it will be to collect speakers from airports and railway stations or to drive them from distant hotel accommodation, as well as those acting as ushers at a large scale conference and those serving refreshments during brief breaks in the proceedings.

All require to be fully briefed on their duties and responsibilities and all must know precisely where they are expected to be at specific times throughout the programme of events.

The Conference Organizer's Assistant(s)

Where the event is a large one it will be essential to appoint assistants, and here it will be necessary to delegate appropriate duties and responsibilities to each for the duration of the preparatory work and for the event itself. Sometimes the allocation of duties will be easily determined, as, for example, where social functions form an integral part of the conference arrangements. Here one person could readily take over all associated duties and arrangements. Similarly, where extensive travel arrangements form part of the work, this, too, would be a good area to delegate.

Budget

Calculating the budget

Anyone embarking on the organization of an event will need to estimate the likely expenditure involved. Sometimes it will be a matter of doing one's homework well in advance and actually costing out projected expenditure. At other times the organizer will be given a budget and will be required to work within it. Either way, a lot of careful calculations are required in terms of the expenditure generated by the event. Offset against this will, of course, be any income which is anticipated from the event and the difference will constitute the profit or loss.

Items to be included in a budget

Everything which goes into the preparation and organization of the event should be included in the budget. These will make up the **fixed costs** of the event and will apply irrespective of how many people actually attend. Additionally, there will be the **variable costs** which will fluctuate according to the number of people actually attending.

Fixed Costs

These include:

- the use/hire of the venue;

- speakers' fees and expenses;
- paperwork, including advertising and postage;
- special printwork;
- transport costs;
- insurance;
- materials – e.g. hire/cost of extra equipment, films;
- flowers, decorations;
- administrative costs – including, for example, overtime payments, overheads;
- contingencies – unanticipated expenses such as last-minute requirements (usually calculated as a percentage).

Variable costs

These include:

- accommodation (unless paid separately by delegates);
- food – all meals and incidental refreshments;
- any special function included in the event;
- special handout materials for delegates – e.g. badges, folders.

The total cost of the event will be the combination of fixed and variable costs, although it is impossible to calculate the final budget until precise attendance figures are available.

Value for money

Given that many conferences are costly in respect of fees, delegates will expect to get value for money, and this needs to be reflected in the accommodation, facilities, service and food provided. People are, in general, much more discerning about what is acceptable in comfort terms, particularly in hotels, and will expect to get what they pay for. Gone are the days when minimal standards were expected and accepted with visitors loath to complain. It is in these circumstances that the little extras such as tea and coffee facilities in the bedrooms, fresh flowers on the dining tables and a complimentary newspaper will make all the difference.

What about Income?

Many events are organized to generate some income as well, and this will come mainly from conference fees and sometimes from sponsorships and trade contributions. In general, conference organizers will calculate a **break-even point** for the event and this will be based on the number of paying delegates needed to attend to cover the fixed expenses. Anything over that point would result in profit, anything below would be a loss.

What about Cash Flow?

One of the principal problems of organizing any event is that there is commitment to expenditure in advance of the receipt of money. For example, advertising expenses have to be met, deposits paid, insurance premiums paid and so on. Although these may be fairly minimal costs for a small event, they can be substantial in terms of a large-scale conference and it may be necessary to cover the shortfall until the income becomes available. This can mean high interest rates and will be particularly relevant in times of high inflation, so contingency plans will be required. It may, however, be possible to secure interim funding and support from within the organization itself or by means of grants from industry or the EEC, for example. In any event, sound budgetary control is essential.

Support facilities and arrangements

There are a myriad things to attend to at a large-scale conference and an oversight can have considerable repercussions later. Assistants are often appointed to help the organizer with all the details. Many conferences and training courses are becoming increasingly sophisticated in the content of their programmes and will utilize hi-tech facilities such as interactive video, so help of a technical nature may also be called for. It is really a matter of good stage management.

Paperwork

The paperwork associated with organizing any event is considerable, and it is important that it suitably reflects the style and image which the organization attempts to project in all its activities. Correspondence and all other printed matter should aim to create the right impression at all times. In terms of the paperwork created within the organization, this can vary greatly, dependent upon whether an organization has a Repro-graphics Department in-house. Many companies now do a lot of their own printing, particularly with recent developments in word processing and phototypesetting techniques, together with the vast improvements in photocopying facilities. However, standard paperwork is likely to include:

- routine correspondence;
- registration documentation;
- supporting information;
- conference papers;

- programmes;
- lists of those attending;
- invitations to special functions;
- menus;
- place cards;
- name badges.

Some of these items will be prepared well in advance of the event whilst others will be required just prior to and even during the event.

Word processing is of great benefit to such activities as each piece of communication to delegates can be personalized and the end product will be of perfect quality and will reflect the standing of the organization making the arrangements. Many conferences will have a logo and this will appear on all printed matter and correspondence and must be consistent throughout the preparations.

All paperwork will have to be processed in some way and it is important to establish simple, logical systems at the outset. Microcomputers with business software can prove invaluable here in terms of storing information and producing invoices, records and other associated documentation. All forms which are used for administrative purposes during a conference should be designed with care to maximize both ease of completion by delegates and staff handling the communications. They should also be of uniform size and may be printed on different coloured paper for ease of recognition. An appropriate filing system should be set up to handle all the paperwork.

Confirm and Assess all Arrangements

Any successful event organizer will have taken steps to ensure that all arrangements made are confirmed, in writing. This includes confirmation on the part of the organizer of all tentative arrangements made, either in person or over the telephone, in respect of accommodation, support materials required and so on. It also refers to the need to receive written confirmation from other parties in respect of their contributions to the event.

Files should be opened to log all confirmations, including those in respect of numbers attending. The organizer should establish a **countdown calendar** (Fig. 47) to monitor deadlines for confirmation of numbers attending. Such information is essential in terms of costing and for finalizing arrangements in respect of facilities and catering.

The countdown calendar will also prove invaluable in assessing the progress of arrangements generally. Many things such as printing will be proceeding over a number of weeks, and it is necessary to monitor

Countdown Calendar	
5th Annual Conference of to be held at during the period of 3–6 May inclusive 1987	

1986	
June	Preliminary discussions Adoption of theme Provisional locations discussed Guest speakers nominated
July	Course organizer to visit three possible venues and report back Invitations extended to guest speakers
August	Provisional assessment made of numbers likely to attend Provisional booking of venue
September – December	On-going preparations, initial printing, etc. Confirmations from speakers Advance notice to interested parties General publicity
1987 January	Programme finalized Details sent out together with application forms and notification of closing date
February	Pre-conference meeting with speakers Contribution synopses co-ordinated
March	Attendance numbers finalized Places confirmed and additional details sent, including travel directions
April	Visit to venue to finalize menus and accommodation, including lecture facilities, technical support and security arrangements Administrative details finalized Staff briefing; delegation of duties
May	Final check of venue, accommodation and support facilities organized

Fig. 47   Countdown calendar

progress and, where necessary, request that the pace of the work be accelerated if it is falling behind schedule. The organization of any large-scale event entails remembering a lot of detail, and it is vital to devise appropriate reminder and follow-up systems to ensure that nothing is overlooked and that a satisfactory assessment has been made of all arrangements undertaken.

Sometimes this may also include allowing time to visit the venue near to the date of the event and to check all arrangements there personally. Time consuming as this may be, it can be time well spent. Also it highlights the interest that is being afforded the event by the organization and will be likely to ensure that those responsible for arrangements at the venue will be on their toes and anxious to create a favourable impression—all of which should help ensure the success of your conference.

Ensure that Security is Adequate

Unfortunately, nowadays, with an increasingly high level of terrorism and crime generally, security arrangements will require to be given sufficient attention when organizing a conference. The level of security required will depend on the nature of the event, upon the identities of participants and upon the location and venue.

Where security is seen as a major aspect of the arrangements it is likely that security specialists will be engaged. It will be their responsibility to liaise with local police and services in the pre-event screening of facilities and in the drawing up of emergency procedures and routines. Events such as the Conservative Party Conference, particularly following the Brighton bombing, require intensive security operations, and arrangements will be underway as much as a year in advance of the event.

Where less elaborate precautions are considered necessary it will still be important to ensure that security is adequate. Security should be seen to include safety aspects as well as security in respect of protection of delegates and their belongings and lack of privacy in respect of information which may, for instance, be of interest to competitors. Points to consider will include:

- the accessibility of the venue to non-participants;
- fire hazard and suitability of escape routes;
- security of belongings – e.g. the provision of safes;
- industrial espionage;
- general standard of safety and security provision – e.g. fire exits, sprinkler systems, presence of specialist security personnel.

From the point of view of the organizer, one of the things which should be included in the conference pack which all delegates receive will be a name badge. Where stringent security arrangements are involved, it may be that delegates and guests, including press representatives, will be required to display security badges at all times as they will be screened by specialist personnel on entry to the conference and within the venue itself.

Supervise the Actual Event

Dependent upon the scale of the conference, there must be sufficient numbers involved in the supervision of the event. Where a lot of energy has gone into the arrangements prior to the event, it is essential that the level of commitment is retained for the duration of the event itself. Supervisory duties will include:

- reception and registration of delegates;
- reception of VIPs and guest speakers;
- bursarial arrangements, where applicable;
- manning an information desk and transmitting messages;
- dealing with press and media representatives;
- liaising with catering staff as regards timing;
- marshalling large numbers of delegates;
- troubleshooting.

Reception and Registration

In terms of these duties the handling of the necessary arrangements will be something which will apply to all sorts of conference, irrespective of duration. It is something which should be tackled as efficiently and as courteously as possible because first impressions tend to linger and will often set the tone for the event as a whole.

It is important that such formalities are dealt with quickly; consequently, at a large conference several desks may be required as delegates will tend to arrive in large numbers. Normally, delegates will be presented with a conference folder or pack which will include:

- conference programme;
- list of delegates;
- site plan of the venue;
- details of the surrounding area and attractions, where appropriate;
- promotional materials from exhibitors, where in attendance;
- advanced circulation of speakers' papers (if required);
- writing paper and pen.

Name badges or security passes will also be distributed during the registration procedure and, once again, it is important that this is done efficiently. All names must be carefully checked against the official conference list.

It is important to remember that, inevitably, some delegates will fail to arrive at the appointed time and so provision must be made to receive latecomers and complete their registration procedures at a later stage. This will probably involve manning the desk until all delegates have been processed.

Also it is possible that there may be last minute substitutions to attend to, at large conferences in particular. This can greatly interrupt the flow of straightforward registrations and it will, therefore, be advisable to arrange for someone to deal specifically with any queries, and to do so at a separate desk.

Evaluate the effectiveness

The effectiveness of any conference will be gauged from many different angles – viz. that of the organizer, that of the delegates and that of those taking part as contributors. From the point of view of the organizer, effectiveness will be measured during the event as well as afterwards when it will be customary to perform some sort of formal evaluation as to how well the event measured up to meeting with the declared aims and objectives.

During the event it will be possible to judge how well things are going by assessing the reaction to the programme and the arrangements. One good indicator will be the number of problems or complaints that require to be dealt with. The fewer of these that there are the more likely it is that things are going well. Another will be the enthusiasm of delegates about the speakers and their readiness to participate in optional sessions and take part in discussion groups.

Sometimes it may be considered worthwhile to issue some sort of evaluation sheet to delegates for completion at the end of the conference. As with any form of questionnaire, great care must be taken in the formulation of questions. The intention will be to see what delegates liked and disliked about the programme and the accommodation with a view to bearing in mind the points raised for any future event. One of the problems of using this sort of technique may be that sometimes it will be difficult to assess the usefulness of a particular programme until sometime later when delegates may have had the opportunity of trying out some of the ideas for themselves. Also, after a long, hard week many delegates may be anxious to get home and will not take sufficient time to complete a questionnaire carefully and accurately, so rendering the answers less useful.

Holding a Post-mortem

An extension of any effort to evaluate effectiveness is to hold a post-mortem after the conference. The principal reason for this tactic is to get answers to the following questions:

- Were our objectives realistic and did we achieve them?
- How was the event received by the delegates?
- How appropriate was the programme?
- How good were our speakers?

- How good were the venue and the accommodation?
- Did we experience any major problems?
- Was the general impression favourable?

If positive responses are gleaned from these questions, the chances are that the event was a success. Where there may have been negatives it will be necessary to pay particular attention to these areas next time around.

Problems and Pitfalls

Like many management problems, one of the main difficulties in organizing conferences and other events is the time-consuming nature of the activity, particularly when it is only one of many other jobs to be dealt with. This is one of the reasons for appointing a conference organizer within a company or even off-loading the work to an outside agency. Problems will come from a range of sources, but are likely to be concerned with the following:

- the timing of the event;
- the selection of the venue;
- achieving a good programme balance;
- keeping within a budget;
- people problems.

Problems tend to manifest themselves in a variety of different ways, and the organizer must try to minimize their impact by having contingency plans available. Some things will, of course, always be outwith the organizer's control irrespective of how well likely pitfalls have been envisaged and catered for.

The most unpredictable element will always be the people involved in that even the best organizer cannot necessarily anticipate **sudden** illness on the part of a speaker. The best that can be done is to have a stand-in available to appear at short notice; alternatively one can ask that all speakers prepare a written paper in advance and agree to have it presented by someone else should this be necessary and/or appropriate.

Other problems in respect of the people aspect of conferences will be the numbers. Sometimes it can be difficult to strike the right balance in terms of delegate numbers. Very often, events will tend to be either under-subscribed or vastly over-subscribed, and either way the organizer has a problem. This is why it is so vitally important that the organizer has done his homework well in advance. Difficulties in relation to numbers will be substantially reduced where the timing, programme content and venue are attractive to likely participants. Also, it is important that the organizer is aware of the timing of competing events, provides an interesting and lively programme and selects a popular location.

Ensuring Success

Effective conference management is an art. It is not something which can be undertaken in a half-hearted manner and it is something which requires a high level of commitment, interest and organizational ability. It will be important to recognize the need to appoint a conference organizer whose duty it will be to undertake all the necessary arrangements leading up to and during the conference. Only by delegating ultimate authority and responsibility for the arrangements to one individual can the efficient co-ordination of a complex event be relied upon. It is also important to appreciate that conferences often tend to bring out the best and the worst in individuals, and it is useful to have a focal person as a point of reference for bouquets or complaints.

Outside Help for Conference Organizers

Conference, exhibition and other event organizing is gathering momentum and many consultancies and other interest groups have grown up in recent years, providing a lot of useful advice in what is, after all, a complex activity and something which can present many headaches for the inexperienced and uninitiated.

February 1986 saw the Third International Confex, held at The Barbican in London. This was a special three-day exhibition designed for all those who organize meetings, conferences, conventions and other special events and exhibitions. As well as providing a wide range of specialist exhibitors, ranging from professional conference organizers to audiovisual equipment hirers, floral contractors and translation services, the event put on a varied and useful seminar programme during the three days.

Some useful addresses for use in conjunction with conference organization are given in Appendix 2.

18
Office Automation

'Office automation refers to an integrated collection of electronic devices which are used to increase office productivity.'

G B Shelley and T J Cashman
Computer Fundamentals for an Information Age

There is a maxim which says 'Nothing is more certain than change', and this is certainly true of the office-based aspects of organizational life. In the last decade we have observed the arrival of the 'electronic office', and, if organizations wish to exercise effective control over the changes which are taking place within the office environment, one of the things they have to examine carefully is the management of office automation. Like any other management activity it should not be allowed to happen in a haphazard way but should be planned, communicated, implemented, monitored and evaluated in a logical step-by-step process if it is to realize its full potential.

Office activities perform a secondary yet complementary function to the *raison d'être* of any organization, and management has more time to devote to the activities of managing when fully aware of the contribution which integrated offices can make to overall effectiveness and increased productivity. This does not merely refer to the introduction of word processing, although for many organizations this will be the first step and very often the only one!

Aspects of Office Automation

Office automation is much more than word processing. It is the total support system (Fig. 48) which draws in all the areas of office activity by which text/data is processed, copied, transmitted, distributed, stored, retrieved and ultimately destroyed. As such, it introduces a different work philosophy with new working specialisms, new job titles and descriptions, new staffing levels and an increased need for teamwork.

For management, this brings with it the need for a revised approach to the treatment of office work, with new systems, procedures and equip-

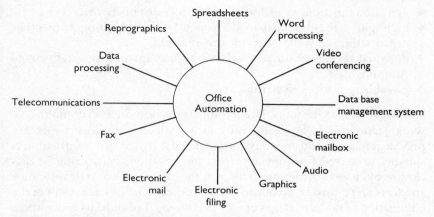

Fig. 48 The office automation support system

ment, whilst for staff it will mean increased work performance and new career opportunities.

Information Flow

Information – which literally refers to all raw data in words, numbers or symbol form which is communicated in written, verbal or visual form – is vital to efficient and effective management. The ways in which it is created, processed and distributed are crucial in terms of increasing productivity and reducing office costs. What office automation can do is provide the capacity to link many of the activities illustrated in Fig. 49, together via a variety of information storage and retrieval media, so providing a smoother and speedier flow of information both within an organization and with the world outside.

Convergent technologies

The first step towards office automation for many organizations was eased by the merger of data processing and word processing. This was evolutionary rather than revolutionary in that it brought with it certain instant advantages:

- improved office efficiency;
- better utilization of staff and equipment;
- direct access to information previously held on an independent system;
- savings of time;
- enhanced storage capacity of information systems;

- increased functions available to word processor operators;
- highlighted the potential to be gained from integrating with other organizations as well within the organization;
- potential savings of office overheads such as space, paper and storage equipment;
- possible reductions in staffing.

Set against these benefits, integration via the introduction of multi-task work stations did, however, introduce problems: security issues are prevalent in any multi-user environment and it is vital that information is suitably protected from unauthorized modification, destruction or disclosure by devices which are built into the system. Also, staff resistance and fears were introduced due to slight reductions in jobs as a result of the elimination of midway stages of work between word and data processing.

Telecommunications

It is this factor which has major significance in terms of assisting management to reach decisions more quickly, to provide a better service to customers/clients, to exchange information more efficiently with business colleagues and to compete more effectively with competitors.

Equipment Factors

Telecommunications provides the means to link one computer device with another, but the problem has always been that computers are digital devices and, as such, are not compatible with the telephone network which operates on an analogue system. To enable integration to take place between the two systems, modems are used to convert digital to analogue, and vice versa. Communications satellites, on the other hand, can transmit or receive digital signals from and to any part of the world but cost has been prohibitive.

Transmission/Receiving Barriers

Not only have devices been different but also problems exist as a result of different machine languages. 'Protocol' is the term used to explain the way in which a message is handled between two items of equipment. Provided the protocols are the same, information can be exchanged between two items of equipment irrespective of the fact that they may have been supplied by different manufacturers and consequently may have many incompatible features. Protocol compatibility is the essential feature for direct intercommunication. Where incompatibility is present, protocol convertors or translators known as 'black boxes' are required to interface between the two devices.

Transmission modes and speeds also produce problems, and it is vital to ensure that these factors are thoroughly investigated and considered at the design stages of a system.

Local area networks (LANs)

'Networking' refers to the interconnecting of items of technological equipment such as word processors, optical character readers (OCRs), phototypesetters, data processing and management information systems in order that centrally held information may be shared or information transmitted from one work station to another.

This has greatly enhanced the potential for decentralizing electronic office facilities, as originally there was a strong tendency to pool all such activities into a centralized location, so often increasing the resistance to change and emphasizing the mysteries which tend to surround anything new.

Networking has brought with it several major benefits:

- literally every office can enjoy the services available via the network – i.e. technology for all;
- it encourages convergent technologies rather than fragmentation between departments, sections and units;
- it calls for strategic planning;
- it reduces the need for duplication of paper records.

In practical terms the introduction of a network will require consideration to be given to:

- cost;
- access;
- type of arrangement;
- message switching procedures;
- control procedures;
- storage implications;
- usage;
- supervision;
- training.

Types of Arrangement

Topology is the term used to describe the physical organization of a network. There are three main possibilities – bus, ring or star.

Bus topology is where all devices are connected to and share a single cable as illustrated in Fig. 50.

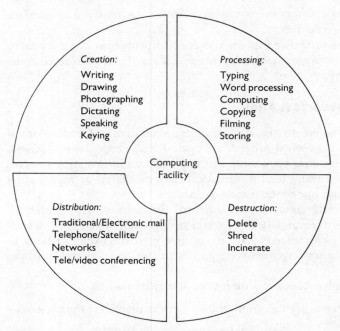

Fig. 49   An overview of the elements of information flow

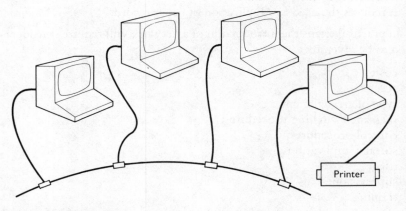

Fig. 50   Bus topology

Ring topology is where all the devices in the network are connected by a single communication cable that runs in a circle as illustrated in Fig. 51. The great disadvantage of this type is that failure of one terminal in the ring renders the entire network inoperable.

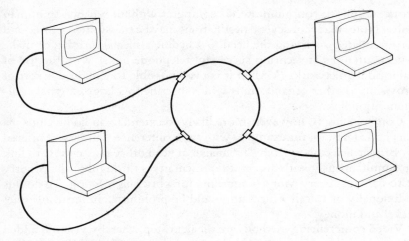

Fig. 51 Ring topology

Star topology is where each terminal or personal computer is connected through a central control unit which receives and routes all messages
from the terminals in the star as illustrated in Fig. 52.

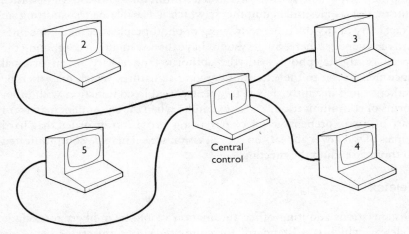

Fig. 52 Star topology

Teleconferencing

Teleconferencing can take many forms but is the term given to the
electronic communication of individuals in two or more separate locations. The locations may be within the same building or miles apart.

At its simplest, it may refer to the capacity of individuals at different work stations to communicate via computer without reliance on human voice. Notes made for several destinations may be transmitted, stored and retrieved later, so saving the need to schedule a special meeting or make several attempts at securing successful telephone links. With the use of value-added networks (VANs) it is even possible to extend this sort of provision to other organizations who subscribe to a large external communication link.

Conferencing is, however, more likely to extend to audio link-ups via telephone lines, as, for example, with the Conference Call service offered by British Telecom whereby a manager at head office may choose to link up simultaneously with his eight representatives throughout the country at 10.00 hours every Monday morning for a briefing meeting. To do this individually or to call a meeting would be prohibitive in terms of time, travel and money.

Video conferencing methods are the next step whereby vision is added to sound. This was first introduced by the then Post Office as Confravision but has since been developed by many other companies.

Facsimile (Fax)

Another important feature of the telecommunications aspect of office automation is facsimile equipment, which is capable of transmitting an exact copy of any document, drawing or photograph over telephone lines to a receiver elsewhere. Such systems have the advantage of combining the speed of the telephone with the authority and clarity of an original document, even to the extent of copying signatures which may then be authenticated instantly. Fax is frequently used in conjunction with other forms of communication, as, for example, when the equipment may form part of a comprehensive teleconferencing provision in order that hard copies of whatever appears on the television screen may be communicated to those attending the meeting.

Teletex

Organizations adopting office automation would be unlikely to exclude Teletex, which is a 'standard' for computer communications based on transmission via telephone lines. It is based on the idea of using the existing public switched telephone network (PSTN), the packet switched stream (PSS) data transmission network and the Telex network as a basis for providing an international text communication network. It is approved by CCITT (the international standards organization to which all public telecommunications authorities subscribe) and is, in fact, described by CCITT, as 'an international service offered by administrations or recognised private operating agencies, enabling subscribers to exchange correspondence on an automatic memory-to-memory basis via telecommunication networks'.

It is, in simple terms, upgraded Telex but has the advantages of being:

- faster;
- more cost effective;
- simpler to operate;
- superior in terms of quality of print out;
- able to offer a full range of characters;
- a non-dedicated terminal;
- compatible with other equipment;
- available from a range of suppliers;
- capable of interworking with Telex;
- potentially able to link with facsimile systems.

The Implications for Management

In a nutshell, management needs to do more than extend its current telecommunications facilities. Both the present and the future have to be considered in order to avoid the dangers of making short-term decisions which might be seriously outmoded in a few years' time.

Identification of needs should be followed by analysis of factors such as:

- telephone usage;
- meeting attendance;
- travelling expenses;
- how information is currently disseminated.

Such information will provide the basis for future developments.

Mailing procedures

A logical extension to any consideration of telecommunication provision will be an analysis of current mailing procedures. It is unrealistic to think that changes will happen overnight and that traditional mail will soon disappear. Increases in the use of electronic mail and mailboxes, together with other means of transmitting text, are still likely to be some way off in terms of replacing the traditional postal services.

Consequently, organizations will be well advised to examine their current procedures with a view to modernizing mail rooms, replacing outdated equipment and improving existing procedures. Many of the criticisms often levelled at mail handling and distribution within organizations are frequently unfounded. This is often a neglected area of development within organizations despite the wide range of sophisticated equipment available.

Aspects such as mail room location and layout are also worth pursuing, together with an analysis of staffing levels and areas of responsibility.

Electronic Mail

This is a term which has been bandied about for some time and an accurate definition is not easy to arrive at. However, basically, it refers to the transmission of data of one kind or another by electronic means. Therefore, copy will tend to be received on screen rather than in hard copy form, with the exception, of course, of facsimile copies which are technically forms of electronic mail. Within an organization this should certainly mean a faster process and will greatly reduce the volume of paper in circulation. Another special advantage of electronic mail is that it enables simultaneous handling and revision of documents to be done by individuals at widely dispersed work stations.

On an inter-organizational basis the main advantages will be the ability to send correspondence to multiple addresses, a reduction in postal charges and, often, a speedier service, given the delays of much second class mail.

The devices used to provide electronic mailing facilities will vary from computer terminals to communicating word processors to Fax systems or Viewdata terminals, and the service is likely to expand with the growth of networking and the increased compatibility potential of modern equipment.

Electronic mailboxes

This is a computer-based message switching system whereby each user is assigned a 'mailbox' into which messages may be sent and held in store until the user chooses to access the information held by making an enquiry at his terminal. Enquiries are made by keying the personal code allocated to each user of the mailbox system and messages are then displayed on the VDU. At it simplest, it passes messages between terminals, but it may also be used via a number of external services – e.g. British Telecom's Telecom Gold.

Sometimes mailboxes are referred to as 'electronic in-tray' because they store the sort of information which would traditionally accumulate in an in-tray.

Reprographics

Another aspect of an integrated office automation system is the reprographics facility provided. Here management must accurately evaluate its present usage by:

- recording the numbers and types of copier currently in use throughout the organization;
- noting the location of each facility;
- calculating the number of copies per month for each machine;
- analysing the type of work carried out;
- assessing the need for special facilities such as reduction and enlargement or automatic collation;
- assessing the number of two-sided copies made;
- considering the importance of speed;
- determining the need for transparency preparation;
- considering the advantages of link-up to word processing.

Misuse of copying facilities should also be evaluated, taking account of:

- the extent of personal copying carried out;
- the amount of waste;
- the volume of excess copies made;
- the level of operational errors;
- the extent of machine breakdown.

Phototypesetting

Consideration can also be given to the advantages gained by introducing phototypesetting. This is very much dependent upon the nature of the organization's work and the extent to which it might be feasible and advisable to contemplate the introduction of an in-house print facility. Basically, the reasons for introducing phototypesetting will include:

- the desire to integrate the facility with word processing and so reduce paper usage whilst producing improved quality material at increased speed;
- the desire to enhance the image of the organization by producing high quality printed matter which is aesthetically pleasing – e.g. there is considerable flexibility with layout and a wider variety of print sizes and styles available;
- the capacity to design and produce all house formats and so save on external printing bills;
- the ability to reduce costs by reducing the size of documents prepared in this way – e.g. it should be possible to reduce a 100-page document to 60 pages by phototypesetting: this not only saves paper but also reduces binding costs.

Records Management

Whether an organization opts for a manual or an automated records management system to integrate as part of its overall office automation strategy, it should be devised to take account of:

- the need to supply accurate and complete information;
- speed;
- cost effectiveness;
- minimal space requirements;
- expansion capability;
- convenience to the user in the provision of a better service;
- ease of understanding and simplicity of operation.

Before any decisions can be reached and any new system devised and implemented it is essential to carry out the following investigations:

- analyse the types of records currently held, in both active and inactive files;
- quantify all records held;
- estimate the amount of additional filing accumulated over the period of one year;
- identify the formats used – e.g. originals, copies, microfilm, micro-fiche, disk;
- analyse the volumes held in the different formats;
- evaluate the classification systems used;
- assess the filing and indexing procedures currently used;
- identify the retention policies in existence both for records which are stored out of statutory requirement and for archival purposes;
- classify all training given to staff;
- analyse supervisory responsibilities;
- survey all equipment;
- estimate the number of records users throughout the organization;
- assess the quantity of duplicated material in existence throughout the organization;
- distinguish between centralized and decentralized records.

Paper-based v microfilm v computer-based systems

In general, investigations of the sort indicated above should enable decisions to be made in favour of a particular type of system or, more commonly, a combination of the options available. Whatever the office system, it will ultimately be a matter of making choices and the choice will be dependent on the nature and size of the organization, the environment in which it operates and the way it is structured internally.

Factors to be borne in mind when making the choice

Paper-based systems will be influenced principally by:

- the volume of material;
- space availability;
- accessibility;
- the number of essential users;
- the degree of confidentiality;
- the speed of retrieval.

The feasibility of microphotography, on the other hand, would be largely dependent on:

- the costs and effort involved in setting up the transfer from existing paper records – i.e. the preparatory work;
- the costs of materials on an on-going basis;
- the costs of essential equipment;
- the potential to link with computer (CIM and COM).

Alternatively, the possibilities of introducing data base management systems would provide the following advantages:

- increased speed of retrieval;
- fewer errors;
- multiple access;
- reduced space;
- less knowledge of filing procedures.

However, set against this would be the need to provide all users with access to a work station from which they could retrieve essential data, together with the accompanying implications which such a step would inevitably involve – e.g. revised layouts, wiring problems, training needs, control mechanisms, security aspects and data protection.

The people dimension

Filing still relies on people whether it is paper based, film based or disk based. Success therefore depends on the quality of the staff handling the records. It is a fallacy to believe that anyone and everyone can file and so have the capability of establishing a workable system.

The ultimate choice of system, or systems, will be influenced by the level of management commitment towards one route or another, the standard or procedures currently in operation and the attitudes of the staff. Where sufficient importance is attached to records management, three levels of staff are likely to be involved in any decision involving changes in the storage and retrieval of information held on file – managers (the administrative level), supervisors (the supervisory level) and the operators (clerical level). Supervisory and clerical level activities in respect of records management can easily be identified and defined but a manager's responsibilities are perhaps less well documented.

Basically they are at company and departmental levels and are concerned with:

- the establishment of operational procedures (in consultation with the supervisor);
- the establishment of retention policies (in consultation with the legal department);
- staff development (in consultation with the supervisor and the training department);
- forms design (in consultation with the in-house print department);
- co-ordination of filing, mailing and messenger services (in consultation with the chief administrative officer and other departmental heads);
- planning and developing systems;
- keeping up to date with procedures;
- designing and preparing a records management manual.

These sorts of responsibilities would be readily associated with personnel at management level in the USA, where considerably more significance is attached to this area of activity. There, good career prospects exist for individuals engaged in records management activities, and the professional qualification – known as Certified Records Manager (CRM) – is attainable by those with three years' full-time experience in records management. The term 'records' does, however, tend to have strong connotations with paper-based systems, and management personnel involved in this area are increasingly referred to as Information Resource Directors.

Perhaps it is time that management in Britain took the issue of records management more seriously. A move towards office automation might be the ideal time to consider it.

Managerial Work Stations

Given the ways in which managers use their time – viz. attending meetings, reading, producing reports, telephoning and originating correspondence (see Stewart (1967) and Mintzberg (1973)) – it is reasonable that a move towards full office automation should give attention to providing managers with better tools for the job. A lot of administrative support can be secured by managers making good use of the office 'professional' as defined on p. 161. However, the manager's effectiveness will be enhanced still further by the introduction of a fully integrated management work station meeting the following specifications:

- compatible with the mainframe;
- with full communications facility – e.g. external Viewdata
- software options availability – e.g. DBMS, spreadsheet, dictionary, diary, calendar;
- user-friendly – e.g. alternatives to keyboards (i.e. touch screens, electronic stylus, mouse).

The only likely barrier to take-up will be finding the time needed to learn to use the equipment to its full potential.

Towards Office Automation – Management's Role

Identifying the features that will figure in an automated environment is one thing, successful implementation can be another. The way will be paved where management is able to demonstrate total commitment to the venture, and this will be largely dependent upon its understanding of the new concepts involved, its appreciation of the benefits to be gained from integration and the quality of the facts at its disposal. Where these three facets are strong, management will be in a good position to lead by example, boost the morale of the workforce generally and ensure a smooth transition.

Management will have many important decisions to make when devising strategies for implementing office automation. They may broadly be categorized as the issues highlighted in Fig. 53 and involve:

- long-range planning;
- seeking the advice and services of consultants;
- equipment selection;
- finance – rent, lease or buy;
- technical support;
- the establishment of internal support teams/units;
- the conduct of feasibility studies;
- how to integrate (if some systems are already in existence);
- how to phase the integration;
- whether to centralize or de-centralize;
- how to deal with staff resistance;
- determining responsibility levels;
- staff selection;
- ergonomic issues;
- health issues;
- training and staff development;
- work measurement;

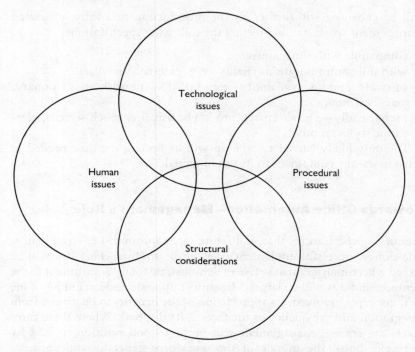

Fig. 53   Features of an office automation implementation strategy

- monitoring progress;
- security issues.

Six Steps in Planning for Office Automation

- **Prepare an existing organizational profile,** establishing the current position and identifying strengths and weaknesses.
- **Identify the pressures for change** – both internal and external.
- **Identify the operational constraints** – e.g. premises, finance, time, staff reluctance.
- **Examine the market and investigate the alternatives,** making use of consultants and considering all the choices available.
- **Draw conclusions and consider recommendations,** making every effort to ensure total participation in the activity.
- **Devise strategies to ensure successful implementation** – i.e. conduct feasibility studies, consider the human aspects, examine the structural considerations and give attention to procedural matters.

Feasibility Studies

A feasibility study is a survey into the total work functions currently performed by management and support staff in a particular area of activity, in order to determine whether or not any change in methods is possible, necessary or desirable. Likely reasons for conducting a feasibility study are:

- the need to increase productivity;
- the need to improve decision-making capability;
- the need to improve staff morale;
- the need to rationalize on equipment purchase;
- the need to integrate additional equipment;
- the recognition that future improvements in office communications are desirable;
- a change in organizational structure;
- the existence of incompatible equipment within the organization.

Any evaluation of what is required must be systematic and clearly related to organizational goals. The development of appropriate procedures is essential in order to assess and/or test viability, impact on work flow, quality and levels of performance. Reaction by staff will be important although hostility to the introduction of change can be greatly reduced by encouraging them to identify their own problems at work and submit proposals for possible remedies.

To prepare for a feasibility study an organization should take the following three steps.

1. Select appropriate individuals to conduct the investigation

Selection could be from within the organization, from outside consultants or from suppliers of systems and equipment. Whichever is decided will have advantages and disadvantages, but where the team is internal it should comprise a cross-section of staff with the necessary range of skills and knowledge. Where external consultants are used, this will add to the expense of the project but the previous knowledge and experience which they are able to bring to the exercise may prove valuable. Suppliers, on the other hand, will tend to be so desirous of obtaining a sale that they will often lack objectivity.

2. Establish a budget

It is important to establish the financial limitations of the exercise at the outset and to bear in mind that final costs are frequently in excess of those estimated during the planning stages. Setting the financial parameters also enables the team to eliminate at the outset systems which are beyond their means.

3. Determine the time scale

It is important to fix a time limit for each stage of the exercise at the outset, otherwise it may greatly over-run to the extent that initial findings may have lost their relevance in the overall scheme of things. Also, it is difficult to budget accurately when there is no time scale, and plans in respect of equipment delivery, installation and staff training will be impossible to finalize.

Feasibility Procedures

- Conduct an overview of the organization.
- Focus on the department or section to be studied.
- Discuss the exercise with senior management personnel.
- Interview staff directly involved in the exercise.
- Carry out more detailed interviews with key personnel.
- Gather all relevant information.
- Collate information.
- Analyse information.
- Prepare a report on the findings of the investigation.
- Present the report for management consideration.

Factors to consider in equipment/system selection

It is part of management's role to authorize the acquisition of appropriate equipment and/or systems. Decisions, however, will be made largely on the basis of recommendations by experts, whether in-house or external. The following factors are likely to influence any decisions reached:

- organizational objectives;
- organizational structure;
- nature of the work;
- volume of work;
- cost;
- staffing implications;
- space considerations;
- 'upgradability' or enhancement potential;
- speed of retrieval;
- retention needs;
- supplier options;
- backup support;
- obsolescence factors.

Whether to Rent, Lease or Buy

Decisions will be made in the light of the total financial picture of the organization and by weighing up the pros and cons associated with alternative methods of financing a major capital acquisition. The ultimate decision will depend on a number of factors.

Where **renting,** the investment is more likely to be considered as a short-time option or there may be some uncertainty about the suitability of the item for the intended purpose. Renting also has the advantage of ensuring maximum support from the supplier whilst minimizing the capital outlay. Also, in accounting terms, rental is viewed as a revenue expense and items are not included as capital expenditure, which may be advantageous in certain circumstances. Rental agreements do, however, tend to be costly when extended over any length of time and any initial benefits may eventually be lost altogether.

Leasing tends to be used to cover longer periods of time and where the organization may wish to build in the option of buying the machine as part of the leasing agreement whilst avoiding the initial large capital outlay required to purchase. The advantage of this, as opposed to outright purchase, is that it does leave the options open – e.g. to change to an alternative system part way through the agreement. Care must be taken to study the 'small print' to ensure that the terms are fully understood. For example, it may be necessary to provide a specific period of notice before any changes may be implemented.

Buying outright requires the necessary capital outlay but does have significant advantages in that it will be beneficial in the long term via tax advantages and depreciation. However, there is the question of obsolescence and the difficulty of trading in equipment should it be thought desirable to change. Software availability, backup and maintenance agreements are other important factors likely to determine the desirability of purchasing technological equipment outright.

Implementation problems

Problems will be different for all organizations, but are generally concerned with:

- tradition;
- structure;
- size;
- people problems – e.g. fears of redundancy, resistance to change, reluctance to re-train;
- health worries.

Tradition and Structure

Office technology used to be the concern of the specialist, with relatively few organizations appreciating the extent to which office automation could contribute to future developments and successes. Organizational structures tended to be devised on functional lines with distinct separation of responsibilities between departments. For example, computing was traditionally in the area of Data Processing or Management Services, and certainly was viewed as 'different' and distinct from any early word processing or other office-based service provided throughout the organization.

Such structures were ill-suited to take full advantage of modern technology as a corporate tool and conflict arose between departments such as data processing and administration when it came to deciding who should assume responsibility for office automation.

Whose responsibility is office automation?

For many organizations this can be problematic because there will tend to be two competing factions – those with the technical know-how and those who will actually make most use of the automated functions. Traditionally, the data processing department has possessed the expertise in that specialists were needed to operate and maintain early computers. Consequently, a mystique has been built up by many such departments, not only in terms of the technicalities of their functions but also in terms of the language they use and often their general attitudes to their role. However, the concept of the automated office is that it should be for 'everyone' in that it should ultimately integrate the functions of all departments. This would suggest a sharing of responsibility but it does not always come easily. What clearly cannot happen is that office automation be hived off as was the case for data processing in that it is essentially user oriented and therefore has to be available to all.

The problem has also been compounded in that managers from many areas have quickly got to grips with many aspects of office technology such as word processing, advanced telecommunications and reprographics facilities, whilst the arrival of stand alone systems which work independently of the mainframe computer have served to distance their need for the expert still further.

Integration is the key

There is a need for a well-planned corporate strategy for introducing office automation rather than haphazard attempts to solve immediate problems as they affect individual departments. This calls for company-wide installations, centrally managed and operated rather than fragmented, incompatible units with little or no potential for future development.

The solution reached by some organizations is to set up some form of steering committee with representatives from data processing and all the other departments involved. This will tend to work reasonably well at the implications stage but will often be less successful at implementation. What is really required is a combination of the discipline of the computer specialist and the resourcefulness of the office manager.

Size

The size of an organization will also have a bearing on implementation, with larger ones tending to respond more readily in that their scale of operations can cope more easily with the investment required whilst also having a greater potential for economies. Also, it is more likely that they will, over the years, already have made use of organization and method techniques, so they will be accustomed to the sorts of investigations which will be necessary.

Smaller organizations, on the other hand, will be more limited in terms of what they can do and will tend to aim basically at improvements in efficiency.

People Problems

People are, by their very nature, suspicious of change. They feel threatened by it and are reluctant to accept it, even when it is inevitable and may serve to enhance the quality of their working life. New systems have always been introduced but the pace with which technology has entered office work has been staggering and in some instances it has been installed before staff were aware of what was happening, let alone have an opportunity to participate in decisions – a recipe for increased problems. Many such fears can be removed fairly easily by early communication and wide consultation.

Problems will also be minimized where attention is given to job design, career opportunities, staff selection and training, as well as to the environment in which new work is carried out.

Health Hazards

A lot of concern has been expressed by both individuals and trade unions about the health hazards of working in an automated office environment, particularly using VDUs. Potential health problems which have been identified are:

- posture problems;
- visual fatigue and eye strain;
- audio problems;
- stress;
- radiation;
- epilepsy;
- headaches;
- nausea.

However, there is little positive evidence to suggest that any of these problems poses a serious threat to the health of those working within an automated environment, provided that all necessary precautions are taken. These include regular medical checkups, eye tests, adequate breaks, ergonomically designed furniture, suitable and sufficient lighting, good acoustics and suitably adapted equipment (e.g. non-reflective screens on VDUs). It is also important that any individual who feels unwell or worried by the effects of operating a VDU or working in a highly automated environment be encouraged to express his or her worries and, where possible, be given alternative work should it be considered advisable on medical grounds – e.g. in the case of a pregnancy or a recurrent eye problem or postural problem.

Concluding remarks

There is a need to design and implement systems with tomorrow in mind, as well as today, and it is the responsibility of management to ensure that they get the sorts of systems which will provide them with the quality of information necessary to maximize management decision making.

Technology must be harnessed if real benefits are to be obtained from the introduction of office automation. This necessitates producing a new breed of managers with a broad range of skills who will be confident and capable of taking the management of their organizations into the twenty-first century.

Glossary of office automation terms

Access time   When the system is available for use; or the duration of time from signalling the computer to receiving information; or the time required to access the data and retrieve it from the disk.

Acoustics   Ergonomic considerations in respect of sound levels.

Active files   Those currently in use.

Administrative support   Job functions of a non-typing nature which assist management.

Anthropometry   The study of human body measurements to fit sizes, heights and shapes of individuals to furniture and equipment dimensions.

Applications software   Software which instructs a computer to perform a specific function.

Archival storage   The high-volume, long-term storage of information.

Archive   To store information.

Artificial intelligence   The field of study by which computer and other electronic equipment can modify and improve operations to more closely simulate the thought processes of humans.

Author   The originator/creator (usually a manager or executive) of a document for preparation on a word processing machine.

Baud rate   The rate of signalling speed in telecommunications, expressed in approximately bits per second.

Bit   The contraction of **bi**nary digi**t**. A bit is the term given to each 1 or 0 in the string of 1s or 0s which comprise the binary or digital code.

Black box   A translator or intermediate interpretation device used with equipment which has different protocols.

Bubble memory   A form of magnetic memory with a very high storage capacity.

Bus network   A network consisting of a length of coaxial cable along which individual devices tap into the communications cable. Signals move along the line in both directions to any station on the cable.

CAD/CAM   Computer-aided design and computer-aided manufacture.

CAT   Computer-aided transcription, which is the capture of keystrokes onto a magnetic medium which is then processed through a computer and printed out.

CBX   Computerized branch exchange – an updated PBX.

Centralization   Location of one or more functions in one place with central support staff.

CIM   Computer input microfilm – a microform-based information storage and retrieval system.

Closed user group   Where only certain users have access to certain frames of a Viewdata system.

COM   Computer output microfilm. Here production is direct onto microfilm or fiche without intermediate hard copy or filming stages.

Communications   Transmission and reception of information.

Compatibility   The ability of one system to handle something designed for another.

Computer graphics Graphical representations on screen, produced by computer.

Convergence The coming together of areas of common interest. Frequently associated with the merger of data and word processing.

CPU Central processing unit – the component which houses the logic and control circuits of a system.

CRT Cathode ray tube – often used in American texts in place of 'VDU'.

Data base or database The compilation and storage of pooled information for future access, retrieval and print-out by multiple users.

DBMS Data base management system – computer software which handles storage and retrieval of records stored in direct-computer data bases.

Decentralization The location of mini computers and terminals with stand alone intelligence capability throughout various departments within an organization.

Digital code Storage transmission and processing of information in digital code form is used and recognized by electronic office systems.

Distributed logic The term used where the intelligence of a computer has been dispersed to several peripherals of the system rather than concentrated in one CPU.

Downtime Time when equipment cannot be used due to malfunction.

EDP Electronic data processing – the manipulation of data by electronic computers.

Electronic blackboard A blackboard developed by Bell Laboratories, which transmits graphics and hand-written communications over telephone lines for viewing on video monitors in distant locations.

Electronic filing The storing of information on machines for computerized access, rather than paper stored in conventional filing cabinets.

Electronic mail Communication between two or more parties using electronic technology to send computerized information, via satellites, cables or telephone wires. Information is displayed visually and need not be translated into hard copy.

Electronic mailbox A computer-based message system. Messages may be left at any time and remain there until the user makes an enquiry.

Ergonomics The science and study of human factors in system design with the intention of adapting machines and other elements of the working environment to the individuals performing the work.

Facsimile (Fax) The means of transmitting an exact copy of graphs, pictures, drawings and other data over telephone lines to a compatible receiver in another location.

Fibreoptics Smooth, glass-like, hair-thin tubes which send out a light source generated from electric power and are capable of carrying information at very high speed.

Full-page display A screen capable of displaying at least 66 lines of 80 characters per line, at the one time.

Gateway An interfacing device by which information may be passed from one network to another.

Global network World-wide integration of many networks.

Hybrid system A mixture of centralized and decentralized word/information processing systems.

Inactive files Those unused but retained for statutory purposes or awaiting destruction according to a predetermined retention policy.

Information processing The integration of data processing and word processing.

Information provider Any organization which leases space within Prestel to set up data bases and disseminate information from them to Prestel users.

Information retrieval The automatic searching and extracting of information from computer data bases.

Integrated software Packages which combine functions such as word processing, electronic spreadsheets and graphics into a single, easy-to-use programme.

Integrated work stations Sometimes called 'executive work stations', these provide both telephone and computer terminal capabilities within a single unit, so enabling both voice and data communication to take place.

Interactive The mode of operation by which a computer-based system can stop and start in reaction to each input from the user – e.g. interactive video.

Interface Used as a noun or a verb, and refers to the connecting of devices.

IPSS British Telecom's International Packet Switched Service for data transmission.

Keypad A compact keyboard of a few digits and control keys.

LAN Local area network – a means of linking electronic devices within a restricted area via a special cable.

Light pen A graphical input device used directly on the display screen to create or modify graphics.

LSI Large scale integration – the process of mass-producing electronic circuits by etching up to 10,000 transistors onto a silicon chip.

Management work station A work area designed to provide all-purpose facilities for the executive – e.g. a computer terminal with text editing features, electronic mail, diary facility, personal files processing capability and other features.

Message switching The technique of receiving a message, but storing it until the appropriate circuit is available and then retransmitting it. Also referred to as 'store and forward'.

Mouse A small light-weight device used as a pointer and moved across a flat surface to control the movement of the cursor and select menu choices.

Network A series of points connected by communications channels.

OCR Optical character recognition (or reader). This enables printed material to be electronically scanned for input into a word or data processing system.

Optical disk A disk which uses laser technology to provide high-density storage of information in either data or image form.

Optical wand A device held in the hand and used to read bar codes – e.g. in libraries.

Originator An individual who creates information or text.

PBX Private branch exchange.

Peripherals Pieces of equipment designed to work with, but not connected to, a word processor or computer – e.g. an OCR.

Phototypesetting The process by which camera-ready data can be reproduced via a sophisticated printing process which prints characters optically by photographing them at high speed.

Protocol The sequence of signals which controls the transmission between different devices; a standardized set of codes used to communicate in machine language.

PSTN Public switched telephone network.

Records management The systematic handling of documents from creation through storage to destruction.

Reduction rate The size ratio between a film image and the original document.

Redundant data The same data stored on more than one file.

Replication The duplication of information in another form.

Reprographics A generic term to describe the various techniques used to reproduce information – e.g. duplicating, photocopying, phototypesetting, COM.

Retrieval The recall of stored information.

Ring network A network whereby devices are interconnected by a ring or continuous loop without a centralized host computer.

Satellite communications Electronic communications via world-wide satellite transmission.

Star network A network whereby all communications pass through a control machine which operates as a 'switcher' at the hub of a star-like configuration.

Stylus A graphical input device used to enter commands which change or modify graphics on a VDU.

System time   The time of day logged by the operating system in the directory where files are created or changed.

Systems analyst   An individual who reviews current operations within an organization and designs new systems.

Systems programmer   An individual responsible for maintaining the computer operating system, making up-dates as they are introduced by the manufacturer, ensuring that the data base and communications facility are operational and generally ensuring that the computer is operating from the software point of view.

Systems software   The programmes which start up the computer, ensure that it is operational and that it can perform a series of utility functions.

Telecommunications manager   The individual with responsibility for the management of the personnel who plan, create, install and maintain networks of communication and monitor the transmission lines for the communications functions of the organization.

Teleconferencing   A system whereby the simultaneous processing of data, messages and visual connections sends pictures and voices through telephone wires to screens and speakers in other locations.

Thimble   An alternative print element to a daisy wheel, used on high-quality printers.

Topology   The physical and logical configuration of networks – i.e. the way devices are linked together.

Total support system   A planned structure integrating all services which were previously considered separate, into one centralized unit operated by support staff under the control of a supervisor.

Transitional approach   A part-way or short-term approach to the introduction of office automation.

Utility functions   Functions performed by the operating system, many of which pertain to file management.

VAN   Value added network. This is the entrepreneurial leasing of communications links whereby cost savings are introduced via the use of a common carrier. It can also be used to link up services such as electronic mail.

Video disk   A television recording on magnetic disk.

Video tape   A television recording on magnetic tape.

VLSI   Very large scale integration – i.e. more than 10,000 transistors on a single chip.

Questions

As the head of a management services unit, explain the selection and training procedures you would adopt when employing and updating staff, taking into account the possibility of occasionally using external consultants.

(ICSA, Summer 1985)

'If managers were doing their job properly, there would be no need for a performance appraisal system administered by the personnel function.' Discuss.

(ICSA, Summer 1985)

Discuss the application of manpower planning to an organization preparing for the introduction of a major new technology to its operations.

(ICSA, Summer 1985)

The first stage of establishing an effective training programme should be to identify training needs. How should these needs be identified with a reasonable degree of accuracy?

(IAM, Summer 1984)

(a) Outline two of the methods commonly used in staff appraisal.
(b) Indicate and discuss some of the more important criticisms that are frequently made about appraisal schemes.

(IAM, Winter 1985)

(a) Outline the main concepts of transactional analysis.
(b) Why are an increasing number of organizations providing courses in transactional analysis for their management personnel?

(IAM, Summer 1984)

(a) Identify the legal requirements in force covering the comfort and welfare of office staff.
(b) Suggest any amendments to current legislation which would improve the comfort and welfare of office staff.

(IAM, Summer 1985)

Discuss the view that 'staff have a right to know how they are progressing in their job at work'.

(IAM, Summer 1985)

Provide a detailed job description for one of the following:

(a) Word Processing Supervisor;
(b) Secretary to the Purchasing Manager;
(c) Receptionist.

(IAM, Winter 1985)

Discuss the scope and justification for providing welfare services to employees in large organizations.

(IAM, Winter 1985)

Your organization has acquired premises 20 miles outside the city centre where it is presently located. Draw up a plan to re-locate its city centre office within a six-month time scale.

(IAM, Summer 1984)

Write a report for your Board of Directors indicating why you would like an open plan office in new premises they are erecting. Include any proposals you may have to overcome possible disadvantages.

(PEI)

(a) Outline how an annual appraisal might be carried out of the clerical staff in the purchasing department of an industrial company. The clerical staff are mostly well experienced in their work and in the age range of 20–35. State any assumptions which you consider to be necessary or desirable.
(b) Assess the contributions that such an appraisal might make to the effectiveness of the industrial organization.

(RSA, 1983)

Your firm is housed in a rather old building, and as part of a modernization scheme it is proposed that the present office layout (i.e. each secretary in her own office adjoining her chief's) should be changed to one of open plan. Your employer, who is not at all up to date with this idea, asks you to give him some information on how you think this will differ from the present layout and list what you consider to be the advantages and disadvantages of such a change.

(PEI)

You have recently been promoted to the post of assistant to a team of four managers and you have been asked to share their fairly small room. At present the desks are arranged in the middle of the room, allowing no privacy, with the filing cabinets next to each desk, making access difficult. There is one large window.

Describe what could be done to make better use of the space, giving privacy to everyone, reducing noise and giving better access to the files.

(PEI)

As secretary to the Personnel Manager, one of your duties is to arrange the advertising for staff. Your employer wishes to compare the respective advantages of using a newspaper advertisement or an employment agency in order to present his recommendation at the next executive meeting which will deal with rising costs. He has asked you to make a list of the steps needed to be taken in each case to arrive at the employment of a satisfactory member of staff. At the close of this list, indicate what costs (both in time and money) are involved.

(PEI)

Explain the British trade union movement. Your answer should include an explanation of the role of the Trades Union Congress, the full-time union official and the shop steward.

(LCCI, 1985)

Mrs Fellows, the Training Manager, has requested your help in setting out formally, for the advice of managers and supervisors at Comlon International p.l.c., a specimen recruitment and selection procedure.

With the aid of headings and written notes, produce this information, starting with 'The vacancy is agreed' and ending with 'Appointment'.

(LCCI, 1984)

Finding the right person for a job is a fundamental problem in every organization. Suggest a systematic procedure to deal with this problem.

(LCCI, 1982)

A Sales Department consisting of a manager, 2 assistant managers, 3 supervisors, 20 sales order clerks and 10 word processor operators is to move into a new building where it is to occupy the following accommodation:

Third floor
One large room 15 ft×30 ft plus two smaller adjacent rooms, each 10 ft×12 ft
Fourth floor
One large room 15 ft×40 ft
(There are two lifts and a staircase connecting the two floors.)
Plan the layout of these rooms, stating how you would place the staff, and indicate, by arrows, the main direction of work flow. (It is possible that partitions could be erected if required.)

(IAM, Winter 1985)

A space, rectangular in shape (40 ft×25 ft) is divided by wooden partitions into ten equal offices, five on each side of a corridor running lengthwise. There are windows in both the long sides of the rectangle. The space is to be taken over as a Personnel Department, and it is suggested that **some** of the partitions may be taken out and an 'open plan' adopted.

Draw a plan of the re-designed office, showing clearly where the work of the department will be performed. Support your plan with written explanations where necessary.

(IAM, Summer 1984)

Most of the thirty staff in your office have joined a union and elected a shop steward. Your manager is uncertain what the shop steward's activities will include, and has asked you to advise him. Describe the role of the shop steward, indicating the advantages and disadvantages to management of his presence in the organization.

(PEI)

(a) What are the main functions of a shop steward?
(b) How can shop stewards be assisted to carry out their duties more effectively?

(IAM, Summer 1984)

Local networks are likely to become more prevalent in providing integrated office systems thoughout an organization. Discuss the effects as far as the production of management information is concerned.

(ICSA, Summer 1985)

'Data base' is a term increasingly used in association with office work.
(a) What does the term 'data base' mean?
(b) Describe one aspect of a data base that would be useful to the efficient operation of the office.

(ICSA, Summer 1985)

The developments in new technology have led to the introduction of computers into most organizations. Describe the impact this has had on people and their jobs, and discuss the likely impact in the next decade.

(IAM, Summer 1984)

(a) What are the problems of effectively and satisfactorily carrying out employee appraisal?
(b) How might the problems vary as between the appraising of different levels and types of employee – e.g.:
  (1) typists in a typing pool;
  (2) the personal assistant to the Research and Development Manager;
  (3) the Marketing Manager?

(RSA, 1984)

The Directors of Comlon International p.l.c. have asked Mr Jackson (Personnel Director) to advise on ways in which general office efficiency can be improved. Mr Landers, the Office Manager, has suggested the following areas for consideration, and you are required to prepare a document discussing the relevant points which Mr Jackson can present to the Directors.

What is the office?

How is the office organized and is the office productive?

Staffing and training

Office buildings, furniture and equipment

Innovating.

(LCCI, 1985)

As personal assistant to the Managing Director of a medium-sized manufacturing company, you are currently sharing office accommodation with two other personal assistants. The company will shortly be moving to new office premises and you have been allocated your own individual office adjoining that of the Managing Director (see diagram below). Reprographic services are being centralized, although the placement in individual offices of smaller, more limited equipment will be permitted where this can be justified on grounds of confidentiality and/or work flow.

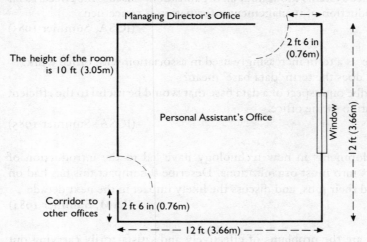

(a) Set out in a diagram your suggested layout for the office, including both furniture and equipment.

(b) Explain why you have included the chosen items of equipment.

(c) What possible (1) advantages, and (2) disadvantages will there be for you in the new work arrangement compared with the existing shared arrangement?

(RSA, 1984)

Offtech p.l.c. is a UK company engaged in the manufacture of advanced office equipment and the preparation of office software. From its head-quarters in Slough, Berkshire, the company markets its products throughout the UK, Western Europe and North America. The Administration Manager has been commissioned by the Board of Directors to organize a two-day conference in Brussels in October 1983 on the theme of 'The Office in the 90s'. The objective of the conference is primarily to promote the company as forward looking and to emphasize the wide geographic base from which the company operates. A subsidiary, but none the less very important, purpose is to establish contact with as many parties as possible in order to facilitate the company's future development.

(a) Outline the problems which might arise in organizing and running such a conference.

(b) Suggest the means which might be adopted towards ensuring the success of the conference.

(c) Devise a programme for the conference suitable for public issue.

(RSA, 1983)

Postscript

'The individual's sense of the future plays a critical part in his ability to cope. The faster the pace of life, the more rapidly the present environment slips away from us, the more rapidly do future potentialities turn to present reality . . . The men who rise in management are expected with each successive promotion, to concern themselves with events further in the future . . .'

Alvin Toffler
Future Shock

Getting to grips with management is far from easy. No two situations are exactly alike, problems are often multi-dimensional and possible solutions inevitably produce unintended outcomes which, again, require positive intervention by managers.

In any event, many management activities take place within organizations which are growing in complexity, particularly as they seek to diversify in order to survive or expand. The greater the diversification, the greater is the complexity, and the greater the pressure for innovation and change.

Time does not stand still, and dramatic changes in the last ten years have seen a major decline in British manufacturing, bringing with it the eclipse of skills and trades which had previously endured for generations. At the same time there has been an increase in demand for new and sophisticated skills in technology, science, computing, marketing and people skills – as the vacancies advertised in the national press will testify.

Many organizations, in both the public and the private sectors, have been forced to improve their performance in order to compete effectively in a highly competitive and volatile market place. In the private sector, predators in the shape of major companies – often multi-nationals – are continually on the look-out for possible 'victims' for take-over in a climate of intense competition, resulting in the formation of even bigger organizations. In the public sector, central government has relentlessly pursued a policy of control over public expenditure through the introduction of mechanisms of accountability aimed at securing 'value for money'.

At the other end of the scale there is the growth of small businesses and the promotion of entrepreneurial activities of all kinds. Relatively young industries such as conference and exhibition management are growing steadily, and advances in information technology have brought with them the need for enhanced facilities, equipment and expertise – all new areas for management activity.

Each of the above points provides an illustration of ever-increasing complexity in the nature of organizations, which are operating more than ever in turbulent settings. These in turn produce levels of uncertainty both for those with functional tasks to perform and for those with managerial duties and responsibilities. Despite the availability of computer technology, forecasting and prediction antennae still have their limitations, so it remains difficult for organizations to determine and control their futures.

Given both the increase in complexity of management and the dynamics of change, it might be expected that management training would be a high profile activity. However, the fact remains that few managers in Britain today have formal qualifications in management, most of them acquiring their skills and expertise 'on the job'. This may have been adequate during periods of relative stability, but is inappropriate in a climate of change.

It has been argued throughout this text that, for organizations to be efficient and effective – i.e. to achieve, or to come close to achieving their goals – strong reliance must be placed on the quality of relationships between the manager or supervisor and individual members of staff. Nothing produces commitment more than encouragement, empathy and recognition of the individual by his immediate superior. But few managers are trained in the art of people skills which are so badly needed in organizations operating traditional hierarchical structures.

As observed in Part II, however, hierarchies are under attack from new collaborative approaches to decision making, such as networks, team building and quality circles. Nevertheless, the fact remains that hierarchies are endemic in organizational structures, having an undeniable strength rooted in the past and consequently are unlikely to dissolve in the face of new and relatively untested alternatives. Only time will tell, but it would seem a safe bet that new management approaches will gradually be implemented, by stealth if not by deliberate policy.

All transition, whatever its form – whether it be in work patterns, practices, traditions, priorities or plans for the future – is bound to have implications for management. What was, not so long ago, but a vision, quickly became a possibility and in many instances is already a reality.

Appendices

Appendices

Appendix 1
Short Courses in Management

The following is a list of typical courses offered recently by three major providers of short courses for management – viz. the British Institute of Management (BIM), Guardian Business Services (GBS) and the Industrial Society (IS).

Course Title	Provider	Duration
Effective Speaking	GBS	3 days
Effective Letter Writing	,,	2 days
Quicker Reading	,,	2 days
Basic Report Writing	,,	2 days
Advanced Report Writing	,,	3 days
Effective Interviewing	,,	5 days
Accounting for Non-financial Managers	,,	3 days
Project Planning by Critical Path Analysis	,,	2 days
Print Buying for Non-specialists	,,	2 days
Producing a House Journal	,,	2 days
Managing Assertively	,,	3 days
Time and Self Management	,,	2 days
Employment Law	,,	2 days
Developing your Managers for the Future	BIM	2 days
The Effective Manager	,,	5 days
Employment Law – an update	,,	1 day
Managing Stress	,,	1 day
The Techniques of Time Management	,,	2 days
The New Assertive Woman Manager	,,	2 days
Career Planning and Development for Women	,,	2 days
Time Management and Personal Planning	,,	2 days
The Manager and the Micro	,,	2 days
Negotiating Skills	,,	2 days
Leadership Skills	,,	2 days
The Influential Manager	,,	2 days
Team Building	,,	2 days
Body Language for Managers	,,	2 days
Leading Effective Meetings	,,	2 days
Getting the Best from your Staff	,,	2 days

Achieving People's Commitment at Work	IS	2 days
Action-centred Leadership: Managers	,,	3 days
Decision Taking	,,	1 day
Delegation	,,	1 day
Discipline	,,	1 day
Target Setting and Performance Review	,,	1 day
Time Management	,,	2 days

Appendix 2
Useful Addresses

Advisory, Conciliation and Arbitration Service (ACAS)
  Head Office, 11–12 St James's Square, London SW1Y 4LA   01-214 6000
British Association for Commercial and Industrial Education (BACIE)
  16 Park Crescent, London W1N 4AP   01-636 5351
British Institute of Management (BIM) (*Management Today* and *Management News*)
  Management House, Cottingham Road, Corby, Northants NN17 1TT   (0536) 204222
Careers and Occupational Information Centre
  Moorfoot, Sheffield S1 4PQ   (0742) 753275
Careers Research Advisory Centre (CRAC)
  Ibbson Press (Cambridge) Ltd, Bateman Street, Cambridge CB2 1LZ
Central Film Library
  Chalfont Grove, Gerrards Cross, Bucks SL9 8TN   (02407) 4433
Confederation of British Industry (CBI)
  Centre Point, 103 New Oxford Street, London WC1A 3DU   01-379 7400
Equal Opportunities Commission (EOC)
  Overseas House, Quay Street, Manchester M3 3HN   061-833 9244
Guardian Business Services (GBS)
  119 Farringdon Road, London EC1R 3DA   01-278 6787
The Industrial Society (IS)
  Peter Runge House, 3 Carlton House Terrace, London SW1Y 5DG   01-839 4300
The Institute of Administrative Management (IAM)
  40 Chatsworth Parade, Petts Wood, Orpington, Kent BR5 1RW   (0689) 75555
The Institute of Chartered Secretaries and Administrators (ICSA)
  16 Park Crescent, London W1N 4AH   01-580 4741
The Institute of Personnel Management (IPM)
  Camp Road, Wimbledon, London SW19 4UW   01-946 9100
The London Chamber of Commerce and Industry (LCCI)
  Marlowe House, Station Road, Sidcup, Kent DA15 7BJ   01-309 0440

Management Centre Europe
   Rue Caroly 15, B-1040 Brussels, Belgium   32/2/516.19.11
Manpower Services Commission (MSC)
   Head Office, Moorfoot, Sheffield S1 4PQ   (0742) 753275
The Open University (OU)
   Walton Hall, Milton Keynes, Beds MK7 6AA
Pitmans Examinations Institute (PEI)
   Godalming, Surrey GU7 1UU   (04868) 5311
The Royal Society of Arts (RSA)
   John Adam Street, Adelphi, London WC2N 6EZ   01-839 1691
Trades Union Congress (TUC)
   Congress House, 23 Great Russell Street, London WC1B 3LS   01-636
   4030
Video Arts Limited
   Dumbarton House, 68 Oxford Street, London W1N 9LA   01-637
   7288
Women in Management
   4 Mapledale Avenue, Croydon CR0 5TA   01-654 4659
Women of Europe
   The Commission of the European Communities, 200 Rue de la Loi,
   1049 Brussels, Belgium
Working Woman
   Preston Publications Ltd, 40 Fleet Street, London EC4Y 1BT   01-583
   2990

In Relation to Managing Conferences

Association of British Professional Conference Organisers
   100 Park Road, London NW1 4RN
Association of Conference Executives
   Riverside House, 160 High Street, Huntington Cambs PE18 6SG
British Association of Conference Towns (BACT)
   International House, 36 Dudley Road, Royal Tunbridge Wells, Kent
   TN1 3LB
British Tourist Authority
   239 Old Marylebone Road, London NW1 5QT
British University Accommodation Consortium Ltd (BUAC)
   Box U 32, University Park, Nottingham NG7 2RD
Expotel Conference Desk
   Banda House, Cambridge Grove, London W6 0BR
The Scottish Conference Association
   Easter House of Ross, Comrie, Perthshire PH6 2JS

Suggested Further Reading

Texts marked with an asterisk (★) have special significance in that they represent what are regarded as classics or major studies. Those marked with a hash (#) provide background and/or general interest reading.

Adair, J (1978) *Training for Decisions*. Aldershot: Gower

Adair, J (1978) *Training for Leadership*. Aldershot: Gower

Adair, J (1978) *Training for Communication*. Aldershot: Gower

Adair, J (1979) *Action Centred Leadership*. Aldershot: Gower

Adair, J (1985) *Effective Decision-making*. London: Pan

Appell, A L (1984) *A Practical Approach to Human Behaviour in Organisations*. London: Merrill

Argyle, M (1979) *Person to Person: Ways of Communicating*. London: Harper & Row

#Argyle, M (1983) *The Psychology of Interpersonal Behaviour*. Harmondsworth: Penguin

Austin, B (1986) *Making Effective Use of Executive Time*. London: Management Update

Back, K and Back, K (1982) *Assertiveness at Work: a practical guide to handling awkward situations*. Maidenhead: McGraw-Hill

Barker, D (1980) *Transactional Analysis and Training*. Epping: Gower

Berne, E (1968) *Games People Play*. Harmondsworth: Penguin

#Berne, E (1972) *What do You Say After You Say Hello*. London: Corgi Books

Birchall, D and Hammond, V (1981) *Tomorrow's Office Today – Managing Technological Change*. London: Business Books

Blaazer, C and Molyneux, E (1984) *Supervising the Electronic Office*. Aldershot: Gower

Blake, R R and Mouton, J S (1964) *Managing Intergroup Conflict in Industry*. Houston: Gulf Publishing

Blau, P M (1973) *The Dynamics of Bureaucracy: a study of interpersonal relationships in two government agencies*. Chicago: Chicago University Press

Brooks, E (1980) *Organizational Change: the managerial dilemma*. London: Macmillan

Burke, W W and Beckhard, R (eds) (1976) *Conference Planning*. Mansfield: University Associates of Europe

★Burns, T and Stalker, G M (1961) *The Management of Innovation*. London: Tavistock

#Burr, R (1985) *The Share Book*. London: Rosters

Child, J (1977) *Organization: A Guide to Problems and Practice*. London: Harper & Row

Clements, R (1980) *A Guide to Transactional Analysis: a handbook for managers and trainers*. Insight Training

#Cooper, C L and Davidson, M (eds) (1984) *Women in Management*. London: Heinemann

Crix, F C (1975) *Reprographic Management Handbook*. London: Business Books

Curran, S and Mitchell, H (1984) *Office Automation: an essential management strategy*. London: Macmillan

Dale, E (1978) *Management Theory and Practice*. New York: McGraw-Hill

#de Bono, E (1982) *Lateral Thinking for Management*. Harmondsworth: Penguin

Derrick, J and Oppenheim, P (1983) *Telecommunications – A Businessman's Guide*. London: Kogan Page

Derrick, J and Oppenheim, P (1984) *A Handbook of New Office Technology*. London: Kogan Page

Deverell, C S (1979) *Management Studies: questions and suggested answers*. London: Gee

Douglass, M E and Douglass, D N (1980) *Manage Your Time; Manage Your Work; Manage Yourself*. New York: AMACOM

Drucker, P (1955) *The Practice of Management*. London: Heinemann

Drucker, P (1967) *Managing for Results*. London: Pan

Farnham, D (1984) *Personnel in Context*. London: IPM

★Fayol, H (1949) *General and Industrial Management*. London: Pitman (first published in French, 1916)

Fielder, F E (1967) *A Theory of Leadership Effectiveness*. New York: McGraw-Hill

#Fogarty, M P et al (1981) *Women in Top Jobs: 1968–1979*. London: Heinemann Educational Books

Gee, K C E (1982) *Local Area Networks*. Manchester: NCC Publications

Goffman, E (1971) *The Presentation of Self in Everyday Life*. Harmondsworth: Penguin

Goodworth, C T (1979) *Effective Interviewing for Employment Selection*. London: Business Books

Grandjean, E (1980) *Fitting the Task to the Man*. London: Taylor & Francis

Hall, R (1977) *Organizations: Structure and Process*. Englewood Cliffs NJ: Prentice-Hall

Handy, C B (1982) *Understanding Organizations*. Harmondsworth: Penguin

Handy, C B (1985) *The Future of Work*. Oxford: Basil Blackwell

#Harris, T A (1973) *I'm OK – You're OK*. London: Pan

#Hennig, M and Jardim, A (1979) *The Managerial Woman*. London: Pan

Hicks, H G and Gullett, C R (1981) *Organizations: Theory and Behavior*. New York: McGraw-Hill

Hirschheim, R (1986) *Office Automation: A Social and Organisational Perspective*. New York: Wiley

Hood, C C (1976) *The Limits of Administration*. London: Wiley

Huczynski, A (1983) *Encyclopaedia of Management Development Methods*. Aldershot: Gower

Hunt, J (1981) *Managing People at Work: a manager's guide to behaviour in organizations*. London: Pan

Inman, M L (1983) *Organization and Management: questions and answers*. London: Financial Training Publications

Institute of Personnel Management (1985) *The Best of Bill Reddin*. London: IPM

#James, M and Jongewood, D (1976) *Born to Win*. Reading MA: Addison-Wesley

Jarrett, D (1984) *The Electronic Office: a management guide to the office of the future*. Aldershot: Gower

Kelley, C (1979) *Assertion Training: A Facilitator's Guide*. Mansfield: University Associates of Europe

Kingdon, D R (1973) *Matrix Organization: managing information technologies*. London: Tavistock

Knight, K (1977) *Matrix Management: a cross-functional approach to organization*. London: Gower

Landau, R M, Bair J H and Siegman J H (1982) *Emerging Office Systems*. Norwood NJ: Ablex Publishing

#LaRouche, J and Ryan, R (1984) *Strategies for Women at Work*. London: Unwin Paperbacks

Lawrence, P R and Lirsch, J W (1969) *Organization and Environment: Managing Differentiation and Integration*. Homewood IL: Irwin

★Likert, R (1967) *The Human Organization*. New York: McGraw-Hill

Locke, M (1984) *How to Run Committees and Meetings*. London: Macmillan

Lockett, M and Spear, R (eds) (1980) *Organizations as Systems*. Milton Keynes: Open University Press

McGregor, D (1960) *The Human Side of Enterprise*. New York: McGraw-Hill

Margerison, C (1978) *Influencing Organisational Change*. London: IPM

#Marlow, H (1984) *Success – Individual, Corporate and National: profile for the eighties and beyond*. London: IPM

#Marshall, J (1984) *Women Managers: Travellers in a Male World*. Chichester: Wiley

Mintzberg, H (1973) *The Nature of Managerial Work*. New York: Harper & Row

Mintzberg, H (1979) *The Structuring of Organizations: a synthesis of the research*. Englewood Cliffs NJ: Prentice-Hall

Mitchell, E (1977) *The Businessman's Guide to Speechmaking and Conduct of Meetings*. London: Business Books

Mumford, A (1971) *The Manager and Training*. London: Pitman

Mumford, A (1980) *Making Experience Pay*. London: McGraw-Hill

Mumford, E (1983) *Designing Secretaries*. Manchester: Manchester Business School

Murrell, K F H (1979) *Ergonomics: Man in His Working Environment*. London: Chapman & Hall

#Naisbett, J (1984) *Megatrends: ten new directions for transforming our lives*. London: Macdonald

Peltu, M (1983) *How to Automate Your Office*. Manchester: NCC

Peltu, M (1984) *Successful Management of Office Automation*. Manchester: NCC

#Plender, J and Wallace, P (1986) *The Square Mile: a guide to the new City of London*. London: Century Publishing

Pritchard, J A T and Wilson, P A (1982) *Planning Office Automation, Electronic Message Systems*. Manchester: NCC

*Pugh, D S and Hickson, D J (1983) *Writers on Organizations*. Harmondsworth: Penguin

Quick, J C (1984) *Organisational Stress and Preventative Management*. Maidenhead: McGraw-Hill

Randell, G A et al (1972) *Staff Appraisal*. London: IPM

Rawlinson, J G (1981) *Creative Thinking and Brainstorming*. Aldershot: Gower

*Reddin, W J (1971) *Managerial Effectiveness*. Maidenhead: McGraw-Hill

Reynolds, H and Tramel, M E (1984) *Executive Time Management*. London: Gower

*Simon, H A (1957) *Administrative Behavior*. New York: Free Press

Simpson, A (1981) *Planning for Telecommunications*. Aldershot: Gower

Smithson, S (1983) *Business Communication Today*. London: ICSA

*Stewart, R (1967) *Managers and Their Jobs*. London: Macmillan

Stewart, R (1970) *The Reality of Organizations*. London: Pan

Stewart, R (1982) *Choices for the Manager*. London: McGraw-Hill

Stewart, R (1986) *The Reality of Management*. London: Heinemann

Taylor, D S (1976) *Performance Reviews*. London: IPM

#Toffler, A (1970) *Future Shock*. London: Pan

#Toffler, A (1981) *The Third Wave*. London: Pan

Tricker, R I (1982) *Effective Information Management*. Aldershot: Beaumont Executive Press

Vinnicombe, S (1980) *Secretaries, Management and Organizations*. London: Heinemann

Vroom, V H and Yetton, P W (1973) *Leadership and Decision Making.* Pittsburgh PA: University of Pittsburgh Press

Waterhouse, S A (1983) *Office Automation and Word Processing Fundamentals.* London: Harper & Row

Welch, W J and Wilson, P A (1981) *Electronic Mail Systems – A Practical Evaluation Guide.* Manchester: NCC

Welch, W J and Wilson, P A (1983) *Facsimile Equipment – A Practical Evaluation Guide.* Manchester: NCC

Whitehead, J (1986) *Planning the Electronic Office.* Beckenham: Croom Helm

*Woodward, J (1965) *Industrial Organization: theory and practice.* Oxford: Oxford University Press

Index